IF IT IS TO BE IT IS UP TO ME

IF IT IS TO BE
IT IS UP TO ME

THE PERSONAL MEMOIRS OF
MARLIN B. REISHUS

KELLER PUBLISHING
Marco Island, Florida

Copyright © 2010 by Marlin B. Reishus

All rights reserved

Composed in Janson at
Hobblebush Books (www.hobblebush.com)

Printed in the United States of America

ISBN: 978-1-934002-16-2

Published by
KELLER PUBLISHING
590 Fieldstone Dr.
Marco Island, FL 34145
KellerPublishing.com
800-631-1952

TO MARGARET (MARG)

My wife, my lover, and my best friend for fifty-seven wonderful years—and still counting. For her unconditional support while I traveled to the four corners of the country to earn our living and to further my career. At times my job required her to be both mom and dad while I was off making another sale or leading my staff to conquer ever increasing goals.

TO KATHY, ERIC, JEAN, AND PAUL

My fabulous children who never disappointed Marg or me. They never cease to amaze us in their achievements and actions.

TO MY GRANDCHILDREN, MY GREAT GRANDCHILDREN, AND MY GREAT GREAT GRANDCHILDREN YET UNBORN

You were my inspiration in writing this book. It is my hope these memoirs will help you to better understand your Grandpa Marlin.

ACKNOWLEDGMENTS

MY LIST OF ACKNOWLEDGMENTS BEGINS with Jim Engh, who provided the research on the Reishus family in his book, *Slægten Reishus* (*The Family Reishus*). With Jim's permission, I recorded some of the information used in this book. His research was invaluable in completing the picture of our family genealogy. He helped me to understand who I am and where my family came from.

I would also like to acknowledge two favorite teachers who made a difference in my life. Miss Florence Willis was my 5th and 6th grade teacher and Mrs. Mary Hatlestad was my math teacher all through high school. Both teachers instilled the desire in me to learn more than I dreamed possible and inspired me for the rest of my life with the philosophy:

"IF IT IS TO BE IT IS UP TO ME."

These outstanding teachers always challenged me to greater heights and to set the bar higher in whatever I endeavored to do.

I would also like to acknowledge my mom and dad, who constantly encouraged me in whatever goals I set for myself. They told me, "You can do whatever you set your mind to."

Finally, I would like to acknowledge my first cousin, Norma Reishus Dovery, who documented the history of Grandma Annetta and Grandpa Knute and their amazing family. Norma's dad and my dad were brothers who shared the same family heritage.

CONTENTS

1	ILLUSTRATIONS	ix
2	FOREWORD	xv
3	HIGHLIGHTS IN THE LIFE OF MARLIN B. REISHUS	xix

PART 1: I ALWAYS COMPETE TO WIN

1	Early Memories	5
2	My Parents	15
3	We Moved to Cottonwood	25
4	High School	37
5	Her Name is Marg	49
6	The Military Beckons	57
7	Officer Candidate School (OCS)	69
8	Gene Fights Polio	75
9	Marriage	79
10	Jump School and the 82nd Airborne	85
11	College Days	97

PART 2: SELLING MYSELF

12	The Babcock and Wilcox Company	107
13	On to Freiden	119
14	Selling Computers for Honeywell	124
15	A Gamble That Really Paid Off	139
16	We Moved Again	145
17	Back To Naperville with R.R. Donnelley	150
18	Our First Store	154
19	The Mid-Eighties	161
20	Reicer INC Expansion Plans Turn to Sale	166
21	Buy, Build, Hold, and Sell	170

PART 3: FUN, FAMILY, AND FRIENDS

22	The Joys of Music	177
23	Vacations	180
24	Katherine Ann (Kathy) Elvin	193
25	Reflections by Kathy	198
26	Eric Marlyn Reishus	202
27	Reflections by Eric	213
28	Jean Susan Reishus (Martin)	217
29	Reflections by Jean	224
30	Paul Brian Reishus	227
31	Reflections by Paul Paul Brian Reishus	234
32	W. (Wallace) Dale Reishus	238
33	Gene Orville Reishus	244
34	Migrating to Marco Island	250
35	Retirement and One Last Move	255
36	Family, Travel, and More	259

PART 4: THE REISHUS GENEALOGY

37	Excerpts From *Slægten Reishus* by James T. Engh	279
38	Excerpts From Sondre Reishby Ingebor, Wife of Sondre	301
39	Excerpts from *Slægten Reishus*	313
40	The Family of Knute T. Reishus and Annette Miller	324

EPILOGUE	337
APPENDIX A: Our Many Moves	343
APPENDIX B: Burger King Stores	346

LIST OF ILLUSTRATIONS

1	Family picture of Mom, Dad, Gene, Marlin, and Dale	2
2	The Swedish Hospital bill for Marlin's birth	7
3	Dale nine, and Marlin age three	10
4	Marlin as a youngster sitting on the sofa	12
5	Dad in his World War I uniform	18
6	Orville and Mabelle Reishus, after their wedding	20
7	Aerial picture of Cottonwood, 1995	24
8	Cottonwood Restaurant menu during the Depression	29
9	Dad driving a 1938 pickup truck in the Cottonwood Golden Anniversary Parade	30
10	Orville and Mabelle Reishus on their 40th wedding anniversary	32
11	Marlin's high school graduation picture in 1948	43
12	Marg, age sixteen months, going topless	49
13	Helen and Earl Olson pose for a studio photograph	50
14	Helen Olson; One of the last pictures of her before she died at age 99	50
15	Earl Olson, Marg's dad on vacation	50
16	Marg as a sophomore in high school	51
17	Silo Lutheran Church	52
18	Christ Lutheran Church	53
19	Marg's hospital bill when she had her appendix removed	55
20	Marlin and Marg's wedding day, February 1, 1953	80
21	Cutting the cake at the wedding reception in the church basement of Christ Lutheran Church	80
22	Marg's 1953 graduation as a registered nurse	82
23	Marg's 1950 student nurse capping ceremony	82
24	Mass paratroopers' jump from C-82s	87
25	Parachuting out of a C-46	88
26	A parachute jump as it looks from the ground	89
27	Marlin as a Second Lieutenant with paratroopers' wing at Ft. Bragg, North Carolina, 1953	90
28	Marlin as a paratrooper on one of his many jumps	94
29	Military emblems worn on Marlin's uniform	95

30	Marlin as a young man just out of service and headed for college	98
31	Marlin in 1968 as a businessman	104
32	Children, Kathy, Eric, and Jean	116
33	Contemporary home in Davenport, Iowa	134
34	Marlin and Marg freezing their buns at Super Bowl VI, Tulane Stadium in New Orleans	137
35	Home on Huntington Court in Naperville, Illinois	150
36	One of Marlin's Burger King Restaurants, including a playground	161
37	Home on Pepperwood Court	162
38	The great room at Pepperwood Court	163
39	The kitchen at Pepperwood Court	163
40	Kris holding Leah, Jenny, Jessy, Lindy, Adam. Kate, Kim, Daniel, and Julie	174
41	Marlin in "Fiddler on the Roof" in 2003	179
42	Helicopter setting down on top of a glacier in Alaska	183
43	Dee Lindberg, Marg, and Marlin on top of a glacier	184
44	Floating in the Dead Sea, Israel	185
45	One of the two pontoon planes that took us to Lake Kagianagami	186
46	One of the sea planes that took us to Lake Kagianagami	187
47	Sons, Paul and Eric, and their cousin Jeff Bergeron, in the center, with the catch that day	188
48	Cabin at Lake Kagianagami	189
49	Plenty for dinner and even brought some home	189
50	Paul with a mess of fish, Geoff Bergeron and Eric in the background	190
51	Marlin's 1992 Vogue motor home with tow car	192
52	The Vogue Motor Home factory in Prior, **OK**	192
53	Son-in-law Doug Elvin	196
54	Doug Elvin and daughter Kathy	197
55	Connor, Jason Roy, Tegan, Kristin, and Coda	201
56	Kathy and Eric saying their prayers	203
57	Giving Eric a haircut in kitchen in Ohio	204
58	Eric, 17, Varsity football at Central High in Naperville	205
59	Eric in high school	207

60	Daughter-in-law Jayne Reishus, married to son Eric	208
61	Granddaughter Kim on the tennis team	209
62	Kim's graduation	209
63	Grandson Daniel with his keychain collection	210
64	Flag girl granddaughter Julie	210
65	Eric and Jayne and their children, Julie, Dan, and Kim	211
66	Eagle Scout Badge	211
67	Grandson Daniel— Eric and Jayne's youngest	212
68	Kim, Julie, and Dan about 1997	212
69	Dan earns Eagle Scout	215
70	Lindy and Jessy	219
71	Sisters, Jessy and Lindy as children	219
72	Daughter Jean about 1998	219
73	Granddaughter Lindy	220
74	Great grandson Dakota	220
75	Granddaughter Lindy	220
76	Granddaughter Jessy	220
77	Great grandson Ryley	220
78	Jessy and husband Eliot Henry with children Rylee and Dakota	221
79	Marg and Marlin at Melinda's (Lindy) graduation in 2006	221
80	Bride and groom, Lindy and Adam Connley	222
81	Parents of the bride, Jean and Cliff Martin	222
82	Adam and Lindy's engagement picture	223
83	Paul in high school	228
84	Paul in Naperville Youth Football league	228
85	Paul in college	230
86	Paul and Jana's engagement picture	230
87	Jana graduates from North Central College, Naperville, Illinois	231
88	Eagle Scout Badge	232
89	Granddaughter Leah	232
90	Grandson Adam	232
91	Kate	233
92	Jana and Paul with their three children: Kate, Leah, and Adam	233
93	Dale's high school graduation picture, 1942	239
94	The USS DALE	241
95	Donna Mae and Dale with Allan, Becky, and David	242

96	Donna Mae and Dale	243
97	Gene's high school graduation picture, 1956	245
98	Gene and his wife Kay	246
99	Condo on Marco Island	252
100	View from condo on Marco Island	252
101	Arrow points to Marco Island condo	253
102	Marlin and Marg	254
103	Monarch Landing Retirement Community	255
104	Clubhouse at Monarch Landing	256
105	Courtyard at Monarch Landing	257
106	Marlin, Gene, and Dale (2000)	259
107	Margaret and Ann	260
108	Kris with her new son and baptismal dress made by Grandma Annetta in 1895	260
109	Marlin and Marg and her sister Ann and Greg, Marg's brother-in-law	261
110	Earl and Helen Olson with Marg and Ann	261
111	Identical twins, Will and Jacob	262
112	Jenny, Kathy's daughter	262
113	Jenn and husband Kyle	262
114	Kris and husband Jason and sons	263
115	Kristy	263
116	Marlin and Marg, Gene and Kay, Dale and Donna Mae	264
117	Presented Miss Willis with a Golden Apple engraved "Teacher of the Century"	264
118	Eric and Marlin playing ball at Field of Dreams with the original cast of the movie *Field of Dreams*	265
119	Reishus reunion at Jerry Reishus's farm just outside of Cottonwood	265
120	Cat Taffy	266
121	Jenny, Kathy, Kris, and Marg	266
122	Family dog Archie	266
123	Jean, Marg, Helen Olson, Marg's mother, Ann, Marg's sister and Kathy and dog Archie	267
124	Vacation home in Galena, IL. President Grant's hometown	267
125	Earl Olson, Marg's dad	267
126	Marlin and Marg, Gene and Kay, Dale and Donna Mae	268

127	Kathy, Paul, Marg, Eric, Jean, and Marlin	268
128	The Reishus coat of arms	270
129	Genealogy of the Reishus Family	271
130	Descendants of Sondre Sondreson and Ragnild Eivinsdtr	278
131	Page from family Bible of Olaf Sondre Reishus	283
132	Map location of Reishus ancestors family farm	285
133	Reishus farm location	286
134	Church in Norway where Sondre and Ragnild were married	288
135	Norwegians living in Minnesota, according to 1880 census	289
136	Norway census, 1801	290
137	Letter from Sondre to Knut, January 28, 1879	293
138	Translation of letter from Sondre to Knut	296
139	Even Olson Reishus and Anna Teigen Reishus	297
140	Descendants of Tobias and Anna Reishus, 1910	299
141	Picture of descendants	300
142	Tobias Knudson Reishus and Anna Kolhei Reishus	322
143	Reishus descendants	322
144	District of New York, Port of New York (passenger list)	323
145	Family of Knute and Annetta Reishus, 1944	326
146	Reishus ancestors	334
147	Page from church records in Norway recording the birth of Even Olsen	335

FOREWORD

ON JUNE 3, 1930, I was born just as the country was entering the Great Depression. My father had been a homebuilder, but the Depression put an end to that. There were no jobs, and as a family, we were beginning to scrape the bottom of the barrel. One Sunday afternoon, I was sitting with my dad on the front porch of our home in Cottonwood as he started telling me what happened one day when I was about four years old. As a teenager listening to my dad, I didn't realize how desperate those times were at the beginning of World War II.

As Dad reflected back to those dark days, I could see the tears welling up in his eyes. He started to shake.

"I returned home from another empty day of job hunting. Your mother gave me a short list of grocery items and asked if I could go to the store for those few things. I had no checking account, no savings, no job, and only seventeen cents to my name."

In those days there were no supermarkets or credit cards. Dad walked the five blocks to Ed Carlson's grocery store, a store that was the equivalent of a convenience store today. Fortunately, Dad knew the owner, Ed, as they were both members of the same Lutheran Church. Dad asked him for credit for some groceries. Ed nodded. "I promise I'll pay you back," he said.

"There was nothing extra in the two bags he sat down on the counter, no frills, just the basics, but more than Mom had on the list," he said quietly, struggling to keep his emotions in check.

"Ed gave me credit when I was really broke, and he believed me when I said I would pay him back. Ed was a great guy."

"Did Mom know you were that broke?" I asked.

"No, she had her hands full taking care of you and Dale. It was ten years before I told her."

That was the first time I saw my dad cry. He had no savings account, no checking account, a wife, two kids, no job and only seventeen cents to his name. I couldn't fathom anyone being that broke. Even little kids I knew had more money than that. I remember feeling afraid as I listened to him.

Through my school years, one might say that I majored in sports and considered academics the extracurricular activity. No matter what the sport, I loved competition. I wanted to play, compete, and win. My competitive spirit just wouldn't quit, and I still have it today. High school sports drilled competition, team play, and the will to do whatever it takes to succeed into my head. That same spirit of competition carried over into the military and my business life.

The summer before my eighth grade year, I met one particular girl by the name of Margaret Olson, whose family moved to Cottonwood. Two and a half years later, in the summer after the tenth grade, there was a key moment that changed my destiny. Four couples had piled into the same car to go to a movie. After the movie, the driver was taking each of us home. That night, Marg's date was Boomer Dahl. My date had been dropped off, and I was sitting in the front seat. Marg, Boomer, and another couple were riding in the back seat. As we pulled up to my house, I turned around to Marg and asked, "Will you go out with me next week?" It was a gutsy move with her date sitting right there. She quickly said, "Yes." The following week, it was my turn to drive. After the movie, I dropped everyone else off before taking Marg home. I walked her to the door and after a little small talk asked, "Can I kiss you goodnight?"

She replied, "No, not on the first date."

That answer was okay with me because that implied there would be more dates. Marg and I dated steady for almost five years before becoming engaged. We were married February 1, 1953.

In 1948, after graduating high school, I wasn't sure what I wanted to do for a career. My parents encouraged me to go to Dunwoody Industrial Institute in Minneapolis. I took their advice and completed a two-year course in heating and air conditioning. Then, like many American men impacted by the North Korean invasion of South Korea on June 25, 1950, I made the decision to enlist. During that first year in the service, an "awakening" occurred that was very important. I was not impressed with many of the officers I encountered, and I was convinced I could do what they were doing and do it better. That "awakening" took me to a higher level of achievement, not just in the military but also through life.

I graduated Officer Candidate School, completed jump school, and received my airborne qualification. After finishing my military service as an officer with the 82nd Airborne Division, I remained in the Reserves for another eleven years. For several years I held the rank of Captain, and would have been up for Major had I stayed in the Reserves. But I had had enough of the military and asked for and received an honorable discharge.

The day after I graduated from Officer Candidate School, Marg and I were married. As I was released from active duty, she completed her training as a registered nurse.

After taking a brief time off, I moved at a rapid pace through the academic subjects at the University of Minnesota and completed a four-year Bachelors Degree in three years. It was now time to get serious about making a living and providing for my family.

In June 1957, the economy was in a downturn, and graduates could not be overly picky about what job they would take. I was fortunate to receive a management position with Babcock and Wilcox Company in their management-training program. I moved up the ranks, but what I really wanted was to be in sales. That opportunity came, and I made the jump first with Freiden and then with Honeywell.

Working for Honeywell was a fantastic experience. I had great success as a sales rep and was elected to their President's Club as well as holding the distinction of "Salesman of the Year." Honeywell promoted me to the position of sales manager and then to branch manager where I exceeded their goals and continued to have great success.

My business career in sales had been good, but I was ready to change direction. In 1980, I started my first Burger King franchise. Six years later on April 10, 1986, my son Eric joined me in our first BK store under the ME Inc. Corporation.

Over the next several years, with hard work and good planning, I bought, built, and operated thirty-six Burger King franchise restaurants. We sold all our stores on January 20, 2006. Eric and I were in business together for twenty years. Later that year, we also sold most of the BK real estate as well.

With years of success in the business world, in the summer of 2006, Marg and I moved to Monarch Landing, a retirement community located in Naperville, Illinois. This has been a fantastic move, one that Marg and I enjoy immensely.

We continue to winter in Marco Island, Florida and enjoy our vacation home in Galena, Illinois, hometown of President Grant.

Life has been good.

HIGHLIGHTS IN THE LIFE OF MARLIN B. REISHUS

June 3, 1930	Born in Richfield Township, Minnesota
June 1948	Graduated high school
September 1950	Joined the Air Force
March 17, 1951	Proposed to Marg
January 31, 1953	Graduated OCS
February 1, 1953	Marriage to Margaret Olson
September 1954	Started University of Minnesota
November 9, 1954	Birth of Katherine Ann
March 5, 1956	Birth of Eric Marlyn
June 1957	Graduated University of Minnesota
July 1, 1957	Started with Babcock & Wilcox
September 11, 1958	Birth of Jean Susan
February 1960	Started with Freiden
August 1962	Started with Honeywell
December 1963	Moved to Naperville
1963	Elected to Honeywell's President's Club
November 2, 1965	Birth of Paul Brian
1967	Marco Island
1968	Promoted to Branch Manager
1980	Opened my first Burger King
April 10, 1996	First BK store under the ME Inc. Corporation
January 20, 2006	Sold our Burger King business and most of our Burger King real estate. After 26 years as a Burger King franchise, I retired.
2006	Moved to Monarch Landing Retirement Community
August 2010	I have finally completed my book. Hope you enjoy.

IF IT IS TO BE IT IS UP TO ME

FAMILY PICTURE OF MOM, DAD, GENE, MARLIN, AND DALE

Part 1

I Always Compete to Win

If one advances confidently in the direction of his dreams, and endeavors to live the life that he has imagined, he will meet with a success unexpected in common hours.

—HENRY DAVID THOREAU

1

EARLY MEMORIES

It is incumbent on every generation to pay its own debts as it goes. A principle which if acted on would save one half the wars of the world.
—THOMAS JEFFERSON

THINKING BACK TO MY EARLY memories, several incidents spring to mind. One of the first was hearing Mom say, "Marlin, you know how you've been having a lot of sore throats? Well, we are going to the doctor to get your throat fixed."

Just before the age of six I was taken to Swedish Hospital in Minneapolis to have my tonsils and adenoids removed. In those days, whether you had sore throats or not, it was quite customary to remove the tonsils and adenoids at an early age to avoid possible problems in the future.

I told my brother Dale who was six years my senior, "I'm going to the hospital to get my throat fixed." I was happy about it. Mother made me think it was a big deal.

At the hospital, I recall Mom walking with me down a long hall and into a very sterile, white, strange room that scared me. Then a stern-faced nurse dressed in white, wearing a funny looking white cap, came into the room, walked over to where I was lying on the bed and put a gas mask on my face. I was fighting like mad, but the ether anesthetic put me out in seconds. When I woke up in the recovery room, my throat hurt like crazy. Mom was in the room with me, and I started crying profusely.

"They are going to get some ice cream for you," Mom softly

told me. When a nice lady brought in the tray with a large scoop of vanilla ice cream, Mom handed the dish to me. "Eat some ice cream, Marlin. It will make your throat feel better." I thought offering me ice cream was a dirty trick and didn't want any part in it. I dearly loved ice cream and had it so seldom at home because Mother was frugal, and ice cream was extravagant, particularly during those Depression days. But I had the worst sore throat of my life, and couldn't imagine swallowing ice cream. I thought it was mean to bring it to me, especially when they knew I wouldn't take it. "Try one spoonful, Marlin. It will make your throat feel better," Mom kept saying.

I didn't know what she meant. I was not a happy camper and was still crying like crazy, which made my throat feel even worse. All I could say was, "No! No! No!" Eventually I tried some ice cream, and my throat did feel better. I guess the tonsillectomy "fixed" my throat, because I no longer had those frequent spells of sore throat.

Having my tonsils out was actually my second visit to Swedish Hospital. I was born at that hospital on June 3, 1930. The hospital bill was quite different than those of today. I have included a copy of that bill to give you a bit of shock therapy. Please note that Mom and I were scheduled to go home after eight and one half days. But for some reason, Dr. O. H. Peterson (a good Norwegian name), decided we should have another day in the hospital. The extra day was probably just another day of rest, which was common, because there were no complications and the doctor just thought an additional day of rest would be better for mother and baby. The original hospital bill was revised to include the $4.25 for the additional day. The cost was $3.25 per day for Mom and $1.00 per day for me.

Because of the way insurance companies work today, a new mother is lucky if she gets to stay in the hospital more than a day or two.

CHAPTER 1 / *Early Memories*

THE SWEDISH HOSPITAL BILL FOR MARLIN'S BIRTH

When I was born, there was no insurance company to give their approval, because health insurance in those days was extremely rare. Most people, including my folks, didn't have it. In today's vernacular "we weren't covered."

MARLIN AGE TWO, LOOKING VERY GROWN UP

My parents lived in a one-bedroom house on 56th Street and 15th Avenue in Richfield Township, an unincorporated area south of Minneapolis, east of the city of Richfield, Minnesota. We had a Richfield address, but when Minneapolis annexed the area into their city, the address changed to Minneapolis. You might say that we went from Richfield to Minneapolis without ever moving.

Our small house had one bedroom and a half bath. The bathroom had a sink and a commode, but no tub or shower. For our bath on Saturday night, we had a large, oblong, galvanized bathtub that was put in the middle of the kitchen on top of the trap door to the cellar, where Mom kept her canned goods. I slept in a crib, and my brother Dale slept on a sleeper sofa in the living room. I hated our sofa. It was upholstered with horsehide, which really prickled my legs when I sat on it. I would do anything to avoid sitting on that thing.

"The reason people upholster with horsehide is because it lasts forever," Dad said to me one day when I was complaining. "Probably because no one would sit on it," I replied.

Our house sat on the back of a rather large lot. Dad always had plans to build a larger house toward the front of the lot when times were better and things were more affordable, but we never did. Dad decided to build a new two-bedroom house on a lot located on 13th Avenue.

As a little kid, I thought our new house was like a palace, especially compared to our old one-bedroom house. We used the basement in our new house as a playroom. The red concrete floor in the basement was not painted red, but had red dye mixed in the concrete.

Dad eventually sold our little one-bedroom house on the large lot. The last time I was in the area, someone was still living in the same little house.

Next door to our house, there was a vacant lot infested with Minnesota striped gophers. My dad set gopher traps because he didn't want them to migrate into our yard and start burrowing and making their usual mess.

Like most normal, inquisitive kids of five, I decided to investigate one of the gopher traps. Suddenly, "Bang!" One of the traps got me. As fast as my feet could carry me I ran crying back to the house with the trap firmly attached to my hand. My cousin Irene, who was old enough to be my aunt, was visiting at the time. My mother and Irene started laughing as they unlatched the trap from my hand. Mother tried to calm me down and that wasn't easy. I couldn't understand why they were laughing as it wasn't a bit funny to me.

I was wearing coveralls made of striped blue jean material that day and my cousin Irene, who was still amused at the incident, announced to everyone that they had caught a striped gopher.

From that day on, Irene called me the striped gopher. Others took up calling me the striped gopher, which I did not appreciate at all. To me it was very painful and totally humiliating.

As youngsters, my brother Dale and I would walk about four or five blocks from our house to the movies . . . or the "picture show" as we called it. Some Saturdays, three or four of our friends went with us. We didn't go to the "picture show" often, but when we did, it was always on a Saturday because the matinee price for kids was only nine cents. We never bought popcorn or snacks because we simply didn't have money for that kind of extravagance.

DALE NINE, AND MARLIN AGE THREE

The following summer after our move, Dale and a friend built a chug in our garage. A chug was basically a soapbox car like those in the Soap Box Derby. It wasn't fancy, but it was functional. I built a couple of chugs too when I was older. Neither Dale nor I ever entered the Derby races, as our chugs were pretty basic, but we did enjoy going to the Soap Box Derby races.

After it was finished, Dale and his friend painted the chug.

CHAPTER 1 / *Early Memories*

As a five-year-old, I was inquisitive, and I'm sure I bothered the heck out of those two eleven-year-old painters as they put on their finishing touch. Finally Dale had enough of me and swabbed his paintbrush across my bare toes. I went screaming into the house looking for sympathy, but got none. The only thing that was really hurt was my pride, but Mom did help get the paint off my toes.

Dale and I slept in the second bedroom and shared a double bed. Even though the paint had been removed the previous evening, when I woke up early the next morning I was still fuming from the paint job on my toes. It was Sunday, and no one was up at that early hour. Dale was flat on his back and still sound asleep. I thought for a bit about how to get even, but didn't think too long before I hauled off and punched him as hard as my five-year-old body would allow. I scored a direct hit on his nose and quickly scampered out of the room knowing Dale was sure to be after me.

My direct hit had turned out better than I had hoped. Dale had a very bloody nose. With his screaming at six in the morning, Mom was up like a flash tending to Dale, so he wouldn't drip blood on the bed or the floor. That was all that saved me from instant retaliation. I was lucky that it was just a nosebleed and nothing more serious. But when I first saw all that blood, I thought I had caused more serious damage than I had intended. In the end, Dale was okay; his nose stopped bleeding, and I felt better about it. I was still a little bit scared, but I felt good. For once, I had gotten the better of my big brother.

That fall, I started kindergarten at Nathan Hale Elementary School. We had a real sandbox in our classroom at school where everyone wanted to play. The sandbox was on legs, so it was waist high to us kindergartners. Another experience for kindergartners was the little store in our classroom where we could pretend to buy cereal, crackers, canned goods, and other items with play money. The boxes and cans were empty, but we didn't care. We each took turns being the customer, clerk, and cashier. The most fun for me was when it was my turn to be the cashier. We sold things in the store and got to handle the play money. I don't think anyone in the class knew how to make change, but we all pretended that we did.

Another memory was when a local bank sent a representative to open a new savings account for all the kindergarten students and funded each new account with twenty-five cents. We were encouraged to bring a nickel or a dime to school each week to deposit in our savings account. Students received their own savings passbook, so we could see how much we had saved. When the school year ended, I had almost three dollars in my account and thought I was rich. The principle was to teach us to save, which was a very important lesson.

MARLIN AS A YOUNGSTER
SITTING ON THE SOFA

On June 1st 1936, after my kindergarten year was over, we moved to Cottonwood, Minnesota, which happened to coincide with my sixth birthday on June 3rd. My parents gave me an Indian suit for my birthday with slacks, a vest with fancy buttons, Indian ornaments, and a headband that had a tail. The headband and tail were loaded with feathers of every color. Only chiefs wore such fancy headdresses. Man, was I cool. I was the best-dressed Indian in town, and I was the only one to have a chief's headdress. I loved that Indian suit. Later, my brother Gene played in that same suit, and still later, when our boys were young, they enjoyed wearing it too. A lot of kids played cops and robbers, but we played cowboys and Indians, and I was the Indian Chief.

My seventh birthday was especially memorable because I was getting a new dresser for my room. The house in Cottonwood was the first three-bedroom house that we had lived in. My folks obtained a used double bed handed down from some relative, so I had a place to lay my head, but no dresser. In the past, I used two painted orange crates standing on their ends with a couple of boards to make the dresser top. Mother made curtains to hide the clothes stored inside. I thought it was fine and looked nice with the curtains in place of drawers. Besides, it was so easy to get things out of the orange crates because I didn't have to open or close the drawer after retrieving my clothes.

But I got excited when Mom got out the Sears catalogue and we began to look at different dressers. I picked the one I wanted, with the guidance of my mom of course, who had carefully taken me in the direction of the one they had already selected. I was ecstatic. Mom and Dad ordered it, and now we just had to wait for it to arrive.

About a week later, Dad's friend George Keltz, who was also the train depot agent, called to say that a piece of furniture had arrived for us via the Great Northern Railway. Dad was working in town that day. When he wasn't on a job out in the country, he always came home for dinner.

The midday meal was sometimes called noon lunch. The last meal of the day was called supper. My brother Gene still calls it "supper." I guess he still has some "Minnesota" in him, which goes along with the saying that you can take the boy out of the country, but you can't take the country out of the boy.

After lunch (dinner) Dad agreed to go down to the depot to pick up the dresser. Dale and I went with him to the station. On the way home, I rode in the back of the pickup holding the crate steady. Dad and Dale carried it up the stairs to my room, then Dad went back to work, saying he would set it up after work when he returned for the evening.

There were two boxes, one for the mirror and one for the dresser. "I can put the mirror on. It will be no problem," Dale announced to Mom and me with confidence. We took the dresser out of the box, and he proceeded to install the mirror on the back. Mother held one side of the mirror, and I held the other while Dale screwed the mirror to the back of the dresser. There was no frame on the round mirror, just little clips holding the mirror to its backing. After mounting the mirror, Dale thought the clips should be tightened a bit. When he got to the second clip, we heard a "**PING**" as the mirror cracked from top to bottom. At first, I didn't understand what happened, as I was still behind the mirror inspecting Dale's handiwork, but then I saw my brand new mirror was cracked.

Dale felt terrible, and I was upset for a short time. But I had a new dresser, with real drawers and a mirror. Sure it was cracked, but for my first seven years I didn't even have a mirror. I lived with that cracked mirror for several years. It just didn't bother me. Since it was an accident, Dale wasn't punished, but he felt really bad. That was punishment enough.

2

MY PARENTS

Charity begins at home, but should not end there.
—ANONYMOUS

MY DAD, ORVILLE REISHUS, WAS the oldest of eleven children. He was born February 25, 1895 to Annetta (Miller) Reishus and Knute Reishus. My grandparents had a farm in Yellow Medicine County west of Cottonwood, Minnesota. The fact that Grandma and Grandpa had eleven children made it easier for Grandpa to expand, adding acres of productive land to his farm. Nine of their first ten children were boys, which provided lots of "free" help. To keep all those boys working, Grandpa Knute had nineteen horses harnessed and ready to work.

When Dad was six years of age, he began his formal schooling at a one-room country school a mile from the farm. He didn't speak a word of English, as Norwegian was the only language spoken at home, church, and in town. Even the store clerks spoke Norwegian, so there was really no need for the children to learn English. In fact, there was no opportunity to learn another language until a child started school.

English was the only language spoken at the one room school. There was none of that "English as a second language." English was the language of the future and immigrants who came to America wanted their children to learn "the new language," even if it meant their Norwegian language would die out.

Dad and his siblings learned English in that little country school, and Grandma and Grandpa learned English from their children when they brought their new language home. Eventually, they all spoke fluent English, but with quite a Norwegian brogue. Many mixed Norwegian and English, which made it even more difficult to understand.

School was taught only six months each year and later on it went for seven months. Farm kids were expected to help out during the heavy spring planting time and the fall harvest. Nowadays, the school year is nine plus months. Country schools and the larger schools in Cottonwood and Wood Lake are now part of the consolidated district, with class sizes of about fifty to sixty students.

Grandpa Knute was always one of the first to get the latest farm equipment. New equipment and good technique allowed him to add additional acres of tillable land. Dad often talked about plowing in the field when he was only seven years old. A kid his age would more than likely use a plow with a seat rather than walk behind the plow, as it would be hard to believe that he could handle a walking plow at the tender age of seven.

It was acceptable for farm kids of all ages to skip school when they were needed on the farm. Farm work came first, and schoolwork only if there was time. After eighth grade, virtually all farm kids quit school to help full time on the farm. That practice continued even into the fifties for some farm families. The thinking was if you were going to be a farmer for the rest of your life, there was no need to go to school past eighth grade. State law now requires students continue their schooling until age sixteen.

Virtually all farm kids today finish high school, and a large majority in Cottonwood and the surrounding area go on to college. Norwegian settlers and their descendants placed a high priority on education. Grandpa and Grandma felt a solid education was necessary and important.

After Dad completed eighth grade he was sent to "Aggie School" at the University of Minnesota, located on the St. Paul

(Farm) campus. School was two years long, but it went only seven months per year. Students attending "Aggie School" were expected to return home to help on the farm in the spring and fall. After months of dormitory and cafeteria food it was a real treat for students to eat home cooking again. Almost all of Dad's siblings went to "Aggie School," but many farmers did not send their kids, as they believed it was unnecessary, too expensive, and besides, they needed their help on the farm. Dad's youngest sister Vivian was the only one who graduated from high school and went on to study business.

When my parents were growing up, horses did all farm work. In the days prior to that time, most farmers used oxen, but horses were more reliable and easier to train. The large breeds of draft horses were even more powerful, and all farm horses were fast compared to oxen. Most farmers in our area had switched to horses. However, as with oxen, the use of horsepower still required a lot of manual labor. Grandpa's farm was considered very large compared to the average farm in those days.

Grandma Annetta and Grandpa Knute's farm property sat on the county line. All the farm buildings were in Yellow Medicine County except the hog house. Grandpa used to kid his Lyon County friends and relatives saying that only the pigs lived in Lyon County, and the people lived in Yellow Medicine County.

Dad enlisted in the Army in 1917, shortly after World War I started, and was assigned to Fort Knox, Kentucky for training. Pay for a private was $21 per month. Dad was assigned to help with the horses and mules because he was the only one in his company who knew anything about them. The Army used horses and mules to pull their supply wagons that were loaded with heavy weapons and ammunition. Dad said, "The horses were fine, but the mules were stubborn and hard to handle," and one day an ornery mule kicked him in the stomach. He was transported to the hospital in serious condition. For several days they didn't know if he would recover from the injury.

When my Grandma Reishus learned Dad was in the hospital, she was definitely concerned. She took the train all the way from Cottonwood to Fort Knox, which was located about fifty miles south of Louisville. That was a distance of some seven hundred miles. Keep in mind that this was the first time in her life that Grandma had ever traveled more than fifty miles from home. Dad recovered from that injury, much to the amazement of his doctors. He sported a huge scar across his belly from the surgery, but suffered no long-term disability.

OFF TO FRANCE. DAD SERVED AS A CORPORAL AND SQUAD LEADER OF A HEAVY 30-CALIBER WATER COOLED MACHINE GUN.

After completing training, Dad received his orders and was transported across the ocean to France, joining the 88th Division, and went straight to the front lines. He held the rank of Corporal and was put in charge of a 30-caliber heavy machine gun crew. The 30-caliber heavy machine gun was water-cooled, and still used in the early fifties during the Korean War when I was in the service. It was a heavy brute and an exceptional machine gun. Dad was in line for Sergeant, but was told by his superior officers that he was too nice of a guy to get the promotion. Apparently they thought to be a good sergeant, you had to be tough, and a nice guy wouldn't qualify.

Salvation Army workers came to the front line trenches to *give* the soldiers hot coffee and donuts. When his company was relieved and dropped a mile and a half back behind the line for rest and recuperation, the Red Cross was *selling* coffee and donuts. Of course the "Doughboys" hadn't been paid for quite some time, as there was no reason to pay soldiers on the front line. Soldiers in combat areas wouldn't have any place to spend money anyway. Because of that experience with the Red Cross, Dad was always willing to give to the Salvation Army later in life, but refused to give to the Red Cross. Thousands of other "Doughboys" had the same experience in World War I and refused to give to the Red Cross later on.

My Mother was born on a farm one mile down the country road from the farm where my Dad was born. Mabelle Ree was the youngest of nine children. When she was six years old, her mother tragically died of typhoid fever. Her oldest sister Hannah became her substitute "mother," teaching her how to cook, clean, sew and tend the garden.

After her eighth grade graduation at the country school, Mother worked on the farm helping out for a year before she decided to go to high school. Mother wasn't really needed on the farm to help, as several of her older sisters were still living at home. She talked to her dad about attending high school, and

MOM AND DAD, ORVILLE AND MABELLE REISHUS SHORTLY AFTER THEIR WEDDING. THEY WERE MARRIED IN THE CHURCH PARSONAGE WITH DAD'S BROTHER CLARENCE AND MOM'S SISTER INGA AS THEIR ATTENDANTS.

he agreed she could go. The question became how to get to Cottonwood to the high school, as the farm was five miles from town, and there were no school busses back in those days. Mom knew some people in town whom she contacted and learned about a family that would take her in. She could do cleaning and cooking for them in return for her room and board. It was a good situation for both her and the family. Mom moved to Cottonwood where she attended high school during the week. Sometimes she would go home to the farm on a weekend if she could get a ride with someone or if her dad picked her up. This arrangement continued for four years, which enabled her to graduate as class salutatorian, number two in her class of eighteen. Mom kept all her report cards from first grade through high school, showing her exceptionally good grades. She graduated high school at age nineteen, due to the fact that she worked on the farm for the year before she enrolled. While living in Cottonwood, Orville Reishus and Mom began courting.

Not long after Mom graduated, she and Dad married in the church parsonage with Dad's brother Clarence and Mom's sister Inga as their attendants. They used to say that they were "standing up for them." Clarence and Inga were the only two that knew of the marriage until after Mom and Dad had boarded the train for Minneapolis immediately after the wedding.

Going into the Building Business

After completing a two-year program at Dunwoody Industrial Institute, where he had studied carpentry, Dad was a building contractor and began building houses on the south side of Minneapolis. He would usually have two houses under construction at a time. As long as sales continued, and bank financing was available, he kept building. He sold mostly two bedroom houses during the Roaring Twenties. Sometime in the mid twenties, he built our small one bedroom house with the half bath. That is where they continued to live for the next several years, including the year I was born.

After the stock market crash of 1929, most homebuilders, including my dad, had trouble selling the houses they had built. Eventually Dad's houses sold, but with the Depression putting a damper on everything, many of these small builders wouldn't, or couldn't start another house. Even if they tried, they couldn't get financing or find a potential buyer and many banks closed. Dad was one of the few contractors who continued to build, but at a much slower pace. Often times he was out of work and couldn't start another house because times were so bad.

As the demand for new houses completely dried up, Dad went out of business the same as the others before him. Every day he went out job-hunting riding on the streetcar as it only cost a nickel, which was cheaper than driving his Model T.

There was a couple of really big builders, who kept on building, but at a pace considerably less than before the crash. Orin Thompson was the biggest. Dad and many other small builders had been in competition with the few big contractors. There was no love lost between these two entirely different groups.

Dad told me, "We were black balled. None of the big guys would hire me, and I wasn't the only one. All of the owners of the small building companies were black balled, and we couldn't start another house because we couldn't get the financing."

It was during this time in about 1934 that Dad reached his lowest point financially—the seventeen cents story I told about in the Foreword of this book. He had returned from a fruitless day of job hunting. Mother gave him a short list of groceries that she needed to feed the family and Dad walked the five blocks to Ed Carlson's store and asked Ed for credit. "Ed, I don't have enough money for any of the groceries on my wife's list, but I promise I'll pay you back." Ed believed Dad was honest and sincere and gave him the credit, and Dad came home with two big bags full of groceries. There was nothing extra, no frills, just the basics, but nonetheless, a lot more than Mom had on the list.

When I was a teenager, Dad told me about that day, "Ed was a great guy, and he gave me credit when I was broke, I mean really broke. I didn't tell your mother for almost ten years. She knew we were poor, but didn't know how bad off we were, and I wasn't about to tell her."

The very next day after getting credit at Carlson's grocery and just seventeen cents from being completely broke, Dad got a job with the Federal Land Bank as an appraiser. Dad never forgot that Ed Carlson had given him credit. From that time on, my parents bought everything they could—groceries or whatever—from Carlson's grocery store.

For his tenth birthday in June of 1934, my older brother Dale wanted a bike. We weren't accustomed to expensive gifts, but this was special since it was Dale's tenth birthday. Dad went to Carlson Grocery and asked Ed if he could get a bike for Dale.

Ed got out some catalogs, and they put in the order. There were other hardware stores in the area that carried bikes, but Dad wanted to give his business to Ed Carlson. Likewise, when we moved to Cottonwood, some one hundred and fifty miles away, whenever we went to the twin cities, Dad would always go out of his way in order to fill up on gas at Carlson's grocery.

Dad farmed for three or four years before he got into the construction business. Primarily he built houses, but he did build some small commercial buildings as well. Now he was offered a position as an appraiser. He was qualified to appraise houses, farms, and small commercial properties. Dad never told me what his salary was, but he did tell me later that the Federal Land Bank paid him more than double what he would have agreed to. Some companies cut their employees' salaries several times, but the Federal Government didn't. They kept the salaries the same as before the Depression.

The Federal Land Bank was so busy with foreclosures that they just couldn't keep up. Guys with experience like Dad's were just what they needed. His new job required some travel, so he needed to buy a more reliable car. Armed with a regular paycheck, he purchased a new 1934 Chevrolet, at a cost of a little less than $600. Having lived during the Depression with no extra money, all of a sudden Dad had a good job, and we had a new car.

With all his contacts in the building trades and some extra time on his hands, later that year Dad built our new house on 13th Avenue. Less than a year later, the Federal Land Bank decided that all their appraisers should have a government car to use. Dad was issued a new 1935 Plymouth. We couldn't justify having two cars, so Dad sold the Chevrolet. It took over a month to sell, so during that time we had one new car, one less than a year old, and lived in a house less than one year old. What a change from just a few years prior. We were living the "Life of Riley."

AERIAL PICTURE OF COTTONWOOD, 1995

3

WE MOVED TO COTTONWOOD

*The more you read and observe about this politics thing, the
more you've got to admit that each party's worse than
the other. The one that's out always looks the best.*
—WILL ROGERS

IN 1936, MANY FARMERS EXPERIENCED foreclosures and their land was taken over by the Federal Land Bank. Because we lived in the area, Dad was offered a job with the Federal Land Bank as an appraiser and received a territory in Southwestern Minnesota. Living in the area meant less overnight travel, which was another plus. He was authorized to appraise farms, houses, and small commercial properties and was the only one in the entire state authorized to appraise all three. The only appraisals he was not qualified for were large commercial buildings.

The Depression was particularly hard on the farmers. Stock and crop prices were constantly going down, but mortgages, real estate taxes and other operating expenses remained constant. Those realities, combined with poor yields due to the drought, doomed the majority of the farmers. Over fifty percent of farmers experienced foreclosure, which resulted in the farmer losing his land. A man living in town may have lost his job, but a farmer lost his land and he lost his ability to do the only job he knew—farming. Farm machinery was sold at auction for pennies on the dollar because there was no one with money to buy even at low auction prices. Many felt hopeless and ran away from the only place they had ever known. Some became so desperate they took their lives.

Dad's job was to appraise property after a loan had been foreclosed. It was particularity hard when he knew the farmer personally, but he didn't know the vast majority since he was appraising all over Southwestern Minnesota.

A few farmers in the area were Dad's relatives. Fortunately, none of them lost their farms to foreclosure. Part of the reason they were successful at farming was because the soil around Cottonwood was very rich and produced bumper crops. They also used good farming skills they learned from Grandpa Knute, and all the way back to Grandpa Tobias. In addition to being good farmers, they were all good businessmen, and that helped.

Just before my birthday in June 1936, we moved to Cottonwood. Mom and Dad were eager to move to Cottonwood, since they both grew up on farms in the area. Cottonwood had a population of seven hundred people and was about ninety miles north of the Iowa border, thirty miles east of the South Dakota border, and one hundred forty miles west of Minneapolis.

We moved into a two-story house located on the edge of town with three bedrooms and one bath. It was one of the nicest houses in Cottonwood. Dad got a home mortgage from the bank with a three percent interest rate. The total price of the house was $3,400. When the town folks learned about the sale, they couldn't believe that anyone would pay so much for a house. When I graduated high school in 1948 we were still living in that house.

One afternoon, Dad and I were sitting on the front porch while Mom was in the kitchen preparing Sunday dinner. Dad started talking about the bad times in the thirties and when he was building houses during the Depression. He was competing against Orin Thompson and the other large building companies. "Thompson and other guys employed only a few people and subbed most of the jobs out. I bid on some jobs, but I couldn't get any," Dad said.

"Why not?" I asked.

"Some guys were so eager to get work that they would bid below their costs. I found out what the bids were and figured that they were getting about fifteen cents an hour. It wasn't enough to pay for the overalls they would wear out on the job," he said, exaggerating the point. He didn't have anything good to say about the big builders, especially Orin Thompson, and absolutely nothing good to say about unions.

Dad continued to build a few houses in the early thirties. Union rules stated that there was to be no work on Saturday, but men needed the work and some decided to break the rule. Dad and the other carpenters who worked on Saturday would park their cars a couple of blocks down the street so inspectors patrolling the streets looking for workers breaking the rule wouldn't know in which house they were working. All of the houses on that two-block stretch were in one stage or another of construction.

One Saturday I was out with Dad and a couple of his carpenters while they were working. I was maybe three or four years old. My job was to stand in the window and let him know if I saw anyone. If I spotted anyone suspicious Dad had the men go to the basement and wait for an "all clear" before returning to work. Once I did spy some strange man snooping around the buildings. Everyone except Dad got in the basement. Dad was careful not to be seen while he watched the guy. That day the inspector walked from house-to-house, but occasionally skipped some. Fortunately, he just walked by the house where Dad and his crew were working, and nothing came of it.

Another Saturday there was a man working at the house next door to where Dad was working who wasn't so fortunate. A small building contractor friend of Dad's was building the house. The builder had subbed out the painting, and the painter was painting the outside of the house when a union guy caught him. Saturday work was an absolute no no. The union position was that if there was so much work that it required someone to work on Saturday, the contractor should hire another union man to work during the week. They wanted more union men working, and no one working overtime on Saturday. Well, this guy was painting the siding, and the union guy picked up a bucket of sand and threw it all over the wet paint.

"Why would the union guy throw sand like that?" I asked Dad. He told me, "They wanted to teach them a lesson." The union guy knew it would be extra work for the painter, and the union wanted to punish him for working on Saturday. Both the contractor and the painter were fined. The union did a lot of dirty tricks like that. Dad was not a fan of the unions, that's for sure.

After working several years as an appraiser, business began to slow down. Dad's job with the Federal Land Bank ceased, as there were fewer foreclosures and fewer appraisals. Dad became an independent appraiser, but it turned into a part-time job because there was not much need for that kind of work anymore.

In 1938, Dad bought Hans Appleton's construction business and was back to work as a general contractor working out of Cottonwood. This continued for a couple years. In January 1940 the construction business was so slow in and around Cottonwood that we moved to Minneapolis where Dad started building. The move back to Minneapolis had been a temporary one, an experiment to test the waters, so to speak. During that time Dad built three new houses.

After six months in Minneapolis, Dad and Mom made the decision to move back to Cottonwood. Before we left Cottonwood we had rented our house, including the furniture, to three schoolteachers. If my parents stayed in Minneapolis, they would need to find housing, which in 1940 was not a problem. But they would need to return to Cottonwood to get our furniture and personal belongings, and rent out the house full time, or sell it.

I was in the fourth grade at Nathan Hale Elementary and Dale was a sophomore at Roosevelt High School. Mom and

CHAPTER 3 / *We Moved to Cottonwood*

Dad asked Dale and me what we wanted to do. I was only ten years old, and it really didn't matter to me. I had grown accustomed to Minneapolis and had a whole new set of friends. Dale had completed his sophomore year and thought Cottonwood was the only acceptable answer. Both Mom and Dad were almost ambivalent. We had been renting a furnished home in Minneapolis for the past few months. It would be easy to return home to Cottonwood.

The decision was made to move back to Cottonwood, and I must say, Dale was the one that influenced the decision, Mom and Dad just granted Dale's wish. When we returned to Cottonwood, Dad started building again. Things began to pick up as the economy slowly began to recover from the Great Depression.

COTTONWOOD RESTAURANT MENU
DURING THE DEPRESSION

DAD DRIVING A NEW 1938 INTERNATIONAL PICKUP TRUCK IN THE COTTONWOOD GOLDEN ANNIVERSARY PARADE ADVERTISING HIS CONSTRUCTION BUSINESS WITH CARPENTERS, DON IVAN ANDERSON, DON OLSON, DON NELSON, AND MARLIN REISHUS. THE HOUSE IN THE BACKGROUND IS THE HOUSE I LIVED IN FROM AGE SIX TO 20 WHEN I JOINED THE SERVICE.

Attack on Pearl Harbor

On December 7, 1941 the Japanese Air Force viciously attacked our country. The lives of all Americans would never again be the same. Dad's carpenters joined the war effort, and it became very difficult to get building material. H. W. Ross Lumber in Cottonwood was less than half full, and Tom Gunderson, the lumber yard manager, told Dad he couldn't get any more. In some ways, it didn't matter because he had lost all his carpenters to the service, and couldn't build anything even if he was able to get building materials.

With construction at a standstill, Dad rented a farm, purchased a couple of workhorses, some used machinery, and hired a retired farmer to help plant crops. He bought a few sows and fifty sheep. We were now in the farming business, raising corn and oats for harvest and pigs and sheep to sell. The profits were pretty meager for all the time and effort it took.

To make additional money, Dad decided to raise chickens for eggs. With used material, he built a twenty-by-eighty-foot chicken coop across the alley on a couple of empty lots he had purchased. When the coop was completed, he bought 2,200 hen chicks. When the chickens were full-grown, they began laying eggs (a lot of eggs). We filled about six thirty-dozen egg cases per day. My parents and I shared the daily job of caring for the chickens. After school, my job was to feed and water the chickens and gather the eggs. Mom usually gathered the eggs in the morning.

Our chickens peak egg laying lasted about two years. When production dropped we sold all the chickens. The chicken coop had been built with the idea of dismantling it at a later date. There was a lot of work involved to disassemble the building and reinstall various parts on local farms. The parts were sold to local farmers. Of course the farmers had to have a foundation and concrete slab, which meant more work for Dad and his crew.

After the chicken coop was removed, the only thing that remained was the slab. I ordered a basketball hoop from the Sears catalog and found a short telephone pole that I put up on one end of the concrete slab. All of this was about to become a basketball court. My friend Roger Larson, a high school classmate, did the same on the other end of the court. We painted the circles and lines on the basketball court for daytime use, but we couldn't play after dark. So we got another longer telephone pole and placed it on one side at mid court. We strung wires from our garage and presto . . . we had a lighted basketball court. All the neighbor kids used that basketball court for years and years.

Sometime in the forties, Dad ran for city council and won. In addition to the normal duties of a city councilman, he was in charge of the city water and sewer system. Cottonwood made a lot of upgrades to their water system during his term as a city councilman. He was also active in the Masons, Shriners, American Legion, Last Mans Club, and Lions Club.

Mother was a Sunday school teacher at Christ Lutheran. I think she taught Sunday school for over twenty-five years, and was active in several church activities and church groups.

MOM AND DAD AFTER THEIR 40TH WEDDING ANNIVERSARY

After the war, the construction began to pick up, but finding carpenters was still tough. Dad's foreman job required climbing up and down buildings on the construction site. His body was beginning to wear out at what he described as "a young man's job." In 1947, approaching his mid-fifties, Dad was no longer able to keep up physically. He made the decision to sell his business to Lauris Gniffke. Lauris was an excellent carpenter who worked for Dad before the war and had the job of bombardier in the war.

Dad continued to appraise land and buildings, mostly for the Veterans Administration as war veterans returned home and began to purchase property on the G. I. Bill. But this job was only part time.

Oscar Naab, the local owner and operator of the Coast-to-Coast hardware store, was looking to sell. Dad heard about it and bought the store. Dad ran the Coast-to-Coast in Cottonwood for twelve years before selling out to a guy by the name of Tritz. After he sold the store, Dad retired from a long career.

In 1964 at the age of 63, Mom died of a coronary thrombosis. Dad had several physical problems and used two canes for walking. When anyone asked him about it, he would always reply, "I'm just wearing out." His hips were in need of replacement, but of course that kind of procedure was in its infancy, and with no health insurance and no Medicare like today, it was cost prohibitive. Three years after Mom died, Dad passed away at the age of 72.

A few facts about Cottonwood:

1. Cottonwood Lake was dry in 1902 and again in the early 1930s.

2. There was a common belief that the drought of the 1930s was sudden. In fact, there was a steady drop in rainfall beginning in the mid 1920s. The lowest amount of rainfall occurred in 1934 and 1936. Parts of the Cottonwood Lake bottom were used for farming, but crops planted in the lake bed were very poor because even the lake bed was too dry.

3. Cottonwood has a contest every winter whereby tickets are sold to allow the recipient to predict when a car will fall through the ice on Cottonwood Lake. The winner, usually the closest by mere seconds, wins a prize. A local charity is the beneficiary.

4. Another contest is the Fishless Derby, which is a fishing contest held yearly to see who catches the least amount of fish. Anyone caught with a hook of any kind on their line is fined and disqualified.

5. In 1867, Halvor Gullickson, a Norwegian immigrant became Normania Township's first white settler.

6. The first white settlers arrived in Lukus (Cottonwood) Township in 1871.

7. In 1880, Silo Lutheran Church was organized in Cottonwood. The Norwegians pronounce Seelo the same as they pronounced Silo like the feed storage facility on many farms. The name was changed to Christ Lutheran Church in 1952. Their first church building was built in 1889.

8. Cottonwood was organized in 1888.

9. In 1898, a telephone system was installed in Cottonwood. A. E. Anderson's phone number was number one and his insurance office phone was number two. In the 1930s, my parents' home phone was number nine, until the dial system was installed in the 1950s.

10. Tobias Reishus, my great grandfather, served as the first Sheriff of Yellow Medicine County.

11. L.T. Reishus served as Mayor of Cottonwood from 1900–1910. Other Reishus family members served as mayors as well.

12. In 1900, Cottonwood's population was 594. In 2010, the population is estimated to be approximately 1200. Cottonwood is one of the few towns in Southwestern Minnesota whose population is growing.

13. In 1900, hail stuck Grandpa Knute's farm, and it was too late to plant another crop. The insurance company paid him only the cost of his seed. From that day forward, Grandpa refused to purchase hail insurance. Over the next fifty years, farms on all sides of him suffered severe hail loss, but Grandpa's farm was spared every time.

14. Boy Scouts started in Cottonwood in 1928.

15. In 1929, the Cottonwood Junior Legion baseball team won the state championship.

16. August 1, 1930 the thermometer reached 107 degrees Fahrenheit.

17. On February 16, 1936 the thermometer reached minus

39 degrees, and for ten days in a row, it didn't get above minus 20 degrees Fahrenheit.

18. George Koeltz, a friend of Dad's was the Depot agent for over fifty years in Cottonwood for the Great Northern Railroad.

19. In 1939, starting with one bus, Wendell Kundson began to provide bus service for school kids who lived on farms. Thirty-three years later when Wendell retired, he operated nine busses.

20. In 1940, an $18,000 bond issue was passed by the city council to install a citywide sewer system, with considerable controversy, I might add. Cottonwood was one of the first small towns in Southwestern Minnesota to install city sewers. The Federal Government under the **WPA** paid a large part of the cost.

21. The Armistice Day Snowstorm on November 11, 1940 caught many by surprise. Many farm animals died in the fields because they could not find their way to the barn. People who were duck hunting on the lakes froze to death before they could get to shore. This did not happen in Cottonwood, but it did in many lakes in Minnesota. It was Cottonwood's most severe storm in history.

22. In 1942, Leslie Larson, Donna Mae's father, won a prize from DeKalb Seed Corn for yielding the highest number of bushels of corn per acre. The average yield was 35 bushels per acre that year, and Leslie got 107.53 bushels per acre, which was an unheard of amount for the time.

23. In 1944, German war prisoners worked on the railroad keeping the rail bed secure. All across the country, German prisoners worked to help our war effort, as so many of our boys were off fighting in the war.

24. In December of 1952, my Dad bought the Retrum's grocery store to expand his Coast-to-Coast Store. A few

days later, Gene contracted polio, so Dad delayed the expansion of the Coast-to-Coast and ran the grocery store for a year.

25. In May 1953, the Lions Club was started in Cottonwood with fifty-eight charter members and it flourishes as the only service club in Cottonwood.

26. In 1957, under the direction of Mayor Wally Olson, Cottonwood installed curbs and gutters and paved streets throughout the town. They were one of the first small towns in Southwest Minnesota to do so.

27. C. W. Reishus Park was dedicated September 14, 1965, in memory of Clarence. He served on the city council and was the Treasurer of the Lions Club for years. He was affectionately known as "Mr. Lion." Clarence, Dad's brother, was born a year after Dad and was close to him all his life. He told everyone who asked that his middle initial stood for "work."

4

HIGH SCHOOL

Never Explain, Never Complain, Just Do It!
—ANONYMOUS

WHEN I WAS FOURTEEN, I started working summers with my dad as a carpenter's helper in his construction company. I earned forty cents an hour, and thought that was a lot of money. Most of the time, he and his crew worked ten-hour days, six days a week. So did I. Occasionally on a Saturday, the crew would quit work at four o'clock, after working eight hours. I liked when that happened because Saturday night was a big night in Cottonwood. There were more people downtown Saturday night than any other time during the week. The high school band would set up on the street corner in front of the bank, and former high school band members brought their instruments and joined in for a one-hour concert. Chairs and music stands were literally on the street. The area was roped off, so people knew not to park in those four or five parking places. After every piece, people in the cars would honk their horns, which was their version of applause.

The summer I was fifteen, Dad gave me a raise to seventy-five cents an hour. Mother thought it was crazy for a kid so young to make that kind of money, but he explained to her that I could do a lot of things as well as the regular carpenters, so he thought the seventy-five cents was just fine. I continued to work summers until my senior year when Dad sold his construction business and bought the local hardware store.

While I was in high school, I didn't pay too much attention to my studies. I majored in sports, minored in girls, and considered academic subjects as extracurricular activities.

Undoubtedly, my primary focus during those four years of high school was on sports. I loved sports. No matter the sport, I wanted to play, compete, and win. I started playing football when I was in the eighth grade. I was much smaller than the older guys, but I did get in for a few plays.

At the beginning of my freshman season, Dad said, "I'll give you $100 not to play. Football is just too rough a game, and I don't want you to get hurt." My brother Dale had played football for years, so I thought I should too.

Dad wouldn't forbid me to play, but he made it clear that he didn't approve. Playing football was more important to me than the money. At the beginning of my sophomore year Dad offered me $200 not to play. At the beginning of my junior year he offered me $300, and at the beginning of my senior year he offered me $400. I continued to play football all through high school because I loved the game.

I wasn't a starter my freshman year, but nevertheless, the coach used me quite a bit. Like most small towns in Minnesota we played six-man football. We didn't have the opportunity to watch the pros or college football teams play on television, so we didn't know there was any other way to play the game except six-man. Our rules were a bit different. If we got a first down, it wasn't first and ten, it was first and fifteen. And there couldn't be a quarterback sneak because there had to be a clear pass in the backfield. The quarterback couldn't just put the ball in the belly of the running back as he went by. It had to be a clear pass, which could be as short as a few inches, but the ball had to be in the air for that brief time. This resulted in more fumbles and more excitement. Everyone was an eligible receiver, so it was a wide-open game. Even the center was eligible to catch a pass, and a pass that didn't go past the line of scrimmage was a live ball. It was treated as if it was a fumble. Like arena football, it was a high scoring game, with the winning team often scoring forty points or more. And the field was only eighty yards long, which contributed to higher scores.

When Gene was a senior, all the six-man teams switched to eight-man teams by adding two guards. A couple of years later, they added a back, and the nine-man rules were the same as eleven-man. The following year they played a couple of games of nine-man and the rest eleven-man. Because of the consolidation of school districts, all schools got larger, and soon every school was playing eleven-man. It is kind of sad to see the era of six-man football fade into history. It was truly an exciting game.

In one game in my sophomore year, our team was ahead by two or three touchdowns. I was on the field with the second team. It was fourth down, and we had to punt. I was the punter and kicked it as far as I could. It went high and looked like a high short kick. The wind was to our back and carried the ball down the field, so to my surprise it turned out to be a really long punt. At least the punt was long for me. The other team took the ball and ran up the sidelines. All of a sudden I was the only guy between a huge 200-pound ball carrier, running behind two rather large blockers and the goal line. All three of them were larger than me, but it was my job to stop them, so I laid out a body block and got all three, saving a touchdown. Unfortunately, they got me too. I broke my clavicle bone and was out for the season. I hated to think what my dad would say. With my arm in a sling supporting a broken collarbone, I went home to face the music. Surprisingly, Dad didn't say much. He knew I was hurting, and guess he thought that was punishment enough.

I broke three ribs my junior year, and in my senior year I broke my nose. There were no face guards on the helmets in those days. After I broke my nose, coach purchased a nose guard and had the local shoe shop and harness maker install it on my helmet. It was good to have the extra protection. However, in those days there was no rule against grabbing the nose guard, so that was bad. In one game I was tackled after catching a pass, and I slid across the grass on my face with the nose guard plowing a furrow in the field. If it hadn't been for that nose guard, it would have been my nose plowing that furrow in the field. My eyes were open, and my face, including my recently broken nose, was only a half an inch from the ground. I think I skidded some two feet or more with the grass and mud flying by my face. When I finally stopped, I thought, "Thank God for that nose guard." I didn't have a scratch on my face, and my nose wasn't touched. Nowadays, grabbing the face guard earns the tackler's team a severe penalty because doing so can easily cause a neck injury.

I played basketball, football, baseball, and ran track. I wasn't very good at baseball, so most of the time I played right field. They always put the poorest player in right field. Almost all players were right handed, and hits would go to the left side of the diamond. I wasn't very fast and ran the 440 and the 880 in track. While I never did win a race, I had a lot of fun. I also competed in the high jump and was pretty good. At least I thought I was until I got to the district tournament and found out how good some of the guys from other schools were.

I was a starter on the football team from my sophomore year on. We had a good team when I was a sophomore, with my teammate Vernon Riggie making All State. He played fullback on offense and end on defense. The opposing teams made a net minus four yards around his end. That's a net minus four yards for the entire season! It was unbelievable he was so good. I think we lost only one game in my sophomore year, and that was the district championship, losing in the closing seconds by three points. My junior year we had an outstanding team too, and lost only one game. Then came my senior year when I was the only returning starter. We won our first and last football game and lost the five in between. We didn't have a good season, but we had fun. In the opinion of most of the team, and the adults too, at least a part of the reason we lost so many games was that Mr. Dainsberg, our new coach, just wasn't any good. The school board must have thought so too. He was not asked to come back the next year.

In my junior year we also had an outstanding basketball team. All the starters were seniors, and I was the sixth man. We lost only three games all year. The first game we lost was to Lynd by only three points. Later in the year when Lynd came to Cottonwood, we lost by two points. Our next loss was in the district tournament to Marshall, a town of over 3,500 and the biggest school in the district. Cottonwood didn't play Marshall during the season and would play them only if we happened to be their draw in the tournament. The next night after we lost to Marshall, Lynd beat Marshall and went to the regional tournament. They won both their games in the region and went to the state tournament where they beat Duluth Denfield by five points and Minneapolis Marshall by fifteen points.

Only one game was left to win and Lynd would be crowned the 1947 State Champs. I should add that Lynd was a town of 212 people. The newspapers announced that after Lynd beat Duluth Denfield in the first game of the state tournament, there were only twelve people left in town. Everyone had gone to Minneapolis to watch Lynd play at the University of Minnesota field house. After Lynd won the second game against Minneapolis Marshall, there was only one person left in town. Two hundred eleven out of two hundred twelve had gone to watch Lynd play in the state tournament.

There was only one tournament in those days. Big schools and little schools all played in one tournament, not like today where there are several brackets, one bracket for each size school. Lynd lost in their last game against Austin, a large school in the southern part of the state. Cottonwood finished the year with three losses by a total of ten points, and two of them were to Lynd, the state runner-up. Not a bad year. Sports fans in Minnesota still talk of the time when little Lynd was the runner-up in the state tournament. We had the best team ever for Cottonwood, but Lynd, a team in our same district had a super team that year.

I loved competition and had a spirit that just wouldn't quit. I still have that spirit today. I want to win. Playing sports, competition, team play, and the will to do whatever it takes to win was in my head. That same spirit carried over into my time in the military and business life.

My first car . . . almost

Louie Varpness lived about a block from us, and he had an old Model T Ford that had been sitting in his back yard. It was up on blocks to keep it out of the dirt and had been there for as long as I could remember. I was earning money working in Dad's construction business during the summer, and I had an itch for a car. I told Dad that Louie Varpness's old Model T was just sitting there, "They don't use it, and I would like to buy it." I was surprised when Mom and Dad said it would be okay. Mr. Varpness offered to sell it to me for eight dollars. It didn't run, and I wasn't sure if I could get it to run. The rims were there, but it didn't have any tires. I bought the car and pulled it home on the rims with Dad's pickup. I knew it needed new plugs and points, and Dad agreed to pick them up when he was in Minneapolis the next week.

I got the car running (barely), but it all ended there. I didn't have enough money for tires, so I kind of dismissed the whole idea and sold the car to Elwood Nelson. Now I wish I had kept it. A Model T in running condition now sells for about ten thousand dollars. Oh, well!

Learning to sail

I was in my early teens when my brother Dale was in the Navy. Dale had a sailboat he kept in Dad's carpenter shop. He had built the 14-foot sailboat in 1941 and 1942 and was very proud of that boat. I used to see the boat in Dad's shop and was eager

CHAPTER 4 / *High School*

MARLIN'S HIGH SCHOOL GRADUATION PICTURE IN 1948

to experiment with learning to sail. I was only thirteen and had no experience with boats of any kind, much less a sailboat.

One afternoon I took the boat out of the back of my dad's shop where it had been stored for quite some time. I hoisted it up on a pair of sawhorses and inspected it. I didn't know if it needed paint or not, but decided to paint it regardless. I did a good job on both the outside and the inside of the boat.

So far I was doing great, but wondered what would happen when I put the boat in the water. Some willing volunteers helped me haul Dale's boat the four blocks down to Cottonwood Lake. I couldn't possibly have managed to get the boat to the lake on my own. When we first put the boat in the water, it leaked. I thought that might happen and hoped when the wood swelled, the leaks would stop, which they did. I was ready to set sail. Well . . . not quite yet. I wanted to get my sea legs, so I fooled around with the boat near the dock for a while, paddling it around and not venturing too far from shore. I felt confident that I was getting familiar with the operation. I was eager to sail, but the mast was still back in the shop.

Over the next few days I managed to get the sixteen-foot mast and the sail down to the front of the shop. Dad offered to help me take the sail home in his pickup for some repairs. I rode in the back hanging on. There was some minor sewing needed to repair a few tears in the sail. Mom gave me instructions on what to do. I finished the job and was ready to give her a try. I called the sailboat "her" because I had named the boat *Sis* after Donna Mae, the girl to whom my brother Dale was engaged. I painted big block letters "SIS" on the starboard and port side of the boat. Donna Mae wasn't quite my sis yet, but she would be after Dale returned from the war. I was just jumping the gun a bit.

Donna Mae's brother, Donald, was a midshipman at the Naval Academy in Annapolis, Maryland. He was home on leave, and I had a great idea. I thought surely he would know how to sail and wondered if I could get him to teach me. I didn't know Donald, other than who he was, so I asked Donna Mae if she would talk to her brother to see if he would teach me about sailing. Donald agreed, and my sailing lessons were about to begin.

All looked good as Donald, Donna Mae, and I set sail. It was a beautiful day with a gentle breeze and clear skies. Donald was the man in charge, telling me things to do and not to do. As the sailboat reached the spot where we changed tack, Donald turned with the wind, instead of turning into the wind. The sail caught a small gust of wind, and the boat went over onto its side, and we were all dumped in the lake. No one was wearing life preservers, as we didn't have any on the boat. And even worse than capsizing, Donna Mae didn't know how to swim.

Donald and I helped Donna Mae into the capsized boat. Well,

not "in" the boat, but "on" the boat, as *Sis* was floating on her side. Donna Mae was safe . . . temporarily. John Smith, one of the town's people from Cottonwood, was out on the lake with his inboard speedboat and saw that we had tipped over, and in short order was Johnny-on-the-spot.

With Donna Mae safely in John's boat we set about getting the sailboat upright, which was accomplished with much difficulty, I might add. John towed us back to shore.

My experience sailing with the Annapolis midshipman turned out to be a real adventure. I could just see the headlines, "Novice sailor drowns his brother's fiancée." Fortunately, it didn't happen, but it could have.

As well as using the boat for sailing, I wanted to use it as a regular motorboat and envisioned myself buzzing around the lake with the mast down (if I only had a motor). I had a friend named Ralph (Sonny) Olson who several years later joined the Air Force with me. Over the years, I had admired the motors Ralph's dad kept in the shed behind their house. I was particularly interested in purchasing one of the older ones. Ralph's dad was not an official motor dealer and owned several newer motors in much better condition than the one I was interested in.

He sold me the old motor for about five bucks and I put it on the back of Dale's boat. It was so old that it didn't have a reverse gear; to back up you had to kill the motor and start it by winding the rope around in the opposite direction. To go forward you had to kill the engine and start the motor again by wrapping the rope around in the opposite direction again. It was extremely noisy, as the exhaust went directly to the air and not under water.

That old Evinrude boat motor was built in 1914 and was actually an antique. I kept the motor for many years and gave it to my grandson Daniel with the condition that he never sell, but pass it on to the next generation with instructions that it never be sold. Just keep it in the family I told Dan. We kept the boat at the lake for the entire summer, so whenever we wanted to go out, it was either tied up at the dock or pulled up on shore.

I sailed many times over the next few years, even taking Marg out with me a few times. Never once did I even come close to tipping it over again, and I found sailing to be great fun.

The boat stayed in the shop until Dale got out of the service and returned to Cottonwood. For several more years, Dale enjoyed using that 14-foot boat that he built.

Dale also built an ice sailboat in Dad's shop. He didn't have any plans or drawings or even a picture of one. He just heard someone explain what one looked like and built it. The boat was T-shaped, with a seat in the back where the sailor sat and the steering skate was controlled. On each end of the T was another non-steering skate. They were about fourteen feet apart. The boat had an eighteen-foot mast similar to a regular sailboat and had a heavy canvas sail. Nylon was just coming into play, but wasn't available to the general public at that time. The boat was made with some two-by-sixes with a one-by-eight board to sit on.

One Sunday afternoon I decided to go ice sailing in Dale's boat. The wind was blowing pretty hard, and I would be able to get some good speed. The boat was already down at the lake with the mast up, so I just needed to get the sail. I took the pickup down to the shop and retrieved the sail before driving down to the lake. In a matter of minutes I had the sail up, and off I went. There was no holding her back. We were flying like the wind and most likely twice the speed of the wind. I had never sailed so fast. Before long the boat was all the way across the lake where I turned around, and lickety-split was back where I had started. I was freezing cold by then, too cold to do it again. I quickly took the sail down and didn't even roll it up. I spread it out on the lake bank and put some heavy chunks of snow on the sail so it wouldn't blow away, and headed for home.

When I got there, I was greeted by my mother asking, "Where have you been?" I told her, "Sailing Dale's iceboat on the lake." She replied, "Do you know how cold it is?" I had to admit that I only knew that it was real cold. She proceeded to tell me, "It's fifteen below zero, and the wind is blowing twenty-five miles per hour with gusts up to thirty-five miles per hour or more." She added, "You're staying home the rest of the day." I quickly agreed. It was too cold to go anywhere. I guess I was sailing at close to fifty miles per hour.

I didn't use his iceboat very much. Maybe I remembered just how cold it was when I was out on the ice. The lake was spring fed, and the ducks kept it open in spots, so no matter how cold it was, one had to steer clear of the open spots of water. I had too many other things to keep me busy and seldom went ice-boating again.

There weren't any mountains or even hills around Cottonwood where we could go snow skiing, and it would cost way beyond our means to travel to where we could mountain ski or even ski down any large hill for that matter. Let's face it; we lived in the plains, and they called it that for a reason. Cottonwood was flat, and one could see for miles. There were no hills in sight. But we were young and energetic and would innovate and make do with what we had. So in the summer, we would water ski behind a motorboat and get up some good speed. In the winter, we would snow ski pulled by a rope behind a car somewhere out in the country. The ditches were anywhere from four to six feet deep and would fill up with snow, so that they were level with the road. We would ski behind a car or pickup and could get up some good speed. I remember falling one time at about forty miles per hour. I didn't get hurt. We usually didn't ski that fast. We took turns driving the car and skiing and had great fun. Everyone fell from time to time, but no one ever got hurt. Falling in that soft snow at that speed was kind of fun. We did that for years, and I think it is still done by the local teenagers.

Cottonwood wasn't famous for anything that I know of, except for the rich farmland, which usually produced bumper crops. However, we did have one thing that no one else had. Cottonwood was one of the first to have a Farmers' Co-op creamery and one of first to have a Farmers' co-op elevator to handle the crops, and the world's first Co-op Oil Company. Farmers used a huge amount of fuel, so why not take advantage of buying in bulk? The World's First Co-op Oil Company is still in operation in Cottonwood. It has now expanded to include fertilizer and is a big operation.

During the war everyone participated in rationing. Pleasure cars had an "A" sticker on the windshield, and owners were given stamps to purchase four gallons of gas per week. Commercial vehicles, which included cars used for business were given a "C" sticker and received stamps to allow for more driving. The speed limit throughout the entire country was reduced to thirty-five miles per hour. Car owners were allotted gas for transportation, but there wasn't enough rubber for new tires. Tires lasted longer at low speeds, so thirty-five mph became law.

Food products were also rationed. All meat products, cheese, sugar, and many other foods were rationed. When we needed meat, my Uncle Norman would pick out his prize steer to be butchered. Dad would take half the steer, and Uncle Norman took the other half. Our half was a bit different than Uncle Norman's, as the butcher was instructed to make more roasts and to grind up all the steak portions into hamburger. Dad thought it was a waste to eat steaks. He felt we should spread the flavor out. I didn't have a steak until I was out of high school, but we had great hamburger.

Dad did the same with the meat we got from my uncle Alfred. Uncle Alfred would pick out a prize hog to be butchered, with each one taking half. This was a common practice by farmers across the country, not only during the war, but also before the war.

We kept the butchered steer and hog at the locker plant in the back of the meat market. This was before we had a home freezer. We always had plenty of meat.

5

HER NAME IS MARG

The heart that loves is forever young.
—A GREEK PROVERB

EVERYONE THAT KNEW HER CALLED her Marg. In 1943, the summer before entering eighth grade, she moved to Cottonwood with her family. Margaret prefers to be called Marg as in Margaret, not Marge as in Marjorie. She used to be quite insistent on being called Marg and not Marge, but over the years so many called her Marge, and still do, that she gave up and now answers to either Marg or Marge. I guess age mellows everyone.

That fateful summer of 1943, none of us knew anything about Marg except that she was going into the eighth grade and was the daughter of the new school superintendent. Her father was

MARG (TOPLESS) AT AGE SIXTEEN MONTHS

Mr. (Earl) Olson, and her mother was Mrs. Earl (Helen) Olson. Marg's little sister Ann was going into second grade. All the boys going into eighth and ninth grades were excited to have a new girl our age in town. Cottonwood was small, with only 700 people, so a new person in town our own age, especially a girl, was a big deal.

HELEN AND EARL OLSON, MARG'S PARENTS

EARL OLSON, MARG'S DAD ON VACATION

HELEN OLSON; ONE OF OUR LAST PICTURES OF HER BEFORE SHE DIED AT AGE 99

Leonard Buysse, a classmate one grade ahead of me, announced to all the boys that Margaret was going to be his girl friend. Of course Leonard had not met her, didn't have any idea what she looked like, or know anything about her. He just decided that Marg was going to be his girl, and all boys going into the eighth or ninth grade were told in no uncertain terms, to back off. He repeated this admonition several times to be sure that everyone understood. Marg knew nothing about this and didn't know Leonard or anyone else in the school. She obviously knew nothing of Leonard's decision that she was to be his girl. Leonard gave everyone the impression that she wasn't just his girl, but his property.

September arrived, and school started. Everyone finally got to meet the new girl, and Margaret got to meet all the other kids at school. On that first day, Leonard made sure that he was close

MARG AS A SOPHOMORE
IN HIGH SCHOOL

to Marg, so he could check her out. After all, he had to learn what his new self-proclaimed girl friend looked like. It didn't take long before Leonard learned that Marg had no interest in him and a while longer to realize that he had struck out before he even got started. Marg had just finished seventh grade, and young boys weren't even on her radar screen.

For several weeks all the guys had fun ribbing Leonard about his being rejected by the new girl in town. Marg still didn't know of Leonard's failed conquest. It was just a guy thing, and like kids that age, we just didn't give up needling him for a few more weeks. At our young age no one was dating yet. The guys hung together in an all guys group, and the gals hung together in an all girls group.

Marg and I were both active at Christ Lutheran Church that was called Silo (pronounced See-Lo) Lutheran Church at that time. We attended confirmation class together and Luther League, which was a high school youth group at church, and both joined the church choir. Silo Lutheran wasn't big enough to support a high school choir, so after confirmation we were encouraged to join the adult choir, which both Marg and I did.

SILO LUTHERAN CHURCH WITH
EAST WING ADDITION

CHAPTER 5 / *Her Name is Marg*

CHRIST LUTHERAN CHURCH, DEDICATED IN 1956

About that same time lightning struck our church steeple. There was a vote by the congregation to decide whether to remove the steeple or repair it. I found it interesting that I was allowed to vote because I had been confirmed, and was therefore old enough to vote on church issues. However, my mother was not allowed to vote because she was a woman. There were just four Lutheran Churches in the entire state of Minnesota that still had the old rule that only men could vote. That rule has since been changed, but Christ Lutheran was the last Lutheran church in Minnesota to finally allow women to vote.

Cottonwood Public School District 15 didn't have a Home Economics, Shop or Agriculture class. The only thing taught was academic pre-college curriculum.

At the start of our freshmen high school year, several new students enrolled in our school, some of whom were farm kids who attended one-room schools out in the country through eighth grade. Our class grew to over twenty. At age sixteen, a few of the town kids quit school, but mostly it was the farm kids who quit because they saw no reason to continue if they were just going to farm. Our class dropped down to sixteen students, which was the same class size when we graduated. Today virtually all students finish high school, and a very high percentage go to college.

At the end of my freshman year when I turned fifteen, I was eligible for my driver's license. I went to Kolhi's Insurance Agency in Cottonwood where I applied. There were just three questions on the application, and all of them were verbal. First Mr. Kolhli asked, "How old are you?"

I replied, "Fifteen," and that was good enough. I didn't need to show them a birth certificate or anything to prove my age. They simply took my word for it. His second question was, "Do you know how to drive?"

"Yes," I answered, and again that was good enough.

Mr. Kolhi's third question was, "Do you know the laws?"

They didn't have what we now call rules of the road. They simply asked if I knew the laws. Again I said, "Yes" and paid the fifty cents for the license. They gave me a signed piece of paper, which was proof that my license had been applied for. The copy of the application allowed me to drive until my actual paper license arrived in the mail about two weeks later. I was now legal to drive. Three months later when Marg turned fifteen, she got her driver's license too.

I had been driving since I was fourteen or maybe earlier and not always with a licensed adult driver with me, I might add. Most farm kids began driving at ten or twelve. They had been driving the family tractor on their farm since about ten or eleven. I know some farm kids who started driving their tractor at seven or eight. This was not uncommon. Many kids of that age would drive either a truck loaded with grain or a tractor pulling a wagon full of grain to the Farmers Co-op Elevator. I never heard of any accidents either. At harvest time all hands were busy, and if a youngster could drive, that was one more pair of hands to help get the job done.

In December of 1945, when she was a sophomore in high school, Marg came down with appendicitis. Now that wasn't so unusual, but what was unusual was that two of her classmates had appendicitis within three weeks of each other. Our class only had nine boys and seven girls, and three of the girls had to have their appendix removed, one right after another.

CHAPTER 5 / *Her Name is Marg*

MARG'S HOSPITAL BILL AT MONTEVIDEO HOSPITAL WHEN SHE HAD HER APPENDIX REMOVED IN DECEMBER 1945. THE ENTIRE BILL WAS $68.08.

After tenth grade the hormones were flowing, and we began to notice the girls more than in the past. During the summer after our sophomore year the kids in our class started to date. It was group dating at first, usually in groups of three, or sometimes four couples. We could easily get four in the back seat and two in the front seat of a car if there were six of us, or four in the front seat if there were eight of us, which happened quite often. The tight squeeze was no problem. In fact we rather enjoyed the cramped quarters. Three sat on the seat, and one girl sat on the lap of her date. It was kind of nice, and each guy jockeyed for position, so that the girl he liked was sitting on his lap. There were no seat belts in those days, and no bucket seats, so the front seat bench had enough room for four.

Frequently, on our group dates we would go to a show in Marshall, which was thirteen miles south of Cottonwood. We called it a show, but now they call it a movie. One Saturday night (as I mentioned in the Foreword), after four couples had been to Marshall, we were all talking about going out the following Saturday night. We had already dropped off my date, and for the life of me, I can't remember who it was. The driver stopped at my house to let me off. There were two couples in the back seat and one couple in the front seat along with me. Marg was in the back seat with her date, Jim (Boomer) Dahl.

Just as we got to my house I turned and asked Marg, who was sitting on Boomer's lap, "Would you go out with me next week?"

She immediately said, "Yes."

I don't know if she was that anxious to date me or just anyone else but Boomer. It was all over so fast that I don't think Boomer knew what had happened. I do know however, that it was the beginning of a long lasting relationship. Marg and I dated off and on and mostly on for almost five years before becoming officially engaged.

The following Saturday night it was my turn to drive, and since I was able to decide whom to drop off first that was a good thing. The driver always wanted to drop his date off last, so they would have a little time with each other without the rest of the gang. I walked Marg to her door, and after some small talk, I asked, "Can I kiss you goodnight?"

She said, "No, not on the first date."

That was okay with me because her statement led me to believe there would be a second, and maybe more dates. When we started dating neither of us dated anyone else for a long time. And oh yes, I did get that kiss on the second date. She later told me she was impressed that I asked her for a kiss on that first date instead of just charging forward without asking.

6

THE MILITARY BECKONS

The Body is a Slave to the Mind. The Mind is a Slave to the Spirit. And the Spirit is STRONG!
—ANONYMOUS

DAD WANTED ME TO BE a tradesman and go to William Hood Dunwoody Industrial Institute in Minneapolis where he had gone after World War I to study carpentry. I didn't want to go to college, or at least I didn't think I wanted to. Mom and Dad said I needed to get some additional training or schooling. Like so many high school graduates, I just didn't know what I wanted to be or do, so I went to Dunwoody and completed their two-year course, studying heating and air conditioning.

Shortly before I completed the course the North Koreans invaded South Korea on June 25, 1950. I had received a job offer in the heating and air conditioning field, but when the war broke out, the offer was almost immediately rescinded. All business employers knew that a twenty-year-old, classified 1-A would be drafted in short order. The same thing happened to several graduates in my class. Companies didn't want to train potential employees only to see them drafted in a few months. I couldn't blame them. I went home to Cottonwood to work in Dad's Coast-to-Coast store for a couple of months until early September when I enlisted in the Air Force.

Because Congress never officially declared war, it was referred to as the Korean Conflict, but we all understood that term was just a political word play. Some 58,000 American military died in that "Korean Conflict." I called it a war, as do most Americans. You can't change facts just because of the words the government uses. It was a war.

When North Korea launched their attack in June 1950 on South Korea, the United States had a small force of 25,000 military personnel in South Korea. Like it or not, we were in a war and our boys were in the thick of it. Because we had such a limited force, things did not go well in the early stages. By September 10, the North Koreans had pushed the American and South Korean forces back to Pusan, a small area on the southern tip of South Korea, and casualties were high.

A successful counteroffensive was begun on September 15 with the Inchon landing. United Nations forces under General Douglas MacArthur pushed all the way to the Yalu River boundary between North Korea and China. On November 26, Chinese forces entered in massive numbers, turning the tide against primarily American and South Korean forces. The winter of 1951 was the bloodiest of the war.

The draft was taking increasingly large numbers of young men to fight in the war. Guys my age knew they would be called, but didn't know when. Several young men from Cottonwood decided not to wait to "get called" and volunteered to join the Air Force. Ralph (Sonny) Olson, a year older than me, Harland Hanson, a high school classmate, and I made that decision in hopes to beat the draft (if truth be told). Four years in the Air Force sounded better than two years in the Infantry. None of us boys wanted to be "ground pounders," which was a military slang term for Infantry. Fellow high school classmate John Olson followed us, joining in December. Americans were still joining in such great numbers that the Air Force couldn't keep up. They didn't supply uniforms to the airmen in John's company until they had been there two weeks. They had to take their basic training in their civilian clothes. Many were joining the Navy or Air Force to beat the draft.

In early September of 1950, the three of us went to Minneapolis to be sworn in. The day after our swearing in, we were on a plane headed to Lackland Air Force Base in San Antonio, Texas for basic training. It was the first plane ride of my twenty years on this earth.

A lot of guys were joining the Air Force in order to avoid being drafted into the Army. Basic training was scheduled to be eight weeks, but one week into our basic training, we were told that our training would be limited to five weeks. New recruits were arriving daily, and the Air Force had no place to house them. There was no choice but to speed up our training. About a week after the last announcement, we were told that our training would be shortened to only three weeks. After the required shots and long hours of training, including Saturdays, all three of us were issued our orders and assigned to Keesler Air Force Base in Biloxi, Mississippi. Keesler had a huge electronics training school, but our assignment was as permanent party, not a part of the school. I was assigned to a maintenance company, and because of my Dunwoody training, I was able to convince them that I should be assigned as a draftsman.

Keesler Air Force Base

Keesler was great. It was a Monday through Friday job, and the hours were nine to four-thirty. Our unit didn't assemble more than once every couple of months, never marched, and didn't parade, as required by so many units. We got up on our own, walked about three blocks to the mess hall and then about three blocks back to the hangar where we had our office. I had my own desk and a drafting table. It was just like having a job in civilian life. Whenever we were not on duty, we could wear civvies, which most everyone did. If we wanted, we could go to town every night, but of course that was not plausible because I only earned $75 per month, and that was before taxes. Yes, we had to pay taxes. I went to Biloxi about once a month. I just couldn't afford to go more often, and would return to base the same night. I wasn't about to pay for a room when I could just catch the free Air Force bus back to base and sleep in my own bunk for free.

Keesler had several squadrons of B-25 World War II medium bombers. Drawings for all the parts necessary to keep the B-25s flying were recorded on microfilm. The Air Force had no way of copying from microfilm to paper. The shop would tell me what part they needed, and I would look it up on microfilm. I would project it on a screen and draw it on paper. It was easy to do, and all in all, it was a neat job. I had always been quite good at drawing, and now I had a chance to get paid for doing what I liked. It kept me busy. Later on, two additional airmen were assigned to do the same job. Both had two or three years of college toward their architecture degrees and had a lot more experience. There were never any complaints on my work, so I must have been doing okay. We now had three guys doing what I had been doing alone. The workload increased, but we could have easily kept up with one full-time and one half-time draftsman. Free time and three-day passes were readily available.

About once per quarter, or sometimes more often, I would get a three-day pass. A couple times, a few of us hitchhiked to New Orleans, but not often, because of the cost to stay in a hotel and all our meals. Rather than use the few passes I had acquired, I saved my three-day passes until I saw a notice on the bulletin board that a plane was scheduled to fly to Minneapolis. I signed up for a "hop" as the Air Force called it, and with a three-day pass in my hand I was on my way.

Since several squadrons of B-25s were based at Keesler, we always flew in a 25. They would arrive in the twin cities early Friday afternoon and were instructed to be back by noon on Sunday.

Once every couple of months a Bird Colonel whose home was in Rochester, Minnesota would check out a plane and schedule a training mission to Rochester. The colonel always had two co-pilots with him. So after dropping him off in Rochester, the two pilots would fly up to an Air Force Base in Minneapolis where they parked the plane for the weekend and refueled for the return trip.

I would have two days to see Marg. The plane was limited to only five in the back as that's all the seat belts there were. I say seat belts, but there really weren't any seats. We would sit on the floor with our legs straight out and our backs against the side of the fuselage. Our parachutes became our seats because they were a lot warmer and softer than the aluminum floor. We only buckled up for take off and landing. In the back, at the altitude we were flying, the temperature was about 20 or 30 degrees. But in the cockpit where the pilots and navigator were sitting, it was a comfortable 70 degrees.

The B-25 had a clear plastic nose where the nose gunner positioned himself. There was a small tunnel that allowed a person to get from the back of the plane to the nose position. We would take turns crawling up there. I loved to be in the nose during landing and take off. A lot of the guys didn't like it in the nose and didn't want to go up there. That meant more opportunity for me to enjoy take-offs and landings at that vantage point. What a sight!

I made five hops to Minneapolis during the eleven months I was assigned to Keesler Air Force Base. On March 17, 1951 during one of those hops, I asked Marg to marry me. She said yes. We knew we wouldn't be able to get married for quite some time as I had my military obligation, and never knew when orders might come sending me to another Air Force base or a base overseas.

Marg had completed two years at Gustavus Adolphus College in St. Peter, Minnesota and was finishing her first year at the Swedish Hospital School of Nursing in Minneapolis. She had a little over two more years before she would complete her

Registered Nurse Training Program, so we knew that marriage was still a couple of years off.

While at Keesler, I applied for Officer Candidate School (OCS). I also applied for Air Cadets to become an Air Force pilot. All branches of service had eliminated their previous requirement of a college degree in order to be accepted to their officer candidate or pilot training programs. Several months later, it became the policy of all branches of the service that one could apply for OCS from any branch of the service to any other branch. I applied for all of them, including the Navy, Army, Marines, and Coast Guard. I had already submitted my application to attend OCS in the Air Force. What convinced me to do this was my observation of the officers that I came to know. Many of them had come through the Reserve Officer Training Program (ROTC) at their college or university. While many were fine officers, sharp guys, and true gentlemen, some just didn't seem to cut the mustard, so to speak. I thought: I can do that, and in many cases I said to myself, I can do better than that. So I applied to all the OCS programs and waited. I met many West Point graduates too, and can honestly say that I never met a "West Pointer" that wasn't exceptional.

All the branches of the service had a point system they used to select their candidates. One would get a certain number of points based on test scores. Another set of points was based on your interview. A third set of points was given based on your years of college. An applicant would get fifty points for each year of college up to 250 points for five or more years of college. No points were given for one year of college. Only those who had two or more years received college credit points. No points were given for the physical. You either passed your physical or you didn't. After all the exams, tests, and interviews, the service told us exactly where we stood.

I was informed that I had 435 points and had been accepted to attend Air Force Officer Candidate School and was in line to get called. People were called up for OCS strictly based on total points, and not how long one had been on the list. Consequently, some guy who had just applied who had 300 points from his interview and tests, plus an additional 200 points because he had four years of college, would be placed ahead of me because he would have 500 total points compared to my 435. If you hadn't been called after six months, you were dropped from the list. One could start over and try again, but it was a futile exercise. There were so many college graduates joining the Air Force in order to beat the Army draft that I didn't have a chance. College graduates started out with the 200 points that I didn't have. I was accepted to the Air Force OCS program, and to the Air Force Cadet Flight Training Program, but not called. Six months passed, and I was informed that I had been dropped, but I still had my application to attend the Army, Navy, Coast Guard, and Marine OCS. I had been accepted in all those programs and simply had to wait to see if I got called before the six months were up.

About that time I received orders that I was being transferred to a new Intelligence Wing being formed at Mountain Home Air Force Base in Mountain Home, Idaho, forty miles south of Boise. The base had been closed after World War II and was in disrepair. People were being shipped from all over the country to form this new Wing, and when all the billets filled, we were to be shipped overseas. We had no idea where, just somewhere overseas.

Then, I received orders indicating that I had been accepted to attend OCS in the Army. The orders stated I was to be in the next class of officer candidates and that further orders would be forthcoming. Shortly after I got the orders for OCS, it came time for the Wing to ship out. The entire Wing was to be shipped to Tripoli, North Africa. I had ten days to get to Fort Dix, New Jersey. On the last day before leaving, I checked with the permanent party office to see if they knew the status of my orders to be discharged from the Air Force and sworn in to the Army to attend Army **OCS**. They said no notice had been received, and I had to leave with the Wing. I had no choice except to head for Fort Dix.

To save money, I took a bus to Minneapolis where I stayed three or four days before getting on another greyhound to Fort Dix, New Jersey. The Air Force gave us six cents a mile and ten days to get there. It was my job to get there and be on time. The Air Force didn't care how we got there. They just said here is some money, and you have ten days. Be on time or you would be **AWOL** (absent without leave), which was a court martial offense. I was able to spend a few days in Minneapolis. I stayed at Marg's Aunt Min's house. Marg had some free time, but had to attend classes, including floor duty as a student nurse.

One day the two of us were in downtown Minneapolis together and passed a window advertising a fortune-teller. The fortune-teller at the store would read tea leaves and tell your future.

Marg said, "Let's go in and see what she has to say."

It was just a fun thing, since neither of us remotely believed that someone could foretell the future by reading tea leaves. I was wearing civvies, but it was easy for her to deduce that I was in the military. Most guys my age were in the military those days. So far, she was right on her first guess.

She then said, "I see travels in your immediate future."

Again she was right. I was on my way to Fort Dix. We were skeptics and were careful not to say anything that would give her a clue.

She then said, "I don't see any water. You will not be traveling over a great body of water."

We laughed and told her, "I am on my way to Fort Dix, New Jersey, and from there I will ship overseas."

I didn't tell her where, just that I was going overseas. But she was adamant. She said, "There is no water, you will not be shipped overseas."

CHAPTER 6 / *The Military Beckons*

I repeated that I had my orders in my pocket, and that I was on my way. She answered, "The orders will be changed. You are not going to pass over a big body of water."

Marg and I left laughing because we knew I was on my way to Tripoli, North Africa.

The tealeaf lady was right. I didn't go over a big body of water. As it turned out, high school classmate John Olson, whom I wrote about earlier, did go to Tripoli, North Africa. If I had gone as scheduled, we would have been on the same Air Force base for some year and a half.

When I arrived at Fort Dix, they told us there had been a change in plans, and the entire Wing of several thousand airmen and officers was to return to Mountain Home. Again they gave us some money (six cents a mile) and ten days to get back to Mountain Home. The new Wing I was assigned to was an Intelligence Wing, the first of its kind in the Air Force. It was a highly secretive mission, and we were under orders not to tell anyone where we were going or what our mission was. I was true to my orders. However, two different sergeants had been interviewed on two separate TV programs and they told the world a few things about our mission and that we were going to Tripoli, North Africa. The Air Force was far from happy. Our entire Wing was shipped back, and the two sergeants were tried in a court-martial and sent to the stockade.

I decided to fly back after riding on the bus for what seemed to be forever. It would cost more money to fly, but I wasn't about to face another week on a bus. I flew back to Minneapolis, and stayed with Marg's Aunt Min while Marg was in the dorm at Swedish Hospital. After a few days I flew to Boise, Idaho and took a bus the last forty miles to Mountain Home. The first day after returning to Mountain Home Air Force Base, I went to the offices of the permanent party and inquired if anything had come in regarding orders for me to go to the Army OCS. They said yes, they had the orders, but replied that I had been shipped overseas.

I said, "Can you send a TWX back stating that I am still here, and I am available to go to Army OCS?"

They sent the TWX, and three weeks later, I received my orders. I was discharged from the Air Force, sworn into the Army the same morning, and given a ticket to fly to Fort Ord, California for Army basic training. Four weeks after my discharge from the Air Force, the entire Wing went to Fort Dix for processing, and then to Tripoli, North Africa. I had truly dodged a bullet. None of the services would ship a guy back from overseas to attend OCS, so I made it just in the nick of time. The tea leaf lady was right. I didn't go over any big body of water.

About 95 percent of the 200 new draftees who reported for basic training at Fort Ord with me were Mormons from Idaho and Utah. They were a great bunch of guys. By this time, I had been promoted to Corporal in the Air Force, and that rank carried over to the Army. Because of my rank, I was selected to be the Platoon Guide. I was the trainee in charge of forty-four other trainees. This gave me a few extra privileges. It was nice.

One of the nicest perks had nothing to do with the Army. At the bottom of the hill, less than one hundred yards from our barracks, was a Frosty Fred, which was something like a Dairy Queen. Their patrons were mostly permanent party soldiers and not your basic recruits, but we did get down there some evenings after dinner. There were four walkup windows on the front and two on each side where we could place our orders. I counted about seventeen people in line at each window. What a gold mine. One day I was in line, and it was my turn at the window, "Hey, I know you," I said to the manager who was taking my order.

It was Jim Retrum from Cottonwood, a classmate of my brother Dale. His sister, Carolyn had been in my high school class. Jim invited me in the back. Frosty Fred's soon became a place to hang out whenever I wanted to slip away from the troops.

Frosty Fred's would get sixty dozen fresh hot donuts

CHAPTER 6 / *The Military Beckons*

delivered every morning in heavy insulated cardboard boxes. By ten o'clock in the morning, before they had a chance to get cold, they would sell out.

Jim showed me a fifty-gallon barrel of yellow mustard sitting in the back. I had never seen so much mustard. They sold hot dogs and put one swipe of mustard on each hot dog. He said that barrel of mustard would be used up in four weeks. I couldn't believe that. Surely he was pulling my leg. Later, when I was hiding out in the back of Jim's Frosty Fred, Jim told me to look in the barrel. It was almost empty, and it had been full some three and a half weeks prior. He had a gold mine, and I had a place to hang out some evenings and weekends. I ate all the soft serve ice cream and hot dogs I wanted for free, but no donuts; because they were all gone before I was able to get there.

I finished my sixteen weeks of basic training and was scheduled to attend leadership school, located on the same base about three blocks from where I attended basic training. I had accumulated quite a bit of leave time, and leadership school wasn't scheduled to start for ten days, so I elected to take ten days and fly home. I caught a hop at no cost to me. On my return, however, I couldn't get a hop all the way to San Francisco, although I was able to catch a hop to Denver. I thought it would be closer, and I would be able to catch a hop from Denver to San Francisco. The plan worked well until I got to Denver. We landed, but the airport soon closed for the rest of the day as they were experiencing a winter blizzard. Nothing was flying in or out of Denver. Commercial planes were grounded too, so I couldn't buy a ticket to go any sooner.

I had the telephone number and the address of the orderly room (office) of the Leadership school. I called them and informed them that I was in Denver, snowed in, and would get there just as quickly as possible. I also sent a telegram stating the same thing, so they would have it in writing. The next day I got a hop back to San Francisco and took a bus down to Fort

Ord. I found my way to the leadership school arriving at about 11 p.m. The guy on duty in the orderly room told me they had been looking for me all day and that I had been reported AWOL. He gave me some sheets and a blanket and instructed me to report back there at 8 a.m.

At 8 a.m. the following morning, I met with the company commander and the company executive officer. They had the record of my telephone call and a copy of my telegram, but it didn't matter. I wasn't there, so I had been reported AWOL. They knew that officially they couldn't punish me because of the circumstances, and I had kept them informed. That first weekend, however, I was put on K.P. duty (Kitchen Police). After cleaning, serving, and working for over twelve hours, I was told to clean the grease trap. It is not necessary to clean the grease trap more than once every six to eight weeks. They decided this was the day, and I was the guy who had the privilege to clean it. About three hours later, after almost sixteen hours, I was finally able to hit the sack. I slept soundly that night. No official punishment, but they found a way. For the entire sixteen weeks of basic training, I never had to pull K. P. because I was the platoon guide. It was one of the few perks for the platoon guide. But from that day forward my official service records indicated that I had been AWOL for one day.

Three weeks into the five-week Leadership Program, orders came for me to ship out to Fort Knox to attend Officer Candidate School at the Armored Division Headquarters. I had about ten days travel time, so I flew home for a few days. Mom and Dad drove me to Fort Knox. I got a free ride, and they got to see the countryside and where I would be training. We stopped at Cave City to see Mammoth Cave, which was a neat experience.

7

OFFICER CANDIDATE SCHOOL (OCS)

Genius is one percent inspiration and 99 percent perspiration.
—THOMAS EDISON

I WAS FINALLY HEADING TO Officer Candidate School. But getting there was the easy part. Not washing out and graduating as a second lieutenant was going to prove to be the real challenge. The question was whether I would be one of the majority to wash out before completing the six month training or be one of the candidates to graduate. I was determined to finish and to prove not only to my friends and family, but more importantly, to myself, that I could do it.

One hundred thirty-five candidates started that hot July day. I told myself once more,

> IF IT IS TO BE IT IS UP TO ME.

Later I learned that the odds were stacked a bit higher for me than I had thought. Of the 135 candidates, 65 were college graduates, another 35 had two years of college or more but had not yet graduated, and 15 had some college but had less than two years. That left 20 candidates, including me, that had no college at all. They told us several times that those who did not have their college degree would have an even harder time completing the course. The TAC officers repeatedly told us it was their job to wash us out. This was their way of motivating us to do better, and they were quite successful at their task, as significantly less than half finished.

Everyone in the class had the intellectual capacity to graduate. The preliminary tests we took to qualify for OCS screened those not capable of handling the material. The TAC officers tried very hard to break us mentally. Could we take the pressure, could we perform under severe and extreme hardship? Most of the guys who washed out did so because they couldn't take the pressure. They were unable or unwilling to perform under the gun, so to speak.

We were up every day at 6:00 a.m. performing twenty minutes of calisthenics before marching off to breakfast. After breakfast we marched to our first class at 8:00 a.m. Classes were not difficult for me or for most of us for that matter. But surprisingly, some couldn't handle the work.

The officers quickly learned who wasn't going to cut it. We had been there just shy of one month when, one Friday afternoon, twenty guys got the dreaded pink slip. In the next three weeks, another twenty guys washed out. Now we were down to ninety-five. Over the next two months we lost another thirty and were down to sixty-five. Ten more guys washed out before Thanksgiving, but five of those were set back to the next class and graduated one month behind our class. By Thanksgiving we were down to fifty-seven or fifty-eight. Three more were set back a month and also graduated with the class behind us. Only fifty-five of the original 135 made it to graduation.

One of the early exercises was a combination cross-country obstacle course run over unusually rough terrain. It included ditches five or six feet deep and six or seven feet across with all kinds of other obstacles to challenge us physically. The run was about two and one half miles long. The first time we ran it two weeks after our class started, I finished fifth. Everyone, including the TAC officers, and especially me, was surprised that I finished so high. Our class still included all 135 of us. I finished high because I was in great physical shape, and I didn't smoke. The smokers, of which there were many, had the most difficult time.

We ran that course once every three weeks throughout the entire six months training. My time improved every time until I finally finished in twenty minutes flat. It had taken me twenty-eight minutes and thirty seconds the first time. However, most everyone's time improved as well, and I finished a bit lower in the class each time. The last time I ran it, I came in twentieth out of the fifty-eight remaining candidates, even though it was the best time I ever ran. I was never a fast runner and to complete it in the top third of the class was a victory for me. I wasn't a racehorse; I was more of a plow horse. I wasn't as fast as some in my class, but I kept plugging when many of the others had fallen by the wayside.

After a two-week break for Christmas, I was back at Fort Knox. On January second I had a horrible cold and reported to sick call. In those days they gave penicillin for almost everything, and that's what they gave me. Within a few days my feet and hands began to swell. I had difficulty walking because the arches of my feet swelled. It turned out that I was allergic to penicillin. The service doesn't have any way to handle people who get so sick they can't report for duty, so they put them in the hospital, and that's where I ended up. They took good care of me, and in six days I was back with the class. I was fortunate too, because if a candidate missed seven or more days, they were automatically set back to the next class. I dodged a bullet. Lieutenant Lawegee knew I had bad feet and tried to make it easy for me for a couple of weeks.

Of the twenty men in my class without college experience, only three graduated: Robert (Pete) Gregg from North Carolina, Al Blankenship from Cave City, Kentucky, and Marlin Reishus. A few days before graduation, the three of us were called into the orderly room to meet with the company commander, Captain Max P. Hutton.

"What did we do to get called in? Are they going to wash us out?" we all wondered. They had led us to believe there would be no more washouts, and that everyone still with the class on January 1st would graduate. However, we knew that seldom was anyone called into the orderly room except for some disciplinary reason.

"Why are they calling the three of us together, and not one at a time?" Pete said.

We were all shaking in our boots, both literally and figuratively, and racking our brains trying to figure out what was going to happen.

I said, "This can't be good." Pete and Al agreed. We all thought the worst.

We reported to Captain Hutton as ordered. He then gave us a little pep talk.

He said, "Remember how I told all of you how hard it would be to finish this class?"

"Yes Sir," we responded in unison.

"Do you remember how the TAC officers and I repeatedly told you and the entire class that it would be even harder for anyone to graduate who didn't have a college degree?"

"Yes Sir," again thinking, here comes the axe.

He then went on to say, "Well, I'm proud of you three guys. You beat the odds. I didn't think any one with less than two years of college would make it. I was wrong, and I am happy to inform you that you will graduate with the class this coming Saturday. We don't post class standings, other than to identify the top five in the class, but I am proud that all three of you graduated in the top quarter of the class."

By this time all three of us were beaming and grinning from ear to ear.

He then said, "Do any of you have relatives that will be coming to the graduation ceremony?"

Al did as he came from Cave City, Kentucky, only thirty miles from Fort Knox, but Pete and I said, "No Sir."

Captain Hutton then said, "Since you two don't have any family coming, I would be honored to pin your bars at the graduation ceremony."

Then he added, "If it is okay with you."

Pete and I said, "Yes Sir!"

By this time our worry had turned to joy. We were all smiles. Things couldn't be better.

At the graduation ceremony the candidate that finished number one in the class was called to the stage first. It was announced that he had graduated number one, and the captain pinned the bars on him. Then they declared all the rest of us second lieutenants. Those who had family in attendance had family members pin on the bars. The captain then came down from the stage and pinned the bars on Pete and me. We were three happy guys.

Before leaving the OCS chapter I should tell the unusual story of Sam Martin. Sam was a guy in the George Company OCS Class II. George II, as they were called, was one month behind us. Their barracks were right next to ours, so we got to see them once in a while. We also had a few classes together. I knew Sam, but not well. Everyone knew of him because of his unusual circumstances.

After two years of college Sam had joined the Navy as a Naval cadet. He was assigned to Pensacola Naval flight training, and after thirteen months graduated as an ensign and earned his pilot's wings. Immediately after graduation, Sam was shipped to Korea. He was flying off an aircraft carrier in the Sea of Japan between Korea and Japan. On his tenth mission Sam was shot down. He crashed right on the front line between the North Koreans and the allied forces. The next thing Sam remembered was a big master sergeant pulling him out of his downed plane, just prior to it blowing up. He was blind for about three weeks, but he did recover, except for some loss of vision. Sam could see well enough to be an officer in the Navy, but there was enough vision loss that the Navy said he could no longer fly. Sam was awarded the Purple Heart.

To become a Naval officer, one had to be a college graduate, unless he was a pilot. Sam had been told that he would never fly again and was no longer a Navy pilot. He couldn't be a pilot, and with only two years of college, he couldn't be a non flying officer in the Navy. The Navy offered him three choices. First he could go to the Navy war college. The Navy would not only pay all tuition, books, room and board, but he also would keep his rank as an ensign and would continue to be paid as a Naval officer while he went to school. He would earn his degree and would stay in the Navy. The catch was that he would also be required to stay in the Navy for four additional years after graduating college. Sam's second alternative was that he could stay in the Navy, but he would have to give up his commission and become an enlisted man. The third alternative was that he could be discharged. After eighteen months in the Navy, Sam decided to take the discharge and go home.

This was early in the war, and the draft boards were quite active. Ensign Martin had been in the Navy only eighteen months, and at that time the draft boards were drafting anyone that had less than two years of service. The objective of this policy was to be able to draft the many guys who had joined the Reserves, spent six months on active duty and were supposed to be completing their obligation as weekend warriors. Many found ways to avoid this weekend duty. The policy of drafting anyone who had less than two years service was to fix that loophole.

Sam's draft board needed bodies, and since Sam had less than two years in the service, his local draft board drafted him. They didn't care about his Naval service. Sam was drafted into the Army, went through Army basic training, leadership school, and Armored OCS. He had been an officer in the Navy, but now was an officer in the Army. I learned that he was one of the few who were shipped directly to Korea right out of OCS. I lost track of him after that and never heard what happened to him other than he did go to Korea. The life of a second lieutenant was oh so short in combat. I just hope and pray that he did survive. Sometimes our government does things that make us wonder. This was one of them.

8

GENE FIGHTS POLIO

It is not good for all our wishes to be filled; through sickness we recognize the value of health; through evil, the value of good; through hunger, the value of food; through exertion, the value of rest.
—DOROTHY CANFIELD FISHER

ALL OCS CLASSES WERE SUSPENDED over the Christmas holidays. This was not to give the candidates a break, but to give the staff time off for the holidays. Anyone who wanted could take up to two weeks leave, and almost every candidate did. I went home to Cottonwood to celebrate Christmas. Marg also had a few days off from her nurses training, so she too was back in Cottonwood for the holidays. There were lots of parties and many good times.

My younger brother Gene was a freshman in high school. He was an outstanding basketball player, and Coach Koplitz took advantage of that. Gene played on the second team and was the star of the team. The first team consisted of all juniors and seniors. Gene was as good as most and better than some on the first team, but played on the second team because he was just a freshman. Gene played for the entire second team game, which was played prior to the first team game. Gene would suit up but not start when the first team played, but the coach used him for at least three quarters of the first team's game. Gene would come home from the games exhausted.

At six feet one and thin as he was, Gene was still growing. His young body couldn't take that much punishment. Dad liked the idea that Gene was such a good basketball player, but didn't like that the coach played him so much. One day Dad went to the school to talk to Coach Koplitz. He acknowledged that he was the coach but laid into him to either play Gene on the second team or the first team, but not on both. Dad told him that he was worried that overusing him was just too much for his growing body. Coach did play him less, but not much less. There were several games just before the Christmas holidays, and Gene and the entire team were exhausted.

On Christmas Eve we had a large family celebration, and the next day, Christmas morning, Gene couldn't get out of bed. Mom had called him several times to come join everyone, but Gene didn't get up. Gene called and asked for help. I went to his room, and he said he couldn't move his legs.

Thinking he was joking around, I said, "Come on Gene, get up!"

He said, "I can't Marlin."

By the look on his face I knew he was serious. I carried him down the stairs, and we raced him to the Clarkfield Hospital where we met Dr. Hauge. The doctor was pretty sure that it was polio. Dr. Hauge ordered a tray of food for Gene, but he didn't want to eat. Finally after some coaxing he took a few bites. A few minutes later when we were in the hall, the doctor told us he ordered the tray of food to see if Gene could swallow. The doctor said it was a good sign when he saw him eat a few bites and swallow. After the brief examination, Dr. Hauge said to get him to Sister Kenney Hospital in Minneapolis as soon as possible. Like, *go now!*

We called Gus Giniffke, a friend of the family from Cottonwood. Gus had a full-size Nash with a front passenger seat that folded back. This made a flat space where Gene could lie down, using the front passenger and right back seat of the car. Gus drove Gene and me to Sister Kenney Hospital in Minneapolis, which was 140 miles away, at speeds of 85 and 90 miles per hour. There were times between towns when we had a good open stretch, and Gus would have his Nash over 110 mph. The state Highway Patrol had been advised and was stationed in every town, flagging us through town at about fifty miles per hour. About forty miles before we got to Minneapolis we met a Highway Patrol officer who escorted us the rest of the way with the sirens blasting to get everyone out of the way. We were flying, and arrived at Sister Kenney Hospital in a little over an hour and fifty minutes. We averaged almost 80 mph through towns and all.

The Sister Kenny people immediately asked me to sign papers giving them permission to do a spinal tap. I said my mom and dad would be right behind us. They assured me there wasn't a minute to spare and needed that permission right then. I signed for the procedure. The spinal tap confirmed it was indeed polio. At least Gene was in the right place. Sister Kenney was one of the premiere polio hospitals in the entire country. Hot packs were started immediately. Mom and Dad arrived and heard the report that Gene did have polio. It was Christmas Day, and Gene had polio. Not a good way to celebrate Christmas. I returned to Cottonwood, as I had to report back to Fort Knox to complete my OCS training.

For the first three days, there was an iron lung right beside Gene's bed. He was observed around the clock, and they were ready to put him in the iron lung if necessary, but wanted to avoid doing so if at all possible because once anyone is put in the iron lung, chances were great that the patient would need to stay in an iron lung for the rest of their life. Three days after Gene arrived they removed it from the room as he had passed the first test. His lungs were able to keep up on their own.

Gene remained at Sister Kenney for seven months before he was able to return home. When he left the hospital, he was six foot one and weighed only 130 pounds.

There are no pictures in this chapter, as Mom would not allow any pictures to be taken while Gene was in the hospital. She didn't want any memories of that chapter in Gene's life.

9

MARRIAGE

There is only one rule for being a good talker: Learn to listen.
—CHRISTOPHER MORLEY

AFTER THE OCS GRADUATION CEREMONY everyone was dismissed for leave. On January 31, I headed to Louisville to catch a plane to Minneapolis. Marg and her dad, and one of her bridesmaids met me at the airport. We arrived in Cottonwood after eight o'clock that evening and went directly to the church for our wedding rehearsal. We didn't have time to stop for a bite to eat as my plane from Louisville arrived late. It was dark and about zero degrees. The rehearsal went off without a hitch, and we were ready for our big day, which was the following day on February 1, 1953.

For years I have joked that it would be a cold day in Hell when I got married. Well, the little town of Cottonwood is a lot closer to heaven than hell. On that cold frosty day in February when Marg and I said, "I Do," it was ten degrees below zero Fahrenheit. The wedding went off as planned. Unlike most of today's weddings, our reception was held in the church basement. The only food was small finger sandwiches and wedding cake prepared by the church Ladies Aid. The strongest drink was black coffee.

On January 30, my dad traded cars and made a deal so he could keep the old car for an additional two weeks. On the afternoon of the wedding, we parked Dad's old car in front of the church with two clearly visible but empty suitcases in the back

CUTTING THE CAKE AT OUR WEDDING RECEPTION IN THE CHURCH BASEMENT OF CHRIST LUTHERAN CHURCH. THE CHURCH LADIES AID PREPARED FINGER SANDWICHES, WEDDING CAKE, AND BLACK COFFEE FOR OUR GUESTS.

MARLIN AND MARG'S WEDDING DAY, FEBRUARY 1, 1953

seat. Dad's new car had been stored in my uncle's garage, so no one knew Dad had a different car. My Uncle Stanley drove the new car to the church and parked it next to Dad's old car. Our luggage was out of sight in the trunk of the new car. We had everyone fooled. Our friends and relatives decorated the wrong car and put a potato in the exhaust pipe. Of course the potato froze in that extreme cold. Marg and I got in Dad's old car to give everyone the thrill of chasing us around the town for a bit. However, the frozen potato caused the car not to start. When we realized that the decorated car wouldn't start, much to the surprise of all watching, Marg and I simply jumped in the new car and drove off, leaving the old decorated car on the street in front of the church. No one understood why we got in this strange new car and drove off. We drove home, changed out of our wedding clothes, and took off.

About ten miles down Route 23, just past Hanley Falls, I was driving about fifty miles per hour because of a light snowfall when Don Keepers, one of the ushers in our wedding party passed us. Don was a Minnesota State Highway Patrol officer. He was convinced that we were on the way to Minneapolis, and he was determined to catch us. When he passed us, he was looking straight ahead and paid no attention to us. He was looking for the wrong car.

Marg had only five days off before she had to return to Swedish Hospital to continue her nurses training, so we didn't have time to go south where it was warm. We didn't have the money to fly anywhere, so we drove to Duluth. That's right, ten below zero in Cottonwood, and we went north for our honeymoon. Go figure.

After returning to Minneapolis, Marg had night duty at the University of Minnesota hospital. I rented a room on the edge of campus for a week so we could have some time together. At the end of the week, we drove back to Cottonwood to pick up my things before flying to Fort Benning, Georgia for my paratrooper

MARG AT HER
STUDENT NURSE
CAPPING CEREMONY
IN 1950

MARG GRADUATED
AS A REGISTERED
NURSE IN 1953.

training. On our way there we hit another snowstorm. The snow was coming down pretty heavy, but the pressure was on for us to get to Cottonwood to get my things and return Dad's new car. Every once in a while we could see a few hundred feet ahead. All of a sudden, I hit a snowdrift right on the highway. The snow came up over the hood as the car came to an abrupt stop. I tried to get the car out of the snowdrift, but it wouldn't go forward or back. I was barely able to open the door and wiggle my way outside. I glanced around and saw a tow truck coming down the road. It wasn't more than thirty seconds after we had hit that snowdrift. A bread truck was stuck in a snow bank further down the road and the tow truck had come to pull the bread truck out. He had to pull us out first because he couldn't get to the bread truck without pulling us out. Luck was with us; he pulled us to the only automobile garage in Plato, Minnesota.

Plato is a town of about 400 people and sits about a half-mile off the highway. The town had a very small mom and pop restaurant, a post office, and a beer parlor. Our car was inside the heated garage. The man who ran the garage told us it would take a day for the snow in the engine compartment to melt. It didn't matter; we weren't going anywhere soon because the highway was closed. We headed for the restaurant to get a bite to eat. A waitress informed us that there was no motel in town, but they did know of a couple that might rent us a room for the night. I looked up the number and called their house and rented the room. I later learned it was the only room for rent in the entire town. Marg had been working nights, and it had been over twenty-four hours since she had slept. She was really tired and needed some rest.

The next day, after a good night's sleep, we learned that over one hundred people were stranded in Plato that night, and we were the only ones that had a bed to sleep in. Everyone else slept in the post office, the local restaurant, or the beer parlor that had been kept open for the stranded motorists. Everyone had to sleep on the floor, if they slept at all. The lady of the house where we stayed cooked a fine dinner and invited us to dine with them. The other hundred plus stranded motorists were eating potato chips, drinking coffee, or as we learned later, many stayed awake all night rather than sleeping on the floor.

Getting stranded never happened when we were dating, but less than two weeks after we were married, it was just my luck that we got stranded.

The next day we got our car that was all warmed up, washed, and ready to go. The snowplows had been through, so the highway was open again. We drove to Cottonwood and spent one night before heading to Minneapolis, so I could catch my flight, and Marg could go back to school.

10

JUMP SCHOOL AND THE 82ND AIRBORNE

When I was a boy I was told that anybody could become president. I'm beginning to believe it.
—CLARENCE DARROW

I ARRIVED AT FORT BENNING mid-February, which was an ideal time to take paratrooper training. It was well known that the cadre really pushed everyone to the absolute physical limits in jump school. In February the weather was cool in Georgia, which would make the physical part of the training a bit more tolerable. Even with the cooler temperatures, some of the men in my training class fell over from heat exhaustion, and some from just plain exhaustion. Most of us were able to keep up because we were in the best physical shape of our lives. At least that was true in my case, having just finished sixteen weeks of infantry basic training, three weeks of leadership, and six months of OCS. Some of the guys in our jump school class did not have that prior rigorous training before they arrived, and couldn't keep up.

A few years before I arrived for training a lot of trainees in summer classes passed out, and some died of heat exhaustion. Congress got involved, some heads rolled, and the physical part of the training was revised. Running was one of many activities in our training. And run we did. They knew some of the men would not keep up the pace. As runners dropped with heat exhaustion, they were picked up by one of the two ambulances that followed along.

Training started with run two minutes, walk three minutes, and run two minutes. We were told they were going to push us a bit more every day, and at the end of our third week at jump school, we would be running eight minutes, walking two minutes, running eight minutes, walking two, and running eight minutes. After one week, we were up to the run eight, walk two routines. The next day, it was run ten, walk two, run ten, walk two, and run ten. We were way past the goal of run eight minutes and walk two, several times in a row. The day before our last day of jump school we ran twenty-four minutes, walked two, ran twenty-five, walked two, and ran twenty-six.

On the last day of training we ran eight, walked two, several times over. They told us at the start of training that we would progress up to run eight, walk two, and so on. They didn't talk about the days in between when we ran seventy-five minutes out of seventy-nine. A lot of guys couldn't make it and were washed out. If they were close and it was felt they could eventually keep up, they were simply sent back to another class to start over again. However, most guys simply washed out and didn't become paratroopers. We never saw them again. No one in our class died or even came close, but only because it was February, and the temperatures were cool. I see how they would lose some if they pushed everyone that hard in the summer heat.

Jump school was only three weeks long. For the first week each day we jumped off the 34-foot towers and would drop down about eighteen feet before the straps would stop us. This was to get the feeling of the opening shock, simulating when the chute opens, after jumping out of a plane flying 120 miles per hour. When the chute opens, the shock is quite severe. The second week we were taken to a 250-foot tower where we were released with the chute already open. We would float down and experience landing. In the third week we jumped out of a plane each day.

CHAPTER 10 / *Jump School and the 82nd Airborne*

Officers in their first, second, and third week of training class were housed in the same barracks. Every Monday night, the guys just starting week one and two would ask the guys in week three what it was like to jump. On the following Monday all the men in my class were to jump for the first time. One night about ten guys including me were gathered around a black chaplain telling about his first jump. Most training jumps were from 800 to 1,200 feet, so it only takes a minute and a half to land after jumping. But this chaplain went on and on for over thirty minutes describing his first jump. Everyone was hanging onto every word because in exactly seven days, we all would be experiencing our first jump.

Finally, after thirty plus minutes of his describing a minute and a half descent, someone asked, "Were you scared?"

The chaplain answered in his southern drawl, "Man, only two peoples knows how scared I was, and dat's da Lord and da laundryman."

With that we all had a good laugh and went about our business, wondering what it was going to be like for our first jump.

Rumors persisted that if a trooper wouldn't jump, they would push you out. Well, that is simply not true. On the first couple

MASS PARATROOPERS' JUMP FROM C-82S

of jumps the jumper goes alone, not in a stick. Each hand is touching the open doorway with the fingers outside of the plane. There is a red and green light on the doorway just above your hand. When the light turns from red to green, that is the signal to jump. They use the three senses—sight, sound, and touch—to tell you that it is time to jump. You know when it is your time, but no one ever pushes you. You have to jump on your own, but it is a court-martial offense to refuse to jump once you have jump orders.

PARACHUTING OUT OF A C-46

There must be a rule written in indelible ink that everyone remembers that first jump. As our plane left the airfield, I volunteered to be the first jumper. The plane was going 120 miles per hour when we reached the drop zone, and the jumpmaster shouted, "Stand in the door!" I assumed the position of toes over the edge outside the plane, both hands and fingers outside the door, and body positioned, ready to push with hands and feet when the green light came on. I heard the jumpmaster shout, "Go!" in my ear and felt his tap on my butt.

Instinctively, I was out the door when the order came. You are supposed to keep your eyes open, but I had mine closed. I said to myself as I went out the door, "Reishus, what are you doing here?" It feels like a truck hits you when the chute opens, and you start bouncing around like a cork in rough water. Then suddenly there is peace and quiet as you float down to earth. The only thing left is the landing, and that is a piece of cake. The sandy soil had been plowed to make the landing soft. On the ground I gathered my chute and proceeded toward the waiting trucks. I had made my first jump and was still in one piece!

A PARACHUTE JUMP AS IT LOOKS FROM THE GROUND

After the initial training jumps, you jump in what's called a "stick." A stick is a line of jumpers who jump right after each other. Only the first man in the stick gets the green light, slap on the butt, and "Go!" in the ear. Everyone else in the stick shuffles, keeping their bellies up to and touching the backs of the guys in front. When the trooper gets to the door, there is no turning back because the guys in the stick behind are shuffling forward. The jumper couldn't stop if he wanted to, and in a sense, the trooper is pushed out.

After jump school, the non-commissioned officers (the non-coms) and the officers in the class stayed for two additional weeks of jumpmaster training. On one of the training jumps we were told the jump would be a cloudy and dark night jump and

SECOND LIEUTENANT WITH PARATROOPERS' WING, FT. BRAGG, NORTH CAROLINA, 1953

we wouldn't be able to see anything. One guy in the back of the room said, "It won't be any different. I haven't had my eyes open yet." That got quite a laugh.

With jump school behind us, my buddy, Pete Gregg, and I were off to Fayetteville, North Carolina to join the 44th Tank Battalion of the 82nd Airborne at Fort Bragg.

When we reported, Pete and I were assigned to the 44th Tank Battalion, but to different companies. There were eight more officers from our jump school class who were being assigned to the 44th and would arrive any day. Only one of us had a car, and we didn't know how we would get to the company every day unless we were assigned the same company, which they approved.

Pete had purchased a new Buick, and at the time I didn't have a car. It was fortunate he had a car because we were assigned to a **BOQ** (Bachelor Officers Quarters) over four miles from our company. I don't know how I would have been able to get to the company every day. Officers who had been with the 82nd for some time occupied the **BOQ** close to the company. There was no **BOQ** for us available any closer.

About all the 82nd did was train for the possibility of being sent somewhere in the world to quell some uprising. The 82nd Airborne is still our country's first line of defense.

About a month after our arrival in Fort Bragg, I had a question for Lt. Roger Jamesmyth, our exec officer. "Is there anyone shipping out to Korea?"

Lt. Jamesmyth had been assigned to the 82nd for quite some time. His reply was, "There won't be anyone shipping out to Korea from the 82nd because our outfit needs to be ready on seventy-two hours notice to go anywhere in the world."

The Division couldn't be ready if there were troopers shipping in and out. I was told, "The only way anyone is shipped to Korea, or anywhere for that matter, is to volunteer, and that won't happen unless they have a replacement."

Until that conversation, I didn't know that signing up for jump school and being assigned to the 82nd assured me that I would not be shipped to Korea. In the back of my mind I kind of wanted to go to Korea. I wanted to do my share. But the good Lord was watching over me, and His plans for me were to not go. Most members of my **OCS** class were shipped to Korea. Unfortunately, I lost track of most of them and don't know their fate.

The 44th Tank Battalion was assigned to the 82nd Airborne. At that time the Air Force didn't have planes that had the ability to carry a tank; our tanks were just too heavy for the largest of the Air Force transport carriers. In war, the tanks would have to come in by land, and the troopers assigned to them would have to come in by land with the tanks. Even though we would never jump in combat, we were required to be jumpers. If you were in the 82nd, you were a jumper. This included the administrative people, chaplain, medical people, mechanics, and everyone else. If you weren't a jumper, you couldn't be assigned to the 82nd in any capacity.

About three months after I arrived, Corporal Willie Washington was going to make his one hundredth jump. Willie was in our company but not in my platoon. The 82nd made a big deal out of it whenever anyone jumped for the hundredth time. In preparations for his jump, it was learned that Willie had never been in an airplane when it landed. He had never flown in a commercial plane and had jumped every time he went up in a military plane. The officers told Willie that he would fly along on the first flight, but not jump with the others. His orders were to come back with the flight crew, land, and go up with the next group and then jump. All went well until the landing. Willie had never experienced landing in an airplane before, and he didn't like it. More than not like it, he was absolutely terrified and refused to go when the plane went back up with another load of troopers. In effect, he was refusing to jump. Once the trooper has orders, he is obligated to jump. To not jump, if you have orders to jump, is a court-martial offense. The jumper's name was on the manifest, and the written orders call for the trooper to jump.

They were trying to give Willie a prize by letting him fly along on the first leg, land, and then go up and jump on the second leg of the flight. The company commander didn't know what to do. They didn't want to court-martial a guy who was about to jump for the hundredth time. Three days later, with consultation from the Battalion HQ and Division HQ, they talked Willie into going up again. They assured him that if he jumped, there would be no court-martial, and he could be released and assigned to a non-jumping division. Willie would never have to jump again, but more important to Willie, he would never have to land again. Finally, Willie went along with it. He made the jump, and everything seemed okay. When I left the Division, Willie had over 110 jumps and still loved it, but said he didn't ever want to land in a plane again.

In May of 1953, I learned that my Uncle Stanley, who sold Dad his new car, had not yet sold Dad's old car. By this time I had saved a few bucks and wanted to buy a car. Learning that Dad's old car was available, and knowing it was in excellent condition, I decided to buy it. I paid $700 for Dad's old 1950 Chevrolet. That was in June of 1953. I didn't have anywhere near that much money, but Uncle Stanley agreed to sell it to me for $700 and accept one hundred dollars per month for seven months. No papers to sign, no note, no interest, just a handshake, so to speak, over the phone.

Marg had a ten-day vacation in early June. She went to Cottonwood, got the car from Uncle Stanley, and she and her classmate, Marion Munson, drove to Fort Bragg, North Carolina. In the middle of her week's stay, the Division had a field exercise. We hadn't had one in about three months, but as luck would have it, we had one when Marg was there. I was sleeping in a tent in the field, and Marg was staying at the officer's club motel.

Part of the exercises was a massive air jump. Marg was sitting in the bleachers set up for spectators and knew the plane I was in and that I would be the first jumper out of the left side of the plane. She picked me out of the hundreds of specks in the sky. After landing, I picked up my chute and walked the couple of blocks right to the bleachers where Marg was sitting. She had spotted me as I jumped, and her eyes followed me as I landed and returned my chute to the waiting truck. I guess it was quite a thrill for her to see me jump and then walk up to her.

Marion, the girl she drove with, flew home, and a few days later Marg flew back to Minneapolis as well. The war in Korea was winding down, and rumors were flying that the Army might let some guys out of the service early. On July 27, 1953

MARLIN AS A PARATROOPER ON ONE OF HIS MANY JUMPS

an armistice was signed, and very shortly thereafter, the Army issued orders that any officer with over two years' service could be released from active duty simply by requesting to be released. In the next few days a whole lot of officers put in their request, and I was among them. Three weeks later the requests were answered, and officers were released from active duty left and right. I was lucky to be one of the early ones to get orders to be released. In a few days I was packed and out of there.

On my drive to Minneapolis, my first stop after fourteen hours on the road was somewhere in Kentucky. It had been 104 degrees that afternoon, and my Chevrolet had no air conditioning. It was cooler at night, so I kept driving until about 11 p.m. before getting a motel. I slept about nine hours, and was on the road again, arriving in Minneapolis just in time for

Marg's graduation from nurses training. Marg was through with her schooling. The war was over, and I was out of the Army. Hallelujah!

MILITARY EMBLEMS WORN ON MY U.S. ARMY UNIFORM

A little more about chutes: Before World War II, troopers packed their own chutes. The chutes were reliable and seldom resulted in a failure. Unfortunately, troopers began to get careless and sloppy in their chute packing, paying little or no attention to detail or just how the chute was packed. They would just throw the chute in, putting pieces of paper in the chute to give the appearance of a streamer. Obviously, this practice resulted in increased accidents and loss of life if a chute didn't open properly. This did not please the Army brass in the least. So they developed a specialist called, "The Chute Packer."

The chute packer was an experienced trooper who had been in the airborne quite some time. His main job was to pack chutes all day long. A skilled specialist would be more likely to pack a chute right.

To keep the chute packers honest and insure that they did an extraordinary job with no exceptions, they instituted the following policy: When a chute packer turned in a completed chute, the officer would ask if that chute was packed correctly. Of course, the answer was always, "Yes Sir." It was reported that the officer took the chute and told the chute packer, "Well, it better be because you are jumping with it tomorrow." The chute was locked up in a holding area.

The next day the officer would meet the trooper just before boarding and getting in his stick. The officer gave the retrieved chute to the Chute Packer and the plane took off. When the plane reached the drop zone, the chute packer would jump with the chute he packed the previous day. It had better work.

Every chute packer personally signed for every chute they packed. This policy reduced accidents and deaths dramatically.

11

COLLEGE DAYS

Never Explain, Never Complain, Just Do It!
—ANONYMOUS

IN SEPTEMBER 1953, I WAS officially out of the Army, and Marg had finished her nurses training. It was too late for me to enroll in college, and besides that, we were broke. We hadn't set up housekeeping yet and didn't have a stick of furniture or any appliances. Our bank account had the grand total of $300. Marg and I had not yet made plans where to go or decided what we were going to do. I had no job and few skills that would enable me to earn a good living. Without much forethought, the two of us decided to go to Cottonwood where I would work in Dad's Coast-to-Coast store and figure out what to do from there. We still didn't know where we would live, or how much money I would earn. I knew I had to do something, and it was up to me to get started on the rest of my life.

IF IT IS TO BE IT IS UP TO ME

We lived with my folks for a few weeks while we searched for a place of our own. The upstairs part of the Cary Dahl house was going to be available to rent in a couple of weeks. We rented it and began looking for furniture. My Uncle Stanley and Aunt Eloise had given us a card table and chairs for our wedding, so we had furniture for the kitchen. We bought a King-Koil hide-a-bed, a King-Koil mattress and box spring, and a bedroom set through Dad's Coast-to-Coast store. In a few weeks they arrived,

OUT OF SERVICE AND HEADED FOR COLLEGE

and we were set. After a few months of living on the cheap, our furniture was paid for. That first bedroom set is now scattered among our kids and grandkids and is still in use somewhere in the family.

A few months working for Dad, I knew one thing for sure. I didn't want to be a hardware store manager or a storeowner for that matter. And after seeing some of the world outside of Cottonwood, I didn't think I wanted to live in Cottonwood for the rest of my life either. Dad had wanted me to learn the hardware store business, eventually take over the management, and ultimately buy the store. There is no question, it would have been a good deal for me had I wanted to stay in Cottonwood. Who other than your Dad would set you up in business and eventually sell it on terms of nothing down and reasonable payments? If we wanted to stay for the indefinite future, this was a great opportunity, but we decided our stay in Cottonwood was not permanent and we already planned to move on.

But for now we had settled in, and Marg was happy with our

situation. I was beginning to think more of college. I convinced her that I needed to get my college degree because, in the long run, having that degree would be best.

I went to see Mr. Brenelson, the Cottonwood superintendent of schools who had replaced my father-in-law, Mr. Earl E. Olson, and told him I wanted to go to college and asked if he would help me. "I don't know where to start," I told him. My grades weren't that great in high school, but I had accomplished quite a bit in the military and felt confident that I could handle college. Mr. Brenelson looked up my grades and gave me a battery of tests.

After getting the test results he told me he would write a letter to the university recommending that I be admitted. He didn't see any reason I shouldn't go to college, and thought I would handle the college material quite well.

The superintendent had moved to Cottonwood while I was in the military. I was very appreciative of the efforts he made on my behalf. His name was Ralph Brenelson, but to me he was Mr. Brenelson. One didn't address the superintendent of schools by his first name.

Gustavus Adolphus in St. Peter, Minnesota is where I really wanted to go. Both Marg and her Dad had gone there, but I knew that was out of the question; I simply couldn't afford it. The University of Minnesota was less expensive, and I could get a part-time job somewhere in the Twin Cities. The more I thought about it, I realized that if I was to go off to college, it had to be the "U." It was the only school that I could afford. As it turned out, the "U" was a good choice for me because their business school was stronger than the business schools at any of the smaller private colleges in the state. I enrolled and was accepted.

In the fall of 1954 we temporarily moved in with Marg's folks in Anoka, Minnesota, which was about twenty miles from the university. Classes started the last week of September, and I was off and running. From that point on,

IF IT IS TO BE IT IS UP TO ME.

On November 9, 1954, six weeks after I started college, our daughter Katherine was born. Having a child made us more eligible for married student housing. We were approved and moved in two weeks later. Married student housing was available to anyone married, but those with children had first choice. All the while I was at the "U," no couples moved in unless they had children.

Married student housing was originally World War II barracks, which were now converted to duplexes. Our unit, like everyone else's, was 20 feet wide by 28 feet long with a total of 560 square feet. It had two very small bedrooms, a bath, and a somewhat larger room with a very small kitchen at one end and the living room at the other end. The only two doors in the place went to the bathroom and to the outside. There were no doors on the closets, bedrooms, or even on the kitchen cabinets. Well, they weren't really cabinets; they were simply shelves with no doors. Everyone put up curtains to block the view of the cupboard's contents.

Every block or so there were two or three 265-gallon drums that held heating oil. We all had a five-gallon surplus military fuel can stored on our front step, and we were free to get all the heating oil we wanted. The units were well insulated and easy to keep warm.

Every time there was a cold snap, Marg's mother would call to see if we were warm enough, which we always were. Our rent was only $35 per month and included all utilities except the phone.

That first school year I got a part-time job working in the wood shop at the Student Union. I didn't earn much money, but it was right on campus and I was able to schedule my work hours around my class schedule. When school ended after my freshman year, I worked as a carpenter. I really wasn't qualified to be a carpenter, but I faked it. A closer job description would have been carpenter's helper. The head of the Carpenter Union's Twin City District Council liked me and gave me a permit to work that summer as a carpenter with full carpenter's wages. I didn't have to join the union, but was paid union wages, which were $2.90 per hour. Most of my classmates, if they were able to obtain a job, made from 75 cents to $1.00 per hour maximum. I was doing well. I worked all summer right up till the Friday before school started in September. We saved a lot of my summer wages and were in pretty good shape financially. Looking back, we were actually poor, but we didn't know it. We believed we were fine.

My job as a carpenter ended when the 1955 fall semester started. I began working at the Roseville Coast-to-Coast store, earning 75 cents per hour with a promise of 90 cents in six months. The job was good, as I could work around my class schedule. I continued this part-time job working two or three afternoons a week and on Saturdays until graduation in June of 1957. I drove to the Coast-to-Coast store to work, but took the intercampus bus to classes every day so Marg could have the car most of the time. She worked as a registered nurse a couple of nights a week at Swedish Hospital and I stayed home with Kathy.

My cousin Arvid Ree was a major in the U.S. Army Reserves, and he encouraged me to consider joining the reserves. It was a wonderful opportunity, particularly for college students. I checked out the reserves and joined along with three other students in the University Grove East married student-housing complex where we were living. The four of us were able to carpool to reserve meetings every Tuesday evening. We were obligated to only one night a week and as officers were paid a little over $50 per month. It was a wonderful part-time job.

I was constantly working on my schedule as to what classes I would need to take for each quarter. I realized that if I went to summer school, just one summer, and took a heavy class load, I could graduate at the end of my third year. I received permission from my advisor, Mr. Smith, another guy whose first name was only known to me as "Mister." I finally did get approval from my advisor, but with a great deal of difficulty, I might add.

In addition to weekly reserve meetings, every summer I had two weeks of active duty at Camp McCoy, near Sparta, Wisconsin. The Army has since changed the name to Fort McCoy, but when I was there, it was called Camp McCoy.

My summer school classes ended just before we went to Camp McCoy. Summer camp was two weeks, and the four of us from University Grove East found an Army leadership class scheduled in the time slot we wanted at Fort Benning, Georgia. The class was three weeks long starting the Monday after Summer Camp and ending the Friday before Fall quarter began at the "U". The schedule couldn't have worked out better. We were all accepted and all signed up for class. We had twelve weeks of summer school, and five weeks of active duty, including the summer training and leadership school at Fort Benning. During this time we were getting officer's pay. It was a good deal. The bank account looked pretty good at the end of that summer.

I graduated in June of 1957 with a degree in business administration after only three years at the "U." Since my GI Bill for college ran out that year in April, it was none too soon, I might add. The GI Bill wasn't much, but it made a whale of a difference. Without it, a lot of veterans, including me, would not have been able to afford to go to college. It paid $95 per month for a single veteran, $120 per month for a married veteran, and $160 per month for a married veteran with additional dependents. It didn't matter how many additional dependents, $160 per month was the max. We had to pay expenses, including books, tuition, room and board, and other miscellaneous items.

During the last year of college I started to run out of money and had to borrow a couple of hundred from time to time from Dad. I owed $1000 at the time of my graduation in June. Even though both Mom and Dad told me that I didn't need to pay them back and to consider it a gift, I paid it all back over the next fifteen months, with interest.

With Marg using the car, most days I rode the intercampus bus. The bus had stops at the St. Paul Campus, University

Grove East where we lived, University Village (the other married student housing facility), and the Minneapolis campus. It was a private bus just for university students and faculty. The total time from University Grove East to the Minneapolis campus was twenty minutes and cost about twenty cents a ride. If you forgot your money, the driver just said, "Remember to pay next time, OK?" It was a very loose and easy situation and an easy low-cost way to get to and from school.

MARLIN AS A BUSINESSMAN IN 1968

Part 2

Business

If a man does not keep pace with his companions, perhaps it is because he hears a different drummer. Let him step to the music which he hears, however measured or far away.

—HENRY DAVID THOREAU

12

THE BABCOCK AND WILCOX COMPANY

I've been rich and I've been poor—and believe me it is better to be rich.
—JOE E. LEWIS / SOPHIE TUCKER

I HAD BEEN RECRUITED AT the placement office of the School of Business at the University of Minnesota. In the winter and spring of my senior year I interviewed with several companies and received a few offers. I accepted the offer from the Babcock and Wilcox Company in Barberton, Ohio for $430 per month. Five hundred was the highest offer of anyone graduating from the School of Business, with one exception, and that was my good friend Paul Lindholm who now owns a bank in Fergus Falls, Minnesota. Paul received the highest offer, and it was no surprise to those of us who knew him well. Paul is one of the smartest guys I have ever known, and truly a great person as well. He graduated with high honors after only two and one half years of college. The average business school graduate in 1957 was offered $400, so I felt pretty good. By the time I graduated we had two pre-school kids. Kathy was two and one-half and Eric fifteen months. I needed to get on with my life, get a job, and earn some money fast.

IF IT IS TO BE IT IS UP TO ME

Since the economy was not too good at that time, not all graduates received a job offer. I was fortunate to be recruited by the Babcock and Wilcox Company as a "Student Engineer." Of the fifty new recruits in the 1957 B & W class of student engineers, five of us were business graduates, and forty-five were engineering graduates. The program of hiring non-engineers to the Student Engineer Management Training Program was an experiment on the part of the company. They thought that some of the future managers should have a business background as opposed to all having engineering backgrounds.

I found it strange to be called a student engineer because I didn't have any engineer training. One of the major reasons I decided to accept the position with B & W was that it had a formal management-training program for newly hired college graduates. It wasn't long before I realized that it was a real plus to be selected to attend the company's Student Engineer Management Training Program. Virtually all of the upper and mid-level management had come through this same management training program in years past. Student engineers were highly respected by management and company employees as well. I learned that it was extremely difficult to get promoted to a management position unless one had been a student engineer. If I decided to stay with the company for the long haul, at least I had some of the right credentials.

During the five-month management training program, the student engineer class traveled to several of the B & W plants. We spent most of the time in Barberton at their boiler factory, but we traveled to Beaver Falls, Pennsylvania for a week at the tube plant and another week in Augusta, Georgia at the refectories plant, and to several others. The tube plant in Beaver Falls had several thousand employees simply manufacturing pipe. I say simply, but it was far from simple. These pipes were to be used in the manufacture of steam boilers and had to be capable of handling heat well in excess of 1000 degrees and over 2000 pounds per square inch of pressure. Every tube and every weld in the entire boiler was x-rayed to see if there were any flaws

CHAPTER 12 / *The Babcock and Wilcox Company*

in the weld or the tube. If a flaw was detected, the weld was removed, welded again, and x-rayed again to insure perfection. It was my hope to be assigned to the tube division because my long-range goal was to get into industrial sales, and I knew that I would be able to get into sales faster with the tube division. I also knew it would be a five or ten year process to get a sales assignment with the boiler division. I wasn't an engineer and to even be considered for sales of these huge industrial steam boilers was a long shot. These boilers stood some ten or twelve stories tall, took at least two years to design, another twelve to eighteen months to manufacture, followed by another eighteen months to two years to erect on the site. It was a long time before one would produce its first pound of steam. The customers were primarily the big public utilities.

As a part of my management-training program I spent six weeks in Kaukauna, Wisconsin where B & W was erecting a black liquor boiler for the Thilmony Pulp and Paper Company. In the process of making paper, a lot of waste and other residue is produced. The industry calls this residue black liquor. B & W designed a small boiler to burn the black liquor. They got rid of the waste and produced steam, which they needed in manufacturing paper. It was a small boiler by B & W standards. Small, if you can call a boiler seven stories tall "small."

All the while I was in the training program we were living in a furnished rental house in Alliance, Ohio. We didn't know which division we were going to be assigned, and B & W was only going to pay for one move. Therefore, everyone in the class rented furnished places until we got our final assignment. During the latter part of the training program, I was in Two Rivers, Wisconsin for about six weeks while I observed the erection of this black liquor boiler. Marg, Kathy, and Eric flew up to spend a couple of weeks with me. I reserved a cabin on a lake near Two Rivers. The plan was for them to vacation while I was at the Thilmony Pulp and Paper site. The day before they arrived, I fell off the dock and hit my head on the bottom of the lake. They hauled me off to the hospital where they said I had a compression fracture of one of my vertebras.

I made arrangements for some people from the resort to meet Marg and the kids at the airport. I'm sure Marg was in a quandary when a couple of strangers met her at the airport and told her they were going to take her to the hospital where I was. All they could tell her was there had been an accident at the lake, and that I was hurt. Being a registered nurse, Marg imagined all kinds of things. It turned out that I wasn't paralyzed and would recover, but I did have to spend a week in the hospital. Marg was at the cabin for one week before I was released from the hospital. We had the cabin reserved for another week, so we got to spend a week together before Marg and the kids flew back. My back has bothered me all my life, but not so I couldn't work. It could have been much worse.

After the five-month Student Engineer Management Training Program, I was assigned to the boiler plant in Barberton, Ohio and not to the Beaver Falls tube plant that had been my first choice. I was the only student engineer assigned to the Materials Department, and I had no title. Many of the non-management employees called me the student engineer and because of my first assignment, some called me the efficiency expert. My first assignment was to look at all the paperwork that kept the 105 employees in the Materials Department busy. A new set of eyes might see a better way to accomplish the task at hand. My assignment was to find a better way to get the job done.

I looked at everything, questioned every piece of paper, asked people why they needed a particular form, why they needed the information on the form, and if they could accept the information in another format. I researched who needed what information and why. After a few months of review, I found there were 29 different forms with much of the same information. Each form required writing and typing the same thing over and over simply because one manager wanted the information listed on a piece of paper one way, while another manager wanted the same information listed another way. Often the managers didn't know that another manager in the same department was compiling the same information but in a different format. When I asked why they did a particular thing the way they did, the answer was, "Because that's the way we do it," or "Because that's the way I want it." I rarely got a legitimate reason for the format, and in some cases why they even needed the information.

In the end, I got rid of all 29 old forms and created three new forms with multiple copies. Some forms had certain information blocked out. I could have gotten it down to two, but some of the information was confidential, and the management didn't want confidential information readily available to so many.

After I made some mock-ups of what information the forms would contain, I presented my ideas to management. Only a few of those affected resisted. Some of those were the older men who were set in their ways and didn't like change. But most of the resistance came from the younger men who felt threatened. (There were no female managers at that time, although that has changed in recent years). They knew there was a lot of duplication of effort and realized that someone, or possibly several, could lose their job. John Jensen, the manager of the Materials Department was behind me, and his support resulted in the project moving along. Everyone knew that John had asked me to come up with an improved system. Since John was behind it, I managed to get the necessary cooperation.

As a result of my findings, John was able to eliminate six positions in the Materials Department. This was handled through normal attrition. Two women employees left to have babies, and intended to be stay-at-home moms, one person retired, and three others were transferred to fill vacancies in another department. The net result was the department now had six fewer people than before, simply because we learned to do things a different way.

No one was fired, and the new system was much more efficient. I was a hero in the eyes of management. Even though I was the new guy who came out of the blue, and began making changes affecting their lives, the rank and file accepted me.

I continued to streamline other aspects of the Materials Department and had similar results. A few months later we were in an economic downturn, and experiencing serious times. B & W hired a new plant manager who was the vice president of the whole 6000-employee plant. It was soon obvious that his assignment was to clean house. He was hired to be a hatchet man. The previous top management team that the company wanted to keep for the long run was assigned to staff positions. They would come back a couple of years later, after the hatchet guy had cleaned house, and the economy had recovered.

Hatchet Man, as he was called by many of the employees, ordered all the departments to get rid of the "Dead Wood," which was his terminology. In a little over two weeks, over 600 employees representing 10.5 percent of the work force were laid off. When Hatchet Man received the updated report a week later reporting "that only" 10.5 percent had been laid off, he called a meeting of all the middle and upper management saying he was very disappointed with so few layoffs. With the economy getting worse and the lack of orders for new boilers, the company required a much larger reduction. He demanded everyone in middle and upper management come back to him with additional 20 percent layoffs. They had only two weeks to get them off the payroll.

The managers were also told that if they didn't comply, they themselves would be fired. He was tough, and everyone knew it. He had been assigned to do this by the top management of the company in Manhattan. When I learned of this, I was afraid for my job because I had only been with the company for a bit over a year. I thought the new kid would be on the chopping block for sure. I had kept Marg informed of the layoffs, but I never let her know that I thought that I could be in the next wave. She had her hands full with two pre-school kids and was expecting a third in a few months. I didn't want to burden her with more anxiety.

Jack Trotter who lived near me in Wadsworth, and with whom I carpooled on occasion, got the axe. Jack had been with the company for nineteen years and seven months. To be eligible for retirement benefits one needed twenty years. Jack was a recovering alcoholic and had missed a lot of work because of his drinking problem. His problem and absences from work happened several years prior, and he had been sober for over four years and had not missed a day during that period. He was a stellar employee. But the company had to let people go, and they were way beyond getting rid of the Dead Wood. They were forced to cut good productive people. Management memories were long, and though Jack had been sober for four years, because of his past, Jack had to go. His previous drinking problem had caught up with him.

Now I was really worried. If they would lay off a guy who had been a manager and had nineteen and one half years with the company, I thought my short tenure of thirteen months would certainly result in my getting the axe too. However, when the next wave hit some two weeks later, and our department was forced to lay off an additional 24 people, somehow I was spared. John Jensen told me that I had to stay on as staff to him to help find ways to get by with only 75 people. There had been 99 on the staff earlier and 105 a couple of months prior to that. My earlier projects of streamlining of the office paid off, and I was allowed to keep my job. Jensen went on to say that I had to find a way to save both his and my job. He was afraid that Hatchet Man could get him too, even though he had 24 years with the company. He had been a student engineer and graduated from the same program I had just completed. This was the only job he had since graduating from the University of Nebraska.

I realized that continuing to produce new ways of doing

things resulted in savings to the company, and my job was "probably" safe. Finding ways to automate, streamline, consolidate, or eliminate meant thinking outside the box. Not finding those new savings could result in my looking for a job in a down economy, which was not a pretty picture. As an optimist, I was a firm believer that the glass was half full, and even if the glass was one-quarter full, I was still optimistic. Over the next few months I found additional ways to bring savings to the company. I remained a hero in Jansen's eyes, and more importantly, I kept my job in a time of high unemployment.

IF IT IS TO BE IT IS UP TO ME

A newly established Systems Department had been formed to help automate anything and everything in the entire company. Ed Bevin, the manager of the new department, learned of my successes in the Materials Department and asked me to come to his office to explain what I had been doing. He asked me to bring my flowcharts and new and old forms, and come prepared to give a full-blown presentation on the projects I had been working on. It was really an interview. He wanted to see if I had the right stuff to help him to automate much of the paperwork throughout the entire division. I guess I passed the interview because Ed wanted me to come to work for him. He told me this was an opportunity to be a part of the Systems Department and to do for the whole company what I had been doing for one department. Ed called me back the next week to offer me the job. I was elated and accepted his offer.

There was a small problem. I was earning $505 per month at my old job in the Materials Department, and with overtime I was getting about $550 most months. While I wasn't getting rich, it was enough to support my wife, two daughters, and a son. We now had three preschool kids.

The first week I was in the Systems Department they asked me to come in on Saturday to work on a new project, which I did. My next paycheck paid at the old rate even though I put in paperwork for overtime pay. I went to my boss, Ed Bevin, who told me I had to talk to his boss who was the comptroller of the division. Before I got a chance to call for an appointment, I received a call from his secretary stating that the comptroller wanted to see me. I had met him before after Ed recommended that I be added to his group. I needed a final interview with the comptroller to get his approval. During my interview, he told me that my new job would be a promotion. However, in this second meeting I was told that I was now an exempt employee and not eligible for overtime pay.

I countered, "How can you call it a promotion when I now earn less money and am no longer eligible for overtime pay?" He did not give me a good answer, but a few days later Ed called me into his office to say that I had received a raise, and my new pay would be $550 per month. I was happy. Working Saturdays or overtime for the Systems Department was rare.

Our house in Wadsworth, Ohio was on Grandview Avenue just seven miles from my office in Barberton. I carpooled most of the time with other B & W employees who lived in Wadsworth. Marg, a stay-at-home mom, had the car most of the week. We drove a six-passenger 1955 Chevrolet station wagon. It was a six cylinder with just the basics, no air conditioning or power anything, but it served us well. In the summer of 1958, the car was over three years old and needed new brakes. I was kind of handy with tools, but knew nothing about cars. Still, I decided to save some money by overhauling the brakes myself. I bought the parts from an automotive store, and one Saturday morning right out on our driveway I installed new brake pads and overhauled the brake cylinder. When I finished and was going to take it for a test drive, Kathy and Eric wanted to go along.

I said, "No, you can't come along right now. If everything is okay, I will come back, and we can all go for a ride."

I wasn't about to take my kids along on that test drive, not

OUR CHILDREN, KATHY, ERIC, AND JEAN

knowing for sure that I wouldn't crash the car. I thought the brakes would work, but I didn't have a lot of confidence in my automotive work. The test drive went fine, the brakes worked like new, and after driving around a few blocks, I went home and took the family out for ice cream cones. The whole job cost me less than twenty bucks. We weren't living from paycheck to paycheck, but almost, and saving a few dollars here and there was important.

That summer we had a scary event that involved missing money. I went with some of the managers to the bank to cash our checks and then to lunch at a restaurant, which we did almost every payday. The next morning I got dressed and was ready to do some weekend chores. Marg asked me to do something that would result in getting kind of dirty. I had on a pair of new khaki slacks, so I changed to some old worn ones. Later that morning I couldn't find the money from my paycheck. We looked high and low. The kids were so small we knew they wouldn't take it, but might have taken the money to play with.

Several traumatic hours later we realized what had happened. Marg had just finished ironing several pairs of khaki slacks, and had put them in my dresser drawer after I had changed into an older pair. The newly pressed slacks were on top of the ones I had been wearing. We had looked in that top pair of slacks several times, but the top pair changed as Marg finished ironing several pairs of slacks. We had looked everywhere we could think, to no avail. It was frightful, as we couldn't see how we could get by without a whole paycheck. We were relieved when we found the money in the slacks that I had put in the dresser drawer sitting neatly on the bottom of the stack. A few hundred dollars at that stage of our life was a huge amount.

One significant project while working in the Systems Department was when I helped Gene Yost, the Freiden Inc. Systems sales representative develop a new way of producing the bill of materials created by the engineers in many departments. The old system was all manual; everything was handwritten, resulting in numerous errors. The same part could be called by many names, depending on the way the engineer elected to describe it. The system we developed required that the bills of material be typed on Freiden Flexowriters. The result was we utilized the automatic typing features of the Flexowriters. This resulted in standardization of nomenclature, uniformity in the way the bills of material were produced, and the way they looked. All this was a direct result of the use of Flexowriters. They also created a paper tape that was sent to the purchasing department to automate the purchase order system, and to the data processing department where the information was automatically entered into the accounting systems. It was a very large project, taking almost a year to develop and another year to implement. The net result was a huge success. The system saved the company a ton of money, improved efficiency, and reduced errors dramatically. The result was a whole lot cleaner operation. The company was very happy with the results.

The improved operation ruffled the feathers of a few of the

Engineering Department old timers who didn't have their minds wired to accept the idea of doing something a new way. After getting the project approved by upper management, they asked me to go to the different departments in many cities to sell the engineers and their managers on the change. In some cases it was a tough sell, but I succeeded, and the project went forward. I was doing the selling internally and Gene Yost, the Freiden Systems salesman, was getting a huge commission. Something had to change.

I saw an opportunity to get into sales, which I had wanted to do for some time. Jutz Mehaelik, the branch manager for Freiden in Akron, Ohio interviewed me. I got the job, and I was about to start a new career in sales. I could now find ways for companies to improve their way of doing things, and if they were successful, I would get the commission. I was off to a new career.

My new job was commission only. That meant that I wouldn't have a salary or expense account. My car expense would be out of my own pocket, and if I were to take a prospective customer out to lunch, it was out of my pocket.

Looking back, this new sales job was a bit of a gamble, as we had three pre-school kids and had purchased a small house just seven months prior. I was responsible for my family and our home. I had better be able to sell.

The branch manager gave me a draw, so I had some money. But the draw had to be paid back out of future commissions. It took a long time to develop a good relationship with prospective customers, so it was quite a while before any commissions were coming my way. But I was confident. The glass for me was always more full than empty, and I kept reminding myself of those ten little two letter words:

IF IT IS TO BE IT IS UP TO ME

13

ON TO FREIDEN

Everything comes to him who hustles while he waits.
—THOMAS ALVA EDISON

WE NOW HAD THREE KIDS, two younger and one in kindergarten and had purchased a small house some seven months earlier, so I was kind of "hanging out to dry." Some of our friends asked if I was crazy, and I assured them the answer was no, and this was an opportunity just too good to pass up. I knew I could sell, and I knew I would enjoy it and was convinced I would be able to better support my family. I bought a new Chevrolet Corvair Monza. I needed a car to drive for the job and couldn't leave Marg without wheels.

I attended a three-week class at Freiden's home office in Rochester, New York. I learned just how little I knew about the Flexowriters, which was an automatic typewriter and forerunner to today's word processor, and Computypers, a billing machine. I had homework every night, learned a lot, and came back to Akron raring to go. I spent the next four weeks following Gene Yost, learning how he sold. After every sales call, we would sit in the car and review the call and discuss what we did wrong, what we did right, what we learned, and wrote down what we planned to accomplish on the next call. Gene had been very successful for several years at sales. He gave me tips, not so much about the product, but about selling. I was ready to go. Boy was I ready.

There was only one systems sales representative in the Akron Office, and that was Gene. The territory was way more than one person could handle, so Jutz divided Gene's territory in two. Gene kept all of the systems accounts except one. The rest of my territory consisted of a lot of companies that were not Freiden customers. They may have been Freiden calculator or adding machine customers, but not Systems customers. In a relatively short period of time I sold Smuckers a Computyper billing machine. Then I sold Rubbermaid an order entry system that required three Flexowriters. I was off to a good start.

A part of my territory included the Goodyear Tire Company and General Tire Company. Gene kept Firestone Tires because he knew some people in Firestone management and thought if we were to get any of the big three tire companies, it would most likely be Firestone. All three of the tire companies' home offices were in Akron and were so large that if we were to break in and make a sale, it was likely to be a big one.

I went after General Tire first. It was smaller than Goodyear and I thought easier to get to the decision makers. I could get the lower level managers interested, but I was having difficulty getting to the guys who were authorized to make the decisions. General Tire was on an austerity program, and chances of a sale were slim. I believed I could sell them, but it was going to be a long sales campaign.

At the same time, I was making some serious inroads at Goodyear. I finally met a man named Jerry who had been assigned by Goodyear to investigate order entry systems. Jerry and I hit it off well. He was a young guy about my age, and was intrigued by the capabilities of the Flexowriter. I spoon-fed him information on the Flexowriter over the next few months. After about six months he was convinced that the order entry system I had proposed not only would do the job, but also was better than any of the competition he was evaluating.

The next step was to sell his management. Jerry was not the decision maker and Goodyear wouldn't let me talk to anyone else at first. Little by little I was able to meet some of the people

CHAPTER 13 / *On to Freiden*

who were authorized. Finally I arranged for a sales presentation, and the decision makers agreed to be there. The big sticks didn't give me any opposition, but it took several months before I got the sale. It was a long and tough sell, but in the end I sold them an order entry system they utilized in all their branch operations throughout the entire United States and Canada. It took me almost a year to make the sale, which was the largest for Freiden in the entire state of Ohio. My commission on that one sale was about two and one half times what I had been earning at B & W in an entire year. Not only did I know now that I had made the right decision to go into sales, but so did those who were close to me. I truly was off and running. I made additional sales and was quite comfortable in my position.

During those years, Marg and I could see that both of our parents were getting on in age, and we wouldn't have them around too many more years. We didn't want our kids to grow up seeing their grandparents just once a year. I had been selling Freiden Systems for two and a half years when Marg and I were vacationing in Minnesota. While we were there I went to the Freiden office in Minneapolis where I talked to Mr. Richardson, the Freiden branch manager for the Minneapolis office. I explained my successes in Akron and wondered if he had an opening in the Minneapolis branch. After interviewing with him and the sales manager of his Systems Sales, they told me that they would like to have me join them.

Back in Akron after our vacation, I told Jutz that I had spoken to Mr. Richardson, the Freiden branch manager in Minneapolis, and explained what they offered. Jutz didn't want to lose me, but he also understood our desire to live near our parents in their last years. He could have made it difficult for me, but that would not be Jutz. He was one of the nicest guys one would ever meet, and he treated his employees like family. A few months later, I had organized and documented everything for the Goodyear order. I was ready for my transfer to Minneapolis.

I moved to Anoka, Minnesota and lived with Marg's parents. Marg stayed in Wadsworth with the kids while our house was listed for sale. After four months, the house hadn't sold, so we took it off the market and rented it to a fellow Army reservist. I went back to Wadsworth, hired a moving van, packed, and we moved. A couple of weeks earlier while I was in Anoka, I found a house to rent near the Mississippi River in Coon Rapids, Minnesota. It was a large two-bedroom house. The master bedroom was quite large, but the second bedroom was even larger. We were able to put up three single beds for the kids, and there still was a lot of floor space for them to play.

I had been at the Minneapolis branch for seven months and was doing some selling, but working for Jutz in Akron was so different than working for Richardson in Minneapolis. The two were complete opposites. Jutz was one of the nicest guys, and one couldn't ask for a better boss. Richardson, however, was an animal. The branch was large, with some twenty sales reps in the office. Nobody liked the guy, and I didn't either.

I called Dick Eickhorn, a former systems sales representative from the Minneapolis branch of Freiden who was working for Honeywell as a sales associate in their Electronic Data Processing Division. He had seen the light and left Freiden a couple of months earlier. I met with Dick and told him of the recent goings-on at the Minneapolis branch of Freiden. He was not surprised. He saw the excessive turnover at Freiden and knew that Richardson was a wild man, and no one could please him. I asked Dick about Honeywell, and he described a great company with a great boss and lots of opportunity. I called Earl Jacobson, the Honeywell Branch Sales Manager in Minneapolis who was responsible for selling Electronic Data Processing and asked for an interview. Dick had recommended me, so he was expecting my call.

Jake and I hit it off right away, and at the conclusion of the interview he wanted to hire me, but first I would need to fly to

Chicago to interview with his boss. Bob Henderson was the Chicago branch manager. Honeywell gave me a plane ticket, and a few days later I flew to Chicago. The interview went well. Bob offered me a position as a sales associate. I flew back to Minneapolis that same day and the following week reported for duty at the Honeywell sales office. I had a salary, benefits, and an expense account. It was a big change from Freiden where I had worked for the last three years. Seven months of that time were in the Minneapolis office working under a real jerk. I realize that there are a lot of jerks out there in the world, but it's different when the jerk is your boss. I was elated to get out from under him.

14

SELLING COMPUTERS FOR HONEYWELL

I am a great believer in luck, and I find the harder I work the more I have of it.
—THOMAS JEFFERSON

AFTER ATTENDING NUMEROUS CLASSES AND completing extensive training on all the Honeywell Computer products, my quest to become a Honeywell Computer sales representative was now at hand and I was raring to go. My experience with Freiden proved invaluable. Most Freiden Systems salesmen sold the Flexowriter simply as an automatic letter writer. They didn't attempt to sell its capabilities to blend it into their data processing system. Every Freiden system I sold was an integral part of the company's automation. In each case we produced a tape that fed into either the data processing department, or the engineering department, or both. I knew the language and was comfortable in the data processing field. Many Freiden Systems salesmen didn't sell the systems approach because it was a much longer sell. They didn't want to wait, and they didn't feel comfortable learning the technology.

For several months I attended classes at the Honeywell offices in Minneapolis, Chicago, Wellesley Hill, Massachusetts, the EDP headquarters, and in Wichita Falls, Kansas at the Beechcraft Aircraft manufacturing plant. Several members of the class were Beechcraft employees. Beechcraft had installed

Honeywell computers, and our instructor, Harriet Lonagren, really knew her computers. Jake had given me permission to fly back home weekends during the three-week class. Three Honeywell employees in the class were from the home office in Wellesley Hills and didn't have permission to fly home on weekends. They were there the entire three weeks along with our instructor.

Harriet, our computer instructor, was a rather large fifty-something woman. She asked the Honeywell guys if she could go golfing with them on the weekend. They came up with excuses of every kind, trying to put her off. Finally Harriet announced, "You Honeywell guys have to let me golf with you. I won't go out as a single in a strange town, please take me with you."

The guys moaned and groaned but finally agreed. They instructed her that if she was too slow, she would have to pick up her ball and speed things up. They didn't want the embarrassment of being held back by a frumpy old woman. Saturday came, and Harriet was ready. The guys reminded her that she would need to keep up the pace. No hanging back. When Harriet went to the men's tees, they explained that she could use the ladies' tees.

Harriet said, "That doesn't sound fair. I'll play from the same tees as you guys."

Well, at the end of the day Harriet shot a 72, one over par, using the men's tees on a course she had never seen before. Little did they know that this much overweight fifty-something woman had won the Illinois Women's Amateur Golf Championship several years earlier, and had been the captain of the Women's Golf Team when she attended the University of Illinois. They were embarrassed, and did they ever take the heat when the rest of the class learned about it on Monday morning. The next weekend everyone wanted to play golf with Harriet.

The territory assigned to me was a part of downtown Minneapolis and the entire state of Iowa. There were six sales reps in the Minneapolis office, and each had what we called an "in territory" and an "out territory." It was organized so that everyone had prospects in the twin cities where they didn't need to travel and could be home in the evening. The "out territories" included the Dakotas, Wisconsin, Minnesota and Nebraska. My out territory was Iowa. It worked so everyone did a little traveling rather than have someone assigned to all outside territories where they would be required to travel all the time. No one would have liked that.

We were selling large mainframe computers that were big-ticket items. If we sensed a genuine interest from the customer after a number of sales calls, we would produce a proposal. It was a combined effort on the part of both the systems analysts and sales reps. My job was to write the sales part of the proposal, usually some 100 pages or more, describing the computer features, their function, and the benefits to the customer. Another part of the preparation by the systems analyst was to diagram the systems approach we were proposing for their applications. The day scheduled for the proposal we would attempt to get all the decision makers to attend the two-hour presentation so we could go through every aspect in detail. In that meeting we utilized professionally prepared charts and diagrams. We weren't the only ones selling mainframe computers. Other companies like IBM, Univac, Burroughs, GE and NCR were doing the same. Seldom would we be competing with all of these at the same time, but we were always competing with IBM. Most of the time, it was just Honeywell and IBM.

After about nine months as a sales representative, I made my first lease/ sale, which was an H-400. The sale was to Donaldson's, a large department store in downtown Minneapolis across the street from Dayton's (now Macy's). Donaldson's Department Store was also referred to as Donaldson's Golden Rule. Closing a deal for one of these large mainframes in less than a year was almost unheard of. Most guys didn't get their first sale until they had been in the field eighteen months or in some cases two years. Almost all the customers leased computers in those days, and this computer leased for about $10,000 per month. Technology was changing so fast that no customer wanted to get saddled with outdated technology and not have the option to upgrade simply because they owned their computer. If they leased, they could upgrade by getting faster peripherals or more memory. It was a win-win situation. The customer could upgrade when necessary, and the sales representative was able to lease additional equipment or replace their equipment with faster more powerful equipment.

The Minneapolis office had been designated as a full branch, and Earl Jacobson had been promoted to branch manager, Earl Anderson, the senior sales rep was promoted to branch sales manager and was now my boss.

I was traveling primarily to Des Moines, Iowa, but I made calls to other cities too. I was spending about two days in Iowa and three days in the twin cities. However as prospects developed, I began spending three days in Iowa and two days in Minneapolis. I would spend Monday and Friday in Minneapolis and mid-week in Iowa, flying on Braniff Airlines to Des Moines on Tuesday morning and returning on Thursday afternoon or evening. I stayed at either the Holiday Inn, which at the time was $8.00 per night, or Johnny and Kay's Motel, a much nicer motel, at $8.50 per night. Often times the Holiday Inn would fill up much before Johnny and Kay's Motel simply because it was fifty cents a night less. I would rent a car to make my sales calls and could do as I wished in the evenings. Most evenings were spent in my motel writing up details of the day's sales calls. It was important to document those notes, while they were fresh in my mind, and they became invaluable when the prospect became really interested in our product. My notes indicated that I had listened to them and observed their operation. Trust was important as I became a part of their team, and my suggestions as to how our computer would help them became more believable and brought me closer to a sale.

About this time Honeywell announced a new computer, the

Honeywell 200. It was in direct competition to the IBM 1401 and the smaller versions of the IBM 360. The H-200 was a faster machine and used the same technology as the IBM machines. But many people were so enamored with the IBM brand; they just couldn't bring themselves to go any other way. We joked that they had "IBM" tattooed on their butts. In some cases no matter how much logic we presented or how much faster our computer was, it just wasn't good enough because it didn't have IBM on the nameplate.

While hitting the streets in Iowa, I found prospects that didn't have that tattoo. Most did, but I was able to find many that were open to new ideas and perhaps even willing to change to the Honeywell brand computer. Over the next year I sold seven H-200s in Iowa in addition to the H-400 I sold to Donaldson's in Minneapolis. I learned that no one in the company had ever sold eight computers over their entire career of selling computers for Honeywell, much less selling that many in one year. Because we had grown so much, I convinced Jake that Iowa should be a sales office on its own. Jake agreed. He went up the line with the request, received permission, and promoted me to branch sales manager over the new Iowa branch sales office. Two years after Des Moines was made a branch office, Omaha and Milwaukee became new branch sales offices as well.

A couple of months before I was promoted to branch sales manager, the Honeywell newspaper announced that I had been nominated to be a member of "The Honeywell President's Club." I didn't know much about the President's Club, but knew that I was among about 120 sales reps throughout the entire company who had been nominated. Only six of us from the Computer Division were nominated. Other nominees came from the Residential, Commercial, Industrial, and Aero Space Divisions. I received letters of congratulation from people all over the company.

About six weeks after my nomination, Margaret received

CHAPTER 14 / *Selling Computers for Honeywell*

several phone calls at home from some guy who wouldn't identify himself, but simply said that he wanted to talk to me. He asked when I would be home. After three or four attempts, one Saturday morning when he called I was there. It turned out that the mystery caller was Jim Binger, president of Honeywell.

Jim said, "I'm calling to inform you that you have been selected to be a member of the Honeywell President's Club. I want you and your wife Margaret to spend a week with me in Jamaica, along with the forty-nine other new President's Club members and their wives." There were no female sales representatives at that time, and we had only one elected member who was single.

As the company president, he was following the company tradition of personally calling the new President's Club members to inform them of their selection to this prestigious club. This was a really big deal. The Jamaica trip consisted of the president and his wife, the vice president of marketing for the entire company and his wife, and fifty new President's Club members with their wives. No other management was present. Out of the fifty, only three of us were from the EDP Division, which had about 650 sales reps at that time. Man it can't get much better than this!

Since we lived in Iowa, which was close to Minneapolis, Jim Binger's secretary called to invite Margaret and me to fly commercially up to Minneapolis and join Mr. Binger and his wife on the flight to Miami in the company plane. The company's twin-engine propeller-driven plane when configured for the airline industry could hold forty-four passengers. This plane was outfitted for corporate travel and held only seventeen comfortably and nineteen max. It had big overstuffed chairs and all the advantages, way beyond first class. I couldn't refuse that kind of offer.

Sales reps and their wives from all over the country met in Miami to spend the night before flying on to Jamaica. After getting settled in our hotel, plans included attending a big banquet where we had a great time getting to know the other forty-nine new President's Club members and their wives, none of whom we had known previously.

The week in Ocho Rios was fantastic. We traveled all over the Island visiting Kingston, the Straw Market, Port Antonio, and Montego Bay. Several of us climbed Dunn's River Falls. What an experience! We all felt we were in seventh heaven.

At dinner the first evening I ordered lamb chops, and they were so good that on the last evening, I said to Marg, "I'm going to have lamb chops again. That was the best meal of the week."

I remarked to the waiter that we had traveled all over the island but had not seen any sheep. Then I asked, "Are the lamb chops imported?"

He replied in his charming Jamaican accent, "Oh, dose not lamb chops, dem goat chops."

That resulted in a big chuckle by everyone within earshot. I still thought they were the best and ordered them again for our last dinner in Jamaica. At least this time I knew I was ordering goat chops, and they were delicious the second time too. Goat chops, lamb chops, or whatever they wanted to call them, they were delicious.

One day while we were in Jamaica we were bussed to Port Antonio on the east side of the island. They took us up the mountain where the temperature was about seventy-five degrees. Upon our arrival, Marg and I got on a twenty-five foot bamboo raft that was about a foot wide in the front and about four feet wide in the back. Each couple had their own raft, along with a Jamaican pole guy who guided us down the river. We sat in the back of the raft on a bamboo love seat just wide enough for two as we watched the pole guy guide the raft down the Reo River. We went through a few rapids, but it was quite smooth for the most part. By the time we got down to where the river emptied into the ocean, the temperature went up to about ninety degrees.

It was a beautifully peaceful hour-and-a-half ride down the river on a bright sunny day with only a puff of cloud here and there to give us a brief bit of shade.

On another day in Jamaica I rented a little sailboat about twelve feet long that you just sit *on* and not *in*. I set sail and was off to the wild blue waters. The rudder had a friction catch, so that if it hit something hard, it would fold up rather than break. After I was out just a little while, I tried to turn around, and just the force of the waves made the rudder pop up. The rudder is necessary to steer, and it wouldn't let me go in any direction except straight out to sea. It just refused to let me turn even a gentle turn. The closest island in the only direction the boat would go was Cuba, a couple of hundred miles away.

I thought, "Boy am I in trouble now, I can't turn around, and there is nothing but open water in front of me." I was going farther out no matter what I tried. Finally I got to a coral reef, which was over a half mile from shore. I hadn't originally planned to go anywhere near that far, but as I said, the boat and I couldn't agree, and in every case the boat won. The coral was two or three feet below the surface, but in some places extended up to the surface. My idea was if I could get out of the boat and stand on the reef, maybe I could turn the boat around, which is exactly what I did. And boy was that reef sharp. I thought I would get my feet cut up pretty bad, but I had to get that boat turned around, sharp reef and cut-up feet or not. Fortunately the waves weren't too high, and I was able to stand on the sharp reef long enough to turn the boat. I made sure the rudder was down as I jumped on and headed back to shore. As long as I didn't make any turns, the rudder stayed down and the boat kept heading for the dock. I sure was happy I was not headed for Cuba.

When I got back to shore, I turned the boat in and tried to explain that the rudder was faulty, that it came up with the slightest increase in pressure. I said that it is dangerous, and they should not rent it until it was repaired. The Jamaican just smiled and shook his head up and down as if he was agreeing with me. He then put the boat with the others for rent. He hadn't understood a word I had said. I tried to explain to another guy who did understand some English, but he just said fine, thank you, and did nothing about it. I was so happy to be on dry ground and not still heading out to sea that I just walked away. It took a while to compose myself. I had been truly scared when I came up to the reef. I knew if I went beyond the reef, I would be gone, maybe forever.

We flew back to Des Moines and returned to our normal life. Mother and Dad had driven from Cottonwood to Des Moines to take care of Kathy, Eric, and Jean while Marg and I were gallivanting around Jamaica. The day after we returned, Mom and Dad drove back home. Two days later, after listening to an evening religious program on the radio, Mom went to bed. Dad had retired earlier. Very shortly thereafter, he heard some strange sounds emanating from Mom. He checked on her, and she didn't respond. The local paramedics and Dr. Borgeson from nearby Hanley Falls, some six miles away, arrived quickly. They did CPR and made a valiant effort, but Mom died of a coronary thrombosis. She was only sixty-three years old.

On the day of the funeral, there was a severe snowstorm. No one could get to the cemetery. Although our pastor advised us not to delay the funeral, we had no choice. It was hard on the family, but we couldn't put Mom to rest until the next day. Several from out of town never made it to Cottonwood because of the storm.

After returning to Des Moines we had a stack of mail to open. To our surprise there was a letter from my mother. She had mailed it from Des Moines to Jamaica informing us what the kids were doing and assuring us that all was well. It didn't arrive at our hotel in Jamaica until after we had departed, so it was forwarded back to us in Des Moines. It was surreal reading a letter from my mother just after we had buried her.

CHAPTER 14 / *Selling Computers for Honeywell*

We moved into our new house in Des Moines after living in a rented house for four or five months while our house was being built. Earl Jacobson, my branch manager, had been promoted to be the regional director in Los Angeles. It was his last trip to Des Moines before departing for LA. We had a going away party for him in our new house and invited all the system and sales guys in the Des Moines EDP Sales Office. It was a great party. During the evening Earl told me that he wanted me to come with him to Los Angeles. He said I would start out as branch sales manager, but assured me that within six months, he would promote me to branch manager.

"*No way!*" Marg said upon hearing it. She reminded me that we didn't even have the curtains up on our new house yet. She wasn't about to move again so quickly. Earl had talked to me before his replacement had been named. A couple of weeks later it was announced that the new branch manager for the Minneapolis office was Bill Devers. When Bill learned that Earl tried to get me to move with him to LA, he too said, "*No way!*" He was new to the Minneapolis area and didn't want to lose his Iowa sales manager so quickly. He didn't need to protest so vigorously since I had already informed Jake that I simply couldn't move my family again so soon.

Every winter the EDP Division of Honeywell had a four-day meeting for those who had achieved Pacesetter status for exceeding their sales quota. Quotas were so tough that only about half the sales reps made their quotas and were declared Pacesetters. The others were either new or on the way out. If you didn't make quota after two years, you most likely were going to be working for some other company because Honeywell wasn't going to keep non-producing people.

The Pacesetters party was for sales people only, no spouses. It was held in a different city every winter, either in Florida or on some Caribbean Island. That first year I made my quota several times over, was elected to the President's Club and named

Salesman of the Year for the entire company. It was a great honor, as Honeywell EDP had over 650 sales reps nationwide at the time. When I left Honeywell after twelve years with the company, I had been a Pacesetter eleven years in a row. Only two other guys in the field had a similar record.

In less than one year, Dick Douglas, the Chicago branch manager, wanted me to take over the western Illinois territory. I would be housed in the Davenport, Iowa office and have sales people in Davenport, Iowa, Rockford, Illinois, and in Peoria, Illinois. It was a lateral transfer, but I would have a much larger territory with more sales representatives. This time, our family moved to Davenport, Iowa just a few weeks after our youngest son Paul was born. We had lived in Des Moines for just sixteen months.

It was 25 degrees below zero the day we moved into our new place in Davenport, which was the coldest day ever recorded for as long as they had been keeping records. With the movers bringing in furniture and boxes, the door was open most of the

OUR CONTEMPORARY HOME IN DAVENPORT, IOWA

CHAPTER 14 / *Selling Computers for Honeywell*

time. We couldn't get the house warm. We put a few pillows in the bottom of the bathtub, and with lots of blankets, made the tub a bed for three-month-old Paul. We kept the bathroom door closed, and it was the only room that was fairly warm. Fortunately he slept most of the day.

I had one car at the airport, having flown back to Des Moines to get my family. I drove the other car to Davenport with the family, so that car was with us at our hotel. At 25 degrees below zero the car would not start. I called a guy at the Honeywell office to come pick us up. He arrived in his Volkswagen Beetle, of all things. With seven people including him, our luggage, and a diaper pail, he had to make two trips. Eric, about ten at the time, had his hands full with luggage and the diaper pail. All of a sudden the metal diaper pail cover came off and went rolling down the lobby. It made all kinds of racket as it rolled across the tile floor. Everyone in the lobby had their eyes on that cover. It was quite embarrassing.

That evening when the movers finished bringing all the boxes and furniture in, we were beat, tired, and hungry. But at least the furnace had a chance to prove that it worked, as the house gradually became warmer.

Neither car would start, and even if they would, they were miles away at the airport and at the hotel. I went next door and knocked on the door softly. "We just moved in, and I can't get my cars started," I said to our new neighbor. "Would you mind giving me a ride to McDonalds (some ten blocks away), so I can get some dinner for my family?"

He said, "Here, take my car," and handed me his keys. He had never met me, but he gave me his keys and asked if there was anything else he could do. He was one nice guy, and proved to be a great neighbor. We had McDonald's for dinner as the house gradually warmed.

The next day one of the Honeywell guys gave me a ride to my car at the hotel and used his jumper cables to get my car started. He took me to the Moline airport, but the second car just wouldn't start. The following day, when it warmed up to about eighteen below, we tried again, and this time it started. We had two running cars, and the temperature was getting a bit warmer. It was still really cold, but at least not 25 below zero. It got to be a balmy fifteen below zero later that day.

We had good sales success in Rockford and Peoria and a fair degree of success in Davenport as well. I had been in the Davenport office for eleven months and had exceeded our quota by a large amount when I received a call from my regional director, Dick Douglas, who asked me to come to Chicago to meet with him.

When I arrived, Dick said, "I want you to come to Chicago to take over a large sales office." I accepted his offer, and this time we moved to Naperville, Illinois. That first year we made our office sales quota in June, which was the earliest anyone could remember a sales office exceeding the annual quota. Sales continued, and I was named Sales Manager of the Year for the Region and for Operations, which covered one third of the country.

In July that year, Branch Manager Bog Koenig, learned of a branch manager opening in St. Louis. Since Koenig had originated in St. Louis, he requested a transfer back to St. Louis. When his request was approved, an opening in Chicago was created and Dick Douglas, my regional director, promoted me to branch manager. This time when I received a promotion we didn't have to move. Hallelujah!

We had been living in Naperville for about seven months when they announced that Honeywell was building a new office building in Lansing, Illinois, and we would be moving our office there. Lansing is a far south suburb of Chicago and a long way from Naperville where we lived. I wasn't about to move again, so I commuted forty-two miles each way for the next three and a half years. This was in the late sixties and early seventies. Traffic wasn't nearly as heavy as it is today, but it still took me fifty

CHAPTER 14 / *Selling Computers for Honeywell*

to sixty minutes to drive each way in my Oldsmobile Tornado, which got eight miles per gallon.

Two years after my promotion to branch manager, my branch had the largest quota of any branch in the Operations. We not only exceeded our quota, but I was named Branch Manager of the Year for the Region and the Operations and runner-up for Branch Manager of the Year for the entire country.

Two or three years later Honeywell bought the computer Division of General Electric. My branch got larger as I added some fifteen GE systems guys and seven or eight GE sales representatives. The GE sales representatives were not as strong as our Honeywell guys, but their systems reps were stronger than the Honeywell Systems reps. General Electric put a greater emphasis on training their technical people. The technical side of our company became much stronger. Not so with the sales side of the house.

FOUR HONEYWELLERS AND THIRTEEN CUSTOMERS FOR A THREE-DAY PARTY IN NEW ORLEANS AT SUPER BOWL VI

While we were living in Naperville, I finally made a decision about my given name. I was born Marlyn, thanks to my cousin Irene who suggested it. Since Marlyn can be either a boy or a girl's name, most people see the "y" and assume it is a girl. For several years, I had been getting three or four letters a week addressed to Miss or Ms. Marilyn Reishus. People would see the "y" and assume it was Marilyn. In addition to the letters, I would get phone calls every week asking to speak to Marilyn. When I answered the phone, they would ask to speak to my wife. When Marg answered the phone, they thought they were talking to Marilyn. In college, at the University of Minnesota, I received two letters asking me to join their sorority. I ignored the first one, but when the second letter arrived, I replied that I would love to join their sorority, providing that I could "live in" and only after I received permission from my wife. I never heard from them again.

I began signing everything M. B. and spelling my name Marlin. The problem was solved. I still use my official name for Social Security and the IRS, but to everyone else the spelling is Marlin.

15

A GAMBLE THAT REALLY PAID OFF

To compel a man to subsidize with his taxes the propagation of ideas which he disbelieves and abhors is sinful and tyrannical.
—THOMAS JEFFERSON

KEN ASHLEY WAS ONE OF my outstanding sales managers. One day Ken asked me to come to see him in his office in Peoria. When I arrived, Ken said he had someone he wanted me to meet who worked at one of the department stores in town. When we arrived at the store, Ken headed for the men's suit department where Kim Kelly worked as a salesman.

Ken turned to me and said, "I would like you to meet Kim Kelly." Ken knew how good Kim was at his sales job and wanted me to consider him as a possible sales trainee. After our introduction and brief conversation at the store, I agreed to meet Kim for a full interview after he got off work.

That evening, Ken and I met with Kim Kelly at one of Peoria's finest restaurants for a rather long interview. During dinner I kept thinking, "Can this haberdasher make the conversion to a highly technical sales job required to sell large mainframe computers?"

There was a lot about Kim Kelly that intrigued me. He had this huge smile that made him very likeable. His suit was impeccable, and he spoke as if he had majored in English. He was obviously intelligent. You could say I liked him; No, I really liked him.

One of the big reasons for my earlier successes was my ability to pick winners for my team. After a rather lengthy interview, I judged Kim to be a winner. I felt confident that we could turn him into a computer salesman, but hiring Kim was somewhat of a risk, and some might say a downright gamble. Getting him ready for sales could take a couple years of training and on-the-job experience, but he seemed to have all the prerequisites. I decided to give him a chance.

After passing the normal background checks, I told Ken to hire him. Looking back, I think, "Boy I'm glad I took that chance. Kim turned out to be a real winner."

We put him through an intensive training program where he attended classes to learn about all our different computers. After several months of training, we gave him a territory. Kim was successful in making a few sales in Peoria and his territory included the state capitol in Springfield, Illinois. Kim did sell a small computer to a company in Springfield, but to really break into the state we felt that he needed to move there. The state utilized a lot of computers and none of them were Honeywell.

We moved Kim from Peoria to Springfield, Illinois with instructions to go after the secretary of state's office. The secretary of state's office was looking to either upgrade their huge Burroughs computer or to replace it with another brand. The severe competition was between their current supplier, Burroughs, IBM, and Honeywell. NCR and Univac were in the competition for a short period of time, but soon dropped out of the race. I guess they weren't willing to put in two years or more and end up with a better chance of losing than winning.

Kim put his life into that prospect. We knew we had a good chance because unlike many government deals, it would be an above board sale. Honeywell never would go for any illegal under the table deal.

The secretary of state's office in Illinois was playing it straight too. They used extreme caution to conduct their business completely above board. One big reason was because about two years earlier, then Secretary of State Paul Powell died rather suddenly, and they found shoeboxes full of cash. Hundreds of thousands of dollars were locked in his office closet. Of course there was no way to trace the money, and no information could be obtained from Secretary Paul Powell because he was dead.

The press was all over the state trying to find anything that was newsworthy. The pressure was on the secretary of state's office to be above reproach. Because of the illicit money, the secretary of state's office was squeaky clean.

The sale for a new computer was going to be won on the merits of the equipment, the equipment supplier, and the sales organization making the proposal. I might just say that Kim had his life on the line because he had all his eggs in one basket, so to speak. He sold that one small computer that was a new-name account in Springfield, but that was not enough to make his quota, much less make it big. I called it a small computer, but it leased for about $4500 per month. That was quite small for the product we were selling in those days.

Kim Kelly needed this secretary of state sale in order to benefit from the two-plus years he had put into this one account. He also needed it for income. Sales representatives made about half their income as salary and half on commissions. Ken had very little in commissions and therefore not very much income. If he were to get that big order, the commission would be huge.

I always gave the people who reported to me as much latitude as they could handle. I liked to delegate, back then, and still like to delegate today. I would give people as much rope as they could handle. I just didn't want to give them enough rope to hang themselves. I was quite comfortable giving Kim some rope, so to speak. I let the reigns go free, and Kim was off and running with instructions to go for it and get that sale from the secretary of state's office. Kim and I were taking a chance and were confident that he could make it big.

Two years after Kim moved to Springfield, he made that

sale ... and what a sale it was! We replaced the largest Burroughs computer in the world and got the largest new-name account in the history of Honeywell. The sale belonged to Kim. It was all Kim's deal. My part in the success was that I had picked the right guy for the job. I knew he could do it and gave him all the rope he needed and instructions to go for it.

The sale was big. I mean really big. It turned out to be about $25 million when it was installed. That's a big number, when you consider it was 1974.

The sale was written up on the front page of the *Wall Street Journal*. The story hit the desks of executives across the country. We made it big time! The world heard about and recognized this huge accomplishment. I couldn't be more proud of Kim and the entire sales organization.

Because of his huge sale, Kim was elected to the Honeywell President's Club. He was the fourth member from our branch elected to that prestigious club. No other branch in the entire company had ever had three members elected to the President's Club. A few branches had two, several had one, and the vast majority of branches had none. As head of the organization, I too had been elected to the President's Club several years earlier. We had a great organization. In fact, Chuck Cerniglia and Ed Shanahan had been elected to the President's Club under my watch. We had more members in the President's Club than anyone else in the entire computer division.

With that sale, our branch had already made its yearly quota, and it was only June. This was the second time we made our quota by June, which was the earliest ever for a branch. It also made me a Pacesetter for the eleventh consecutive time. Only two others in the entire computer division had made it eleven times.

The Director of Operations for the center third of the country was Ken Fisher. Ken had come along when Honeywell bought General Electric's Computer Division. There were just a few managers at any level who joined the Honeywell organization, and Ken Fisher was one of them.

CHAPTER 15 / *A Gamble That Really Paid Off*

Ken was hell-bent on changing the organization. His first move was to replace my boss Jean Larken, the Central Region director, with a General Electric guy. Jean was a very capable guy who had repeatedly been a Pacesetter and had built a great sales organization. His demise was followed by several other changes, and in all cases, they were replaced by GE guys.

General Electric's philosophy had been that management should be strong technically, and that sales could be taught. Honeywell, on the other hand, felt that strong sales was paramount, and that it was difficult and near impossible to make a strong technician into a good salesman. Ken was replacing strong sales types with technical people. This was happening at all levels. After several months, my old boss found a mid-level management job in New Jersey where he remained until his retirement. This undoubtedly was not to Ken Fisher's liking.

It was no surprise that I was replaced next. Ken wanted me out and replaced me with Jim Jordan. Jim did not have much in the way of sales credentials, but he had his masters degree from the University of Chicago, Ken Fisher's alma mater. To Ken, that was paramount. Ken thought an advanced degree was more important than the sales record. My replacement had never sold a new-name account, and hadn't even been a branch sales manager, but he had his masters from the University of Chicago. It was also known by all, that Jim was strong technically, but weak in sales.

I was now in a staff position, so no longer qualified for sales bonuses. Ken was trying to get me to quit. It didn't matter to him that I had made my quota for eleven straight years.

Honeywell was having other problems as well. They had a fantastic huge computer, but sales of the small and medium sized computers that made Honeywell the leader in computer technology were getting beat out by our competitors. Other computer companies were upgrading their technology at Honeywell's expense. Many "Honeywellers," including some of the very best, were leaving the fold. I saw the writing on the wall. It was time to make a change.

Putting my feelers out, I sent letters to the presidents of five-hundred large companies, and got quite a number of hits and several interviews. One company in particular that seemed interesting was Diebold in Canton, Ohio. They were looking for someone to head up their TABS (Total Automatic Banking Systems). I interviewed for the position and was hired. My job as director of sales and marketing included all products that were computer driven. Ken Fisher got his way. I resigned.

Diebold had recruited me to an upper level management position as their director of sales for the companies up-and-coming Electronic Banking Systems. Diebold was very strong in banking products, safes, vaults, safe deposit boxes, remote drive-thru equipment, and other banking products. They were truly number one in their industry. Their outstanding Engineering Department had developed an automatic teller, and I was to recruit and develop a national sales force to sell electronic, computer-driven products. Their existing sales force was good at handling their conventional products, but were not computer savvy and not equipped to handle the new generation of computer-driven products.

Shortly after I resigned from Honeywell, Ken Fisher got the axe. I guess the executives of our division headquarters in Wellesley Hill, Massachusetts realized Ken was dismantling a great field organization by replacing key people with less capable people. Most of Ken's replacements had come from General Electric. When I heard that Ken had met his demise, I had a smile on my face from ear to ear. About a year later, I was approached by Honeywell to come back. They offered me a branch manager position with a promise to be a regional director within six months. I declined.

16

WE MOVED AGAIN

I think there is only one quality worse than hardness of heart and that is softness of head.
—THEODORE ROOSEVELT

AFTER ALL THOSE WONDERFUL YEARS with such a professional company like Honeywell and living in the fantastic town of Naperville, Illinois, we were off to new experiences. Our move to North Canton, Ohio included adjustments for the family. We were in a new town, a new house, and new schools for the kids, a new church, and a new job for me.

We moved into a very small rental house for about three or four months while our new house was completed. Most of our furniture was stored in the basement or the garage of the rental as all the rooms in that house were so small. The kitchen was the only large room in the house, so that's where we put the piano. We all managed to live in that small house because we knew it was temporary. The house didn't have city water, and we had to rely on well water that stunk of sulfa something terrible. It was the beginning of a less than desirable year of our lives.

After about three or four months in that little rental house our new house was complete, and we moved in. We were very happy with it. That first summer I built a huge deck on the back, and all was well. We found a Lutheran church not too far from our house where the pastor and members welcomed us with open arms. It turned out to be a great church, and we lived in a great neighborhood of wonderful people. But all was not well at work, and the move to North Canton, Ohio was one I would later regret.

Eric had taken early graduation and was hired as an orderly at Canton McKinley Hospital. He wanted to get some hospital experience because he thought he wanted to go to medical school after college. Eric had already been accepted at Northwestern University for fall enrollment.

After several months working in the emergency room, he came home one day with an announcement, "I will never own a motorcycle." Working in the emergency room opened his eyes to the fact that auto accident injuries could be minor or severe. "In motorcycle accidents, they bring victims to the hospital in a bushel basket. There are no minor motorcycle accidents," he said sadly.

We were happy with his announcement because his mother and I would have never approved of his owning a motorcycle. Most parents find that after their children become "of age," they might not have much to say about their decisions. We were glad that his thinking was in tune with ours.

Diebold's engineering people developed state-of-the-art products that were superior to the competition, but it only took a month on the job at Diebold before I realized that I had made a mistake in agreeing to work for them.

I reported to Joe Carron, who was the vice president of sales for the entire company. Joe had eleven field sales offices spread across the entire country reporting to him. It was a "good old boys' network." Joe and virtually all of his field organization didn't want anything to do with anything that was computer-based and didn't want my staff or me for that matter near their customers. It was an unbelievably unprofessional group. After a few months with the company, I came home and told Marg I was going to find a new job, "I've had enough with Diebold." I was earning a good salary, and we enjoyed the neighborhood and our church, but they were a very unprofessional bunch of guys and I didn't enjoy working for the company.

CHAPTER 16 / *We Moved Again*

Another very important factor that weighed heavily in my decision to leave Diebold was the North Canton school system. If I had known the school system was so out of touch with reality, I would never have taken the job with Diebold and subjected our daughter Jean and young son Paul to such a poor school system.

The schools were overcrowded to the point that the elementary school gym had been divided into four classrooms. The walls were made of pipes holding up curtains. The only thing between the classes was a piece of cloth that only went up about six feet. The teachers and students didn't have a chance, with the noise from the other three classes. It was extremely difficult. The cafeteria had been converted to classrooms as well. Paul was in elementary school and caught the bus well before daybreak because the school was on split shifts. Jean was a freshman in high school and caught the bus to go to school at 11:00 a.m. After school, the bus dropped her off at 6:30 p.m., long after sunset those winter days. During lunch, the students had to sit with their lunch on their lap, sitting on every other step of the stairway, or on the floor in the halls. Under these conditions, the school district still failed to pass a school referendum for the sixth consecutive time. The day after the school bond issue failed, I told Marg, "Were getting out of here. Our kids deserve more." And thus I started another job search. I didn't care if I had to take a job earning less money. I wasn't going to subject our kids to a substandard education, and there was no doubt in my mind that the North Canton school district was indeed substandard. We were going to move. I didn't have a clue where we would go, but I knew we were moving someplace else. I concentrated my search in the Chicago metro area. It would be nice to go back to Naperville.

That summer, Paul started little league, and I volunteered as an assistant coach. I wasn't going to make the move to Canton a complete waste. We tried to live as normally as possible while I laid plans for other employment and initiated my search.

I started another letter writing campaign to chief executives of several hundred companies. Soon after I started my search, I received a letter from R. R. Donnelley. They were following up on my letter to their president some eighteen months earlier. They wanted me to come to Chicago for an interview right away. There was a snowstorm predicted that night, and I didn't think I would be able to get to the airport in the morning. I asked my neighbor Jim Wolf if he could give me a ride to the Holiday Inn that evening in his four wheel drive pickup. Jim had built our house and was a really nice guy, and I knew I could count on him. Jim's four-wheeler made the trip fine. The Holiday Inn where I spent the night was only four miles from our house. It is a good thing I went to the Holiday Inn, as the neighborhood streets where we lived were blocked for two days. The main roads and the road to the airport were open. I made my flight.

After a day of interviewing and testing at R. R. Donnelley, they asked me to stay one more day for an interview with Chuck Lake, the company president. I was happy to stay for the interview. After my interview with the president, I was offered a position as Director of Electronic Graphic Sales. They agreed to pay the realtor expense for selling my house and all moving expenses. I arrived back home that night just as the neighborhood streets were getting cleared. Due to the snow, virtually all offices in the area were closed for the two days I was gone, so I didn't even miss a day of work.

The next day with the job offer in hand, Marg and I asked Paul and Jean if they would like to move back to Naperville. They were ecstatic. They had lived there previously for over seven years. The entire family was extremely happy. We couldn't wait to get back to Naperville and to their great school system. And I couldn't wait to get away from a bad employment situation.

With the economy soft, Diebold was having a tough year. They were laying people off and offering incentives to get people to take early retirement or just to resign. I went to my boss and told him, "In these troubled times with the company downsizing, you really don't need me. Why don't you give me four months' pay, and I'll leave and go find employment elsewhere?"

He went to the chief executive officer of the company with my request and came back with, "We'll give you two months pay to leave early." It was a good deal for Diebold because they were trying to downsize. People in their blue-collar, white-collar, middle-management and executive personnel, it didn't matter, they needed to get rid of people. I had made it easy for them. I took the deal and started with R. R. Donnelley immediately. I got double pay for January and February. Not a bad deal for getting out of a terrible situation at work and a chance to leave a very unsatisfactory school system. I was a happy camper, and I had a chance to restart my career. The Naperville school system was rated as one of the top school districts in the state of Illinois and has been year after year. We were going back home.

17

BACK TO NAPERVILLE WITH R.R. DONNELLEY

My reading of history convinces me that most bad government results from too much government.
—THOMAS JEFFERSON

I HAD BEEN RECRUITED BY R. R. Donnelley to be their director of electronic graphics sales. Previously their print sales representatives had handled electronic graphic sales. In some cases reps did very well, but most didn't have the technical knowledge or the desire to learn.

Donnelley was, and still is, the world's largest commercial printer. Most of the telephone books in the country and 150

OUR HOUSE ON HUNTINGTON COURT IN NAPERVILLE, ILLINOIS

different magazines are printed at Donnelley. A couple of their plants print only books.

Their sales reps could make more money selling printing than they could learning the technical computer jargon necessary to sell electronic graphics.

The company's upper management realized this and decided to establish a new division specifically to handle electronic graphics. I was recruited to head that new division. The service we sold was converting documents to film in order to make a plate for the printer. We accomplished this process with computers. Our job was to sell this service all over the United States.

I studied the printing and electronic graphics process and started learning the technology. Since I had a good background in computers, the transition wasn't too difficult. It didn't take long before I was ready to handle this highly technical service.

Donnelley was a great company when I worked there and still is today. It had great management, and they treated their employees very well. They are the world's largest printer and enjoyed a solid reputation in the industry. I had found a great company to work for, and in many ways it felt like I was back at Honeywell again, working for a highly professional and ethical company.

I recruited sales people from several companies who had one thing in common: they were highly successful at selling in the computer field. I hired two of my former sales managers. Ken Ashley had been my Honeywell sales manager in Peoria, Illinois, and Chuck Cerniglia was a Honeywell President's Club member. Chuck had been a Honeywell sales manager for me in Chicago. Both were very successful at Honeywell.

Like so many employees at Honeywell, they too saw the writing on the wall. Honeywell was in a steep decline. This was the only reason they were tempted to leave the company that had been so good for them over the years.

In the five years I was with Donnelley I built a great sales force, and increased sales by 1600 percent. The downside of the job was that I was frequently out on the road for periods of time traveling to sales offices across the country and living out of a suitcase. It was taking its toll on me. I felt my family was beginning to suffer the effects too.

The president's position at Donnelley was going to open up in one year. Jim Sullivan was one of two executive vice presidents in contention for the position. The current chairman, Chuck Lake, was scheduled to retire, and Donnelley's current president was groomed to move up to chairman.

One of my sales reps in Chicago had a client in the Chicago area. Donnelley couldn't compete in getting documents converted from manuscript to an electronic media, which was largely a clerical task. Our competitors had lower labor rates than Donnelley.

It looked like the best solution to that situation was to get a competitor to do the labor-intensive portion and Donnelley would do the technical and more profitable portion. After the conversion was made to magnetic tape, Donnelley was highly competitive, and could produce a better end product faster and at a lower price than the competition.

I understood there was a risk getting a competitor involved. I received my boss's approval and his boss's approval before we made our proposal. Our client was a huge Donnelley print customer. At our meeting with him, he didn't like the fact that we brought one of our competitors in to present a joint proposal.

That following week, Donnelley had a huge golf outing for their big print customers. Jim Sullivan, the executive vice president was teamed up with our client on the golf course. The client asked Jim about our joint proposal, and Sullivan went crazy.

Sullivan didn't care if I had my boss's approval and his boss's approval; he insisted that I be fired because we were treading on one of "his" print customers.

I was fired because of that incident. Getting fired was something new for me. I talked to my boss about it at great length, but Sullivan had his mind made up and wouldn't budge. Roger Missemer, who was my boss, said he couldn't do anything about it. I was history.

Getting fired wasn't the end of the world for me. After traveling so much as part of my job, I was ready to settle down. A brand new door was about to open in my life.

I made a decision to go into business for myself. I was confident that I had the discipline to run my own company. Over the next several months I looked at several companies. Finally, I decided to buy a franchise. My first choice was a McDonald's franchise, but that meant I would have to move, as there were no franchises available in the Chicago area. My second choice was Burger King. They welcomed me with open arms. I was elated that I would no longer have to report to a boss or work at a job that involved a lot of travel. I was ready to give it a try.

It would take some time before my first store would be ready to open. In the meantime, I decided to start a placement service. Working out of an office in my basement, I lined up several companies that were looking for either sales reps or systems reps in the computer field. I put ads in the *Chicago Tribune* and began to develop a client list. Over the next nine months I placed quite a number of individuals. I earned more in that nine-month period than any nine-month period in my life. It also filled the time period prior to opening my first Burger King restaurant.

My first Burger King was located at the Fox Valley Mall on Route 59 on the border between Naperville and Aurora, Illinois.

I still think very highly about R. R. Donnelley. They are a truly professional organization. I just ran up against Jim Sullivan, and I lost. About a year later, John Walters was the new president at Donnelley. Jim Sullivan had burned too many bridges in his quest to become the president. He left the company, and I had a big smile on my face. I just hope that my firing was one of those bridges that Jim burned in his quest for the presidency.

18

OUR FIRST STORE

Nice guys finish last.
—LEO DUROCHER

BECAUSE THE ECONOMY WAS SO unstable we had some difficulty trying to open our first Burger King store. Every week or two interest rates would go up a quarter of a point, or in some cases half a point. I had enough money to handle the business, but not the business and the property. I had arranged to have a developer construct a building to our specifications. The developer was also my future landlord. He kept delaying construction because the interest rates kept rising. After three or four months of delay I decided to get a loan and do it myself. Within three weeks I had obtained a loan at fourteen percent, and it cost four points. I had contacted several banks and mortgage brokers and found the interest on the loan was the best I was going to find. The interest rate was high, but the money was there, and I was ready to proceed.

There was a slight problem; I didn't have enough money for the down payment on the business and the down payment on the real estate. I could handle one or the other but not both. I called my friend Chuck Cerniglia who had worked for me at both Honeywell and at Donnelley. "Chuck, how would you like to go into the Burger King business?" I asked. After two or three rather long meetings over the next week, we came to an agreement. We were going to be partners. I would run the business and draw a salary, and Chuck was simply the investor.

CHAPTER 18 / *Our First Store*

I wanted 51 percent for me and 49 percent for Chuck, but he insisted it be fifty-fifty. I took the deal because without him I couldn't proceed, and Chuck wasn't going to budge. Chuck and I settled as fifty-fifty business partners under the name of Reicer Inc. and fifty-fifty on the real estate under the name of Reishus and Cerniglia Partnership. We were off and running, or I should say more like crawling.

I made a mistake in choosing a builder who had a lot of experience, but had never built a restaurant of any kind, much less a Burger King restaurant.

The building turned out fine when it was finished, but it took him way too long to build.

On January 22, 1980 we were finally ready for our first customers. I was forty-nine years old and starting my own business. On opening day the temperature outside was about zero degrees, and with no landscaping, it didn't look like we were open. Our prospective customers stayed away in droves. The cold spell continued for the next couple of weeks, and sales remained very soft.

Some of my grandkids and several friends have asked me how I was financially able to start in business for myself. I have to say it was because I saved. I wasn't lucky enough to inherit. I earned the money myself and I was fortunate to choose Margaret as my wife and partner. Margaret is a very frugal person and has kept me in check for fifty-seven years. Neither Marg nor I are big spenders having both grown up during the Depression. We just weren't accustomed to many of the frills, and saving money came natural. Paying our debts always seemed like the right thing to do.

First I had to pay back the money I had borrowed from my dad during my last year of college when I could no longer make it on my limited income. I paid Dad $50 to $75 per month at the rate of about fifteen percent of my gross income, and finally paid the loan back in full. Both Mom and Dad told me that it wasn't necessary to pay the college loan back and to consider it a gift, but I felt I should pay it back, which I did, with interest. After Dad was paid off, I began accumulating money for a down payment on a house. About four and a half years out of college we had enough saved ($1000) for a down payment. Our first house cost $13,500 and the house payment was $98 per month, which included taxes and insurance, on the FHA loan.

Immediately after closing on the Wolf Avenue house, I began making extra payments. Later I did this on all the houses we owned. This enabled me to me to build equity more quickly. It was my method of forced savings.

Congress passed a law that allowed automatic savings using the 401k plan. This law opened the doors for millions of Americans to save for the future. There was no IRA, Roth IRA or 401k at that time. They all came later.

While I was at Honeywell, management recognized there should be a way to encourage personal saving, and established a stock purchase plan. Everyone in the company was eligible and encouraged to participate. In the beginning, one could invest up to five percent of pre-tax income. Honeywell matched that with an additional two and one half percent. I immediately signed up for the maximum. Later Honeywell allowed us to invest up to ten percent and Honeywell matched it with an additional five percent. I signed up and was saving ten percent of my money and received a bonus of five percent. Later Honeywell allowed us to invest up to fifteen percent and the match remained at five percent. I was essentially saving twenty percent: fifteen percent from my money and a match of five percent from the company. It helped that Honeywell stock gained significantly over the next few years. It wasn't long before I had saved enough to open that first store. The rest is history.

I was dabbling in the stock market but wasn't doing very well. I just didn't have the interest to follow the stock market game every day or every week or every month for that matter. It has been said that we are all ignorant, only in different subjects. I learned that the stock market is not one of my strong suits. I now have my money invested in the market, but I leave it to my financial advisor to make the calls to sell or to buy.

I encourage young people, and people of all ages for that matter, to save. Invest in your company's 401k to the max allowed. If your company doesn't have a 401k, invest in an IRA, or better yet in a Roth IRA. Everyone can save; you just have to decide to do it. Learn to live on less than you earn.

And you know what happened to us? We learned to live on our new take home pay. The fifteen percent was never seen, so we didn't miss it. It wasn't long before the savings account was large enough to enable me to open that first store. After that first one it got easier, and in the end, I owned and operated thirty-six Burger King restaurants.

Marg and our son Paul worked in the BK kitchen. Marg was our only hamburger maker with five years of college. Paul was fourteen at the time. It was legal to employ fourteen and fifteen year olds, but only for very restricted hours. We made sure we complied with the law. Marg worked from ten to two during our lunch rush. Employee nametags had first names only; so many customers and some of our employees didn't know that Marg was my wife. This continued for the next several years. When the new hires came on board, they simply knew her as Marg, and the existing staff went along with it. Sometimes it would be two or even three months before they found out that Marg was the wife of the owner. They would exclaim in great surprise, "Oh my God, you're related to Marlin?" and then was almost always followed by, "What have I said?" or "What have I done wrong?" They were afraid that Marg would bring home things that someone had said or done that would not put them in a favorable position. However, Marg didn't bring the kitchen stories back home to me. She would only tell me if something serious had happened and felt I should know. We kept it that way, and it worked quite well.

We hired three fourteen-year-olds to work at our first store.

Our son Paul, his friend Mark Hauge, and Lishan Aklog, all worked at the store. Paul's friend Lishan was a tall kid who had been brought to this country from Ethiopia by our church. He attended eighth grade at Lincoln Junior High School. When the school was deciding what subjects Lishan would take, he agreed with their suggestions, but asked about calculus. His school advisor told him that calculus was taught only in high school to advance placement seniors. Lishan replied, "Well I'm half way through the course, and I have all A's." This really surprised everyone. They tested him and determined he was right. Naperville sent a bus to Lincoln Jr. High to pick Lishan up every day to bring him to Central High School where he could join the advance placement seniors in their calculus class. At the end of the year, he got an A in calculus, just as he did in all his classes.

Lisa was another employee who worked for us who was a junior at Central High School. One day she asked me if I knew anything about algebra. I told Lisa that Lishan was coming to work in a few minutes and to ask him. "He's just a freshman, what does he know?" Lisa replied. "Trust me; I think he will be able to help you out." A few minutes later, Lishan came lumbering down the stairs to the crew room. I told him that Lisa needed some help with her algebra. He said he was glad to oblige. Fifteen minutes later when I walked by, Lisa said to me, "I can't believe this guy. He's amazing."

The Burger King managers had a hard time believing that Lishan was capable of doing more. He was an extremely quiet and unassuming guy. They had put him on the broiler, the easiest job in the store and had kept him there for seven months. I told the managers to train him at other positions in the store, which they did. They soon realized that this fourteen-year-old black kid from Ethiopia was undoubtedly the smartest person in the building. He truly was amazing.

Lishan's advisor told him that he had accumulated enough credits to graduate after his sophomore year. He "aced" everything they could throw at him. But his parents who were both medical doctors in Ethiopia, said no. It was their personal belief he was too young to go to college, so he stayed at Central one more year.

Lishan graduated at the end of his junior year at age sixteen. He received a full scholarship to Harvard. After four years at Harvard he graduated with highest honors and received a full scholarship to the Harvard Medical School. He is currently the head of Cardiac Thoracic Surgery in San Diego. We all knew he would end up with an important job.

Mark Hauge, the other fourteen-year-old I hired has been a Youth Pastor at several churches since he got out of college. The third was our son Paul. He works as a registered architect and a senior designer for a large Engineering and Architectural firm.

I guess I did pretty well in picking my first fourteen-year-olds. They turned out just great, don't you think?

Business was slow, and we were losing money every month. I decided to talk to Bob Lucky, the president of Chart House, Inc. from whom we were franchising our Burger King restaurant. We were franchisees of Chart House and sub franchisees of Burger King. I called Bob and told him I wanted to see him. He agreed and invited me to come to Lafayette, Louisiana, the home office of Chart House. His secretary told me they would send a car to pick me up at the airport. To my surprise, Bob Lucky himself picked me up, and drove me to his home. He said, "We are going to have a cookout here at the house if that's okay with you." We had several cocktails before a fantastic steak dinner. It was getting late, and I was concerned about getting to my motel. Bob was getting to the point where he was in no condition to drive. They had a huge house that included a guesthouse. He asked me if it would be okay with me if I was to stay in the guesthouse. After having a nice dinner and evening together, this was fine with me.

The next morning after a big breakfast, we were off to Chart

House's corporate offices. I explained that Chart House had put me in a location that just wasn't ready for a Burger King. Maybe it would be ready in a couple of years, but not now. I told him we were doing everything right, and we had good scores from our Chart House district manager, but sales just weren't there in sufficient volume to support the store. After spilling my tale of woe and answering a lot of questions, Bob turned to me and said, "Ma Lin," he always called me Ma Lin, "what you need is another store." He went on, "I have been told that you run a good store, and you simply need time for it to develop." (About one third of the stores in the Chicago land area were Chart House Company stores). "We'll sell you a store and give you a good price. I'll have the guys in Chicago work something out for you, and we'll have some suggestions for you next week."

I went home feeling pretty good, but I wasn't sure if I had been had, or had just been given a real opportunity.

19

THE MID-EIGHTIES

Governments tend not to solve problems, only rearrange them.
—RONALD REAGAN

BY THE MID-EIGHTIES, THINGS WERE going quite well. We had four stores, and all were profitable. The Fox Valley store came around and was putting up some big numbers, as was Hoffman Estates. We survived the road construction on Ogden Avenue in front of the Naperville store, and once the road opened again, it too began to show some big numbers. Our West Chicago store was the only one not bringing in as much business. As we had

ONE OF MY BURGER KING RESTAURANTS,
INCLUDING A PLAYGROUND

forecasted, it did make a profit, but remained average at best for all the time we owned it.

Our son Paul was the only one still living at home. Eric, Kathy, and Jean had married and were living elsewhere.

Our house in Naperville was a large two-story Georgian house. Marg and I started thinking about how nice it would be to live in a ranch-style house. We were getting tired of the stairs. We searched for and found a lot in a heavily wooded area not too far from where we were living. It was in the same high school district, so the move was fine with Paul. We didn't even consider looking at lots that would have resulted in Paul's changing schools. Our kids had gone through enough moving as a result of my job promotions. So long as Paul would still attend Naperville North High School, we decided to go for it. This was a move that *we* wanted and not a required move for my job, as had been the case for so many of our moves.

I bought the lot and designed the house. After many renditions, I was finally satisfied that it was what we wanted. I took the plans to an architect and asked him to make it legal. When he was finished, I almost felt cheated because he made so few

OUR HOME ON PEPPERWOOD COURT. THIS RANCH STYLE HOUSE THAT WE DESIGNED WAS OUR FAVORITE HOUSE OF ALL. WE LIVED THERE FOR 18 YEARS.

CHAPTER 19 / *The Mid-Eighties* 163

THE GREAT ROOM ON PEPPERWOOD COURT

MARG PREPARED A LOT OF WONDERFUL
MEALS IN THIS KITCHEN.

changes. However, he did document all the specifications and made a few really good suggestions. The following year we had the house built and moved in. Marg and I still agree that it was the best house we ever lived in. We enjoyed living in that house for eighteen years, a record for us.

When Paul graduated from high school and started college, we were officially empty nesters and started making plans to do some traveling.

We bought a brand new 34-foot Winnebago Elandin motor home and headed out on our first trip, a long weekend trip to Galena, Illinois. We had never been to Galena and had heard so many good things about it that we decided to check it out. We were novices and didn't realize one should always pull a tow car when camping with a motor home. It is just too tough to unhook the water, the sewer, and electricity just to go get a loaf of bread, run any errand, or go sightseeing for that matter.

After getting all hooked up in a very nice campground on the west side of Galena, we decided to drive to downtown Galena, about four miles away. We didn't have a car with us, so this meant unhooking and taking the motor home. What we didn't realize when we began driving around town is that Galena, whose population was about 3000, was also the hometown of President Grant. Every year on the weekend closest to Grant's birthday the Boy Scouts have a tri-state rally, and this was the weekend. There were over 6000 Boy Scouts in Galena from Iowa, Illinois, and Wisconsin. They were camped everywhere. As we were driving through town in that big coach, I believe all 6000 of them were walking the streets downtown. We drove about three miles per hour looking for a place where we could turn around. We ended up driving back through the middle of town again at three miles per hour and finally arrived back at our campground. We had been gone for over an hour and a half and didn't even get out of the coach to see downtown Galena.

Not long after that first trip in our new Winnebago, we picked up our friends, Molly and Bill Elsass in Wadsworth, Ohio where they had a home. We first met Bill and Molly when we lived in Wadsworth after accepting my first job out of college. Somewhere in Northern Florida the four of us stopped to camp for the night. But first we decided to go out to dinner at a very popular local fish house. As we drove down this road, there were cars parked on both sides of the street, and the Gulf of Mexico was just beyond the cars. We came to the end of the road where there was a circle turn around. The restaurant was obviously popular; patrons had parallel parked their cars the whole way on both sides of the road and around the circle as well. I tried to make the turn, but there was no way I could get that big motor home around the circle. We ended up waiting until the owners had finished their dinner and drove their cars away. If they hadn't moved their cars, I would have still been there. This experience was another reason to always have a tow car.

We finally arrived on Marco Island and were welcomed by my partner, Chuck Cerniglia who owned a condo on Marco. Chuck and Cathie were just finishing their vacation and were about to leave. Chuck had invited us to stay in his condo for a few days, which we did. A year later, we stayed in his condo again for three days. After our second trip to Marco, we decided that we liked Marco enough to buy our own condo. That fall we flew down and bought at the "Riverside Club," which was the same complex where Chuck and Cathie had their condo.

On our 40th wedding anniversary, we rented three additional condos at Riverside, and all of our children and grandchildren joined us. It was a great time. Paul and Jana had no children at the time, so they stayed with us. The other three families each had their own condo, so it worked out well.

We owned that condo at the Riverside Club for eleven years. We enjoyed Marco Island so much, we sold our condo at the Riverside and bought at the Princess del Mar, which is a much larger condo right on the beach where we enjoy watching Marco's beautiful sunsets.

20

REICER INC EXPANSION PLANS TURN TO SALE

The art of government consists in taking as much money as possible from one class of citizens to give to the other.
—VOLTAIRE

BUSINESS CONTINUED TO BE GOOD. The economy was recovering, and banks were eager to lend money. We had a good record, paid all our bills on time, were showing a nice profit every month, and had money in the bank. As a result, banks looked on us with favor.

We had good deposits and were in a period of "easy money." If one of our businesses had a slow period during the first couple of years, we always, and I mean always, would pay our bank loans on time. If we were strapped for cash at times, we might pay one or some of our suppliers a few days late, but never the bank, or any institution that had loaned us money. This policy bought us good favor with the financial institutions. We could get money for expansion whenever we wanted. It also enabled us to get more favorable rates than most of our fellow Burger King owners.

I was always looking for a good lot to build a Burger King restaurant and had my eyes on several. Chuck and I decided to go for two that we both liked. One lot was in Warrenville, a town bordering on Naperville's northwest side, and one was in Hoffman Estates in a new shopping center that was being developed on Golf Road. Our plan was to build Hoffman Estates first, and follow immediately with the Warrenville store when Hoffman was up and running.

Hoffman Estates

As things moved forward, we realized it was not going to be quite as simple as we had hoped it would be. The local governmental bodies in Hoffman Estates had a different idea than ours. The Hoffman Estates City Planning Board and City Council were extremely difficult to deal with. It didn't seem to matter what we presented to them, it wasn't good enough. They didn't want us. They simply did not want any fast food restaurants of any kind.

Warrenville, on the other hand, wanted us very badly. Our store would provide $25,000 plus in real estate taxes, $70,000 in sales tax revenue and 40-plus jobs would be created. Both the Planning Commission and the City Council were very easy to deal with, and as a result, we received quick approval to build. At the same time as the Warrenville deal was moving ahead, the Hoffman Estates city fathers continued to drag their feet.

The Warrenville store was built and up and running for several months before we finally received approval to begin building at Hoffman Estates.

Warrenville opened with a big bang. Sales were even better than we had expected. It turned out to be a home run.

During the construction of Hoffman Estates, John Jansen, a former executive at Chart House, approached us. John had the backing of an extremely wealthy gentleman, and they wanted to buy our stores. Neither Chuck nor I wanted to sell, but we both had entertained the idea of buying each other out. Chuck wanted to buy me out, and I wanted to buy Chuck out. But neither of us could come up with a good plan to fairly price the transaction. It seemed like a good idea to string John Jansen along to see how high he would bid in his attempt to buy our stores.

Our Hoffman Estates store wasn't even finished, and we

therefore had no sales data on which to establish a selling price for that store. John was very bullish on the store's location and agreed to plug a very high number for our sales calculation. His number was much higher than we were projecting.

We went back and forth for a couple of months, and with each negotiation session their offer price went higher. Finally, Chuck and I realized they weren't going any higher. At the price they were willing to pay, Chuck said to me that he wouldn't give me half of their price to buy me out, and I said I wouldn't give him half of their offer to buy him out. We then both said at the same time, "I guess we just sold our stores." We both agreed the deal they offered was too good to pass up and decided to take the money and run.

This was bittersweet for me in that I really didn't want to sell. What I really wanted was to buy Chuck out and own it all. The price to buy him out was just too high. I felt that everything we made would be going to the bank for at least five years, and if sales were soft, we might not make it. It was too big of a gamble. The sale to Jansen was imminent.

Our attorney and Jansen's attorney negotiated back and forth for about a month before completing the documents. The contract was finally done and ready for signatures. We were selling the business for all six stores, but retaining the real estate for the four of the six. Burger King Inc. owned the real estate on West Chicago and the old Hoffman Estates stores. We then established new leases for the buyer at a higher negotiated lease rate. We were going to have a great lease for years to come.

We signed the contract and turned it in to Burger King Inc. for their approval. We didn't think we would have any difficulty getting BKC's approval as the buyer already had two Burger King restaurants along with some twenty TCBY yogurt stores. They were extremely well financed, and John was a former Chart House executive and had been in the Burger King business for a long time. He was eminently qualified.

CHAPTER 20 / *Reicer INC Expansion Plans Turn to Sale*

Now we had to wait. Normally approval is received in three weeks and sometimes less. This time, however, they took the entire thirty days as specified in our franchise agreement. Then they came back with a request for additional information. After we supplied the additional documentation, the clock started over. They had an additional thirty days.

Finally after twenty-eight additional days, we received notice that Burger King was exercising their right of first refusal. Burger King was going to buy our stores. Jansen was out. The reason it took so long was not that they needed additional information, but simply a delay tactic to allow them time to get board approval. Pillsbury was the parent of Burger King, and the deal was big enough that it took approval from the Pillsbury Board of Directors. The contract wouldn't change. Pillsbury had to live up to the original contract we had negotiated with Jansen. This turned out to be a good deal for us as we now had Burger King on the hook for the contract. With our approval Burger King changed the terms of the contract to make each lease agreement a twenty-year deal. The deal was simply getting better.

Burger King bought the businesses, and we had new twenty-year leases on the four pieces of real estate that we owned. We were happy campers. As it turned out, a few years later Burger King sold all their stores in Illinois, and we now had a new tenant. However, Burger King was still on the lease. The tenant paid rent to Burger King, and BKC paid us. About four years later, the Burger King operator went bankrupt. Not a worry for us. Even though the operator went bankrupt, it was only a minimal concern to us; even though three stores were shuttered (Warrenville remained open). We continued to receive our rent per the terms of our lease agreement. They had about twelve years to go. Several months later, we allowed BKC to buy out of their lease agreement, and we rented to others. It's been several years now, and we continue to enjoy a nice income stream.

21

BUY, BUILD, HOLD, AND SELL

*Politics is perhaps the only profession for which
no preparation is thought necessary.*
—ROBERT LOUIS STEVENSON

IN 1986, TWO YEARS BEFORE Chuck and I had sold our Reicer Inc. stores, Eric and I had purchased two stores from Marty Saladin, and they were doing well. Eric was comfortable in handling the day-to-day operations, and I was comfortable with Eric running the operation. We organized under ME Inc., and Eric and I were the sole owners.

But in 1988 I had an itch; I didn't know what to do with myself. I approached Eric with an idea, "Let's build some stores." He agreed with the plan. I was eager to start searching for sites. I had a nice rental income on the stores we had leased to Burger King, and knew that developing some additional stores was good business.

Dick Sampson, head of Burger King development for Illinois told me of a site in the town of Streator. He said, "I think this site has some real potential. Why don't you take a look at it?" I checked the site out and it looked promising.

We put together all the demographics, and they looked good. Our findings included the number of people living within one, two, three, and five miles of the site. The demographics also told us the area's average income level, education level, and much more. The Highway Department furnished statistics of the number of cars that used the streets or highways around the potential site.

My nephew Jeff is a pilot, and he provided us with an aerial photograph of the Streator site and surrounding area. The aerial picture also showed the location of all the competing stores in the vicinity. The site location passed all the hurdles, and we were ready to proceed. We submitted the paperwork to Burger King for approval.

Eric and I worked in tandem gathering all the information. It was my job to line up financing. I had done this for the six Ricer Inc. stores and the stores that Eric and I had purchased from Marty Saladin, so I knew what the financing institutions were looking for. I spent a great deal of time preparing our financial request, which the banks greatly appreciated. The package we presented was so professional that it got to the point where the banks were bidding for our business. They told us they seldom received such a professionally completed package. The effort paid off handsomely and resulted in better terms for our loans.

Streator was about seventy miles out in the country, so it would be a little inconvenient to manage, but the projected numbers looked real good. Now I had the challenge of convincing Burger King that we were the right franchisees to develop the site.

I told Dick Sampson's boss, who was the head of development, that I wanted to develop the site. He responded that if I did develop Streator, I couldn't develop in the greater Chicago area, and it would limit me to only develop country sites. It had to be city or country. It was a known fact, that there was so much turnover occurring at **BK** Corporate, that I suspected he wouldn't be around very long. I agreed to his restriction, and we developed the site. Streator turned out to be a home run, much better than we had forecast.

Shortly after we opened the Streator store, we learned that a store in Elmhurst was for sale. The development manager we originally dealt with was no longer in the picture, so the requirement to build or buy either in the city or country was no longer applicable. I had predicted correctly. The old head of Development was history, and his successor didn't have the same restraints. The franchisee owned two stores that he wanted to sell. But he wanted to sell both to one operator and we wanted to buy only the Elmhurst store. The other store was further north, which made it a bit more difficult to operate and it didn't have the sales volume. There were additional problems with the second store that caused us to turn the offer down. In addition to being so far away, it had a lot of congested city traffic while traveling from Palos Heights and the Lockport stores. Since the seller wanted to sell both, I arranged for another buyer to purchase the second store, and we were able to complete the deal. The seller was so skittish about the other buyer that he required us to close the transaction at the exact same time in the same room. He thought there was a good chance that the second deal would fall through, and he would end up selling Elmhurst to us and not sell his other store. That was not acceptable to him. It was a long closing, almost all day, and it was touch and go at times, but we got the deal done, although our lawyers' clock was ticking all day long.

Every deal was not a big winner. We bought Richton Park, which, in retrospect, we should have taken a pass on. We remodeled it, improved the operations, and we increased sales, but not enough to make it an average store. Several years later we built Chicago Heights, a new store just a few miles from Richton Park, but in the same general area. Neither store was in a good area. We packaged Chicago Heights with Richton Park and were able to get rid of both stores. We were happy to be rid of Richton Park, and as we had suspected, Chicago Heights was no panacea either.

We continued to build and buy a few, including purchasing two in St. Louis. We then built two new stores in St. Louis as well. Though we had an absolute home run with one of the stores we built in St. Louis, the market proved difficult to handle, as it was a five hour drive away. After a few years we sold our stores in the St. Louis market, and we continued to concentrate our expansion plans in the Chicago market and outlying towns not far from Chicago.

Over the next few years, we continued to build and buy a few more stores. But in January of 2006, both Eric and I sold our interest in all the stores except one. A few months later Eric bought my interest in our one remaining store in Naperville. He continues to operate the Naperville store, which we built in January of 1998. It turned out to be a high volume store and it continues to be a high volume store today. It was our best store. Oh, one more thing, Eric really picked a winner when he picked the Naperville site.

Up to the time of selling my stores, I continued to search for sites and arranged for and negotiated the financing. Eric continued to handle the operations. When we sold out, he had three district managers who reported to a director of operations, who reported to Eric. Kathy had three or four clerical people reporting to her and was responsible for all the books, human resources, payroll for some 650 employees, insurance issues, and the like. She did a fantastic job. I don't know what we would have done without Kathy. She was irreplaceable. She too reported to Eric.

Paul designed and built our 8200 square foot office building. Viking Development and ME Inc., the Burger King operations, used half of the building, and we rented out the other half. When we sold our businesses, we sold the office building to a different buyer.

It had been 26 years since I started my venture in the fast food business. I owned and operated 36 stores over that 26-year period. It was time for me to retire, and retire I did, and I love it!

OUR TEN GRANDCHILDREN. KRIS HOLDING LEAH, JENNY, JESSY, LINDY, ADAM. KATE, KIM, DANIEL, AND JULIE

Part 3

Fun, Family, & Friends

Work Like You Don't Need the Money. Love Like You've Never Been Hurt. Dance Like No One Is Watching.
—ANONYMOUS

22

THE JOYS OF MUSIC

Light travels faster than sound. This is why some people appear bright until you hear them speak.
—AUTHOR UNKNOWN

I HAVE ENJOYED SINGING ALL my life. In high school I sang in the mixed chorus, the boys glee club, the mixed octet, and boys quartet. I also sang in the church choir. Our church didn't have a high school choir, so after my confirmation, I was encouraged to join the adult church choir. As teens, Marg and I both sang in the adult choir.

When I was a student at the University of Minnesota, I started to sing with the mixed chorus, but quickly dropped out when I learned how much they practiced. I had a part-time job working about twenty-five hours per week and attended the Army Reserves every Tuesday evening. With my family, work, Reserves, and studies, I decided there just wasn't time for the chorus.

In high school, I played the trumpet in band, and enjoyed the honor of first chair my junior and senior year. The old trumpet that my folks bought for me when I was in grade school was all beat up. My junior year they bought me a new "Super Olds" trumpet. It was a great horn, costing $225. My old horn was still worth $35 as a trade-in. Too bad the horn player wasn't as great as the new horn.

I kept that "Super Olds" trumpet for many years. Not long ago, I donated it to the Collier County (Florida) School District, so it could be used by one of the many poor students in the district. I was told it had a current value of about $350.

About two years ago, Nick Bliss moved into Monarch Landing, the retirement home where Marg and I now live. Nick was a retired professional trumpet player. I was telling Nick about my Super Olds. He knew the horn well and said it was worth somewhere between $2000 and $2500. He added that if it was in good shape, which it was, it was probably worth close to $3,000. Oh well, I'm sure some kid is enjoying a great horn.

When we were living in Naperville, Jon Swanstrom invited me to an "Auditions for Admissions," which was an evening at the DuPage Valley Barbershop Chorus. They were a chapter of the Society for the Preservation and Encouragement of Barbershop Quartet Singing in America (SPEBSQSA). I was a baritone and auditioned for the group. They invited me to join, which I did. That was the start of a long relationship with the Barbershop Chorus, a hobby that I enjoyed immensely.

There were about forty or forty-five members in the chorus when I joined. Two years later we had grown to about fifty. Many of us thought we should even have a much larger chorus. The president of the chorus asked me to be on the board of directors. My job was to take responsibility for membership as membership vice president, but I told the board that they had to back me. Over the following two years I wanted to grow the chorus to seventy-five members or more. The board gave me their total support. We changed the name of our recruiting night from "Auditions for Admissions" to "Guest Night," because the word "audition" scared some potential members away.

When I organized an all out membership drive we totaled about fifty-five members. We prepared for the "Guest Night" for about a month. Thirty-five guests came, and we had a great program. Over the next several weeks, seventeen of those "guests" joined the chorus.

We were off and running. I continued to host "Guest Nights" every few months, and after another two years, we had grown to one hundred seventeen members. Our chorus had the capability of becoming one of the Illinois District's top choruses. We had eighty-nine members on stage for our spring shows and fall contest. The spring show was held at the Downers Grove North High School auditorium with a capacity of almost 1000 seats. The two evening shows sold out, and we were more than half full for the afternoon matinee. Every spring we made enough money from those three shows to pay the chorus's expenses for the entire year. That trend continued for the next several years. Times were good with the DuPage Valley Barbershop Chorus. We placed second in the Chicago land area and fourth in the Illinois District out of about fifty choruses. We were invited to sing on the stage of McComich Place Theater. It was neat singing to an audience of 5,000 people. The next summer we were invited to sing the National Anthem at the start of a Cub's game at Wrigley field, which was another wonderful experience.

I sang barbershop for seventeen years. When we began to spend the winter months in Florida, I knew that it wouldn't be fair to the rest of the chorus to be gone for so much of the year so I dropped out. When we are in Florida, Marg and I both enjoy singing in the choir at the Marco Lutheran Church where we are members. Music has always played an important part in both our lives, and it continues to be important even to this day.

MARLIN IN "FIDDLER ON THE ROOF" IN 2003, PRESENTED AT THE MARCO LUTHERAN CHURCH

23

VACATIONS

Plan for this world as if you expect to live forever, but plan for the hereafter as if you expect to die tomorrow.
—IBN GABIROL

IN 1993, MARG AND I went on an Elderhostel trip to Denmark, Norway, and Sweden. Six of our good friends accompanied us. Our group included Bob and Jo Sutherlin, Dee and Lee Lindberg, and Wes and Sonia Swanson.

Elderhostel is one of the largest educational travel organizations in the world and goes to all fifty states and ninety countries.

One of many grand adventures happened in Norway when our bus stopped so we could walk around one of their beautiful parks. Forty of us in the group understood that when we finished our tour, we were to meet at the other side of the park. That is, everyone except Bob, who somehow managed to get lost. When he didn't show up at the designated location, we had all the authorities searching for him, even checking with all the hospitals.

Finally, the group continued without Bob to our next stop, which was in Oslo to see the ski jump used in the 1952 Winter Olympics. The ski jump was about thirty miles away from where Bob disappeared. After Bob realized the group had moved on without him, he found his own way to our next stop. Many Norwegians speak fluent English and were able to tell him how to catch a bus to the ski jump.

Some people in our group were looking down the mountain

CHAPTER 23 / *Vacations*

from the top of the ski jump and saw a little speck at the bottom they thought looked like Bob. Well, it was Bob, and we were able to corral him back into the group.

Since Sonia and I were the only true 100 percent Norwegians, I was ordered by the King of Norway to deal with Bob, and rid the country of this Scottish American who had caused so much disruption to his Royal subjects.

The next day, on orders from the King, I presented Bob with the "Royal Order of The Noose," which was a rope that was to be fastened around Bob's neck with the other end firmly fastened around Jo's wrist. It came with instructions from the King of Norway that the "Noose" was not to be removed until they left the country. Bob had caused so much commotion and so many hours of needless searching for him that the King stated emphatically that the "Noose" was to remain firmly around his neck until he crossed into Sweden.

Shortly after that episode, we left the country and headed for Sweden, where our Elderhostel trip ended. We rented a large van in which all eight of us could comfortably ride. The driver and one other person sat in front, with two more rows behind the driver that each held three passengers. A large area for luggage was in the back. It was good to have all the bodies together in one vehicle with no chance of getting separated from the other.

We made plans to meet my friend Curt Ulle when we arrived in Stockholm. Curt spends about four months during the summer in Stockholm and eight months in Naples. When Curt learned that we would be coming to Sweden, he offered for all of us to stay at his place. I said, "Curt there are going to be eight of us," to which he replied, "Well, we have thirteen beds."

We appreciated his hospitality, but with so many of us, we thought it would be better to stay in the Grand Hotel in downtown Stockholm.

Curt came to our hotel later to meet our group and take us on an unbelievable tour that only a native who really knows the city could do.

On our third day in Stockholm, Curt arrived at our hotel to escort us back to his home on the Baltic Sea, which was located twenty-five miles from our hotel. As our van approached the entrance to his place, there was a thirty-foot flagpole with an American flag flying to welcome his American guests. Curt's son and his girl friend Helene were there to meet us. Down at the dock where he kept his forty-foot boat, there was another thirty-foot flagpole with a Swedish flag flying. After a warm welcome we all boarded his boat for a trip to the archipelagos islands, located about fifty miles away. When the boat tied up at the dock, we had the opportunity to walk around the area and explore. When we arrived back at the boat, Curt had prepared a delicious meal for us.

After our boating adventure to the archipelagos we arrived back at his house where Curt's cousin and helper had prepared a fabulous dinner for us. Curt's attorney and his wife had been invited to join us. They were wonderful people. There were eleven of us seated at the dining room table that had been specially made from trees cut down from his land. The spacious table had room for two or three more. It was beautiful.

Before dinner we used Curt's private sauna located in a little building at the edge of the sea. Since it was summer, we didn't go rolling in the snow like you see in pictures, but we all enjoyed skinny-dipping in the Baltic where the water was downright cold. We bravely ventured in up to our necks. After several trips back and forth from the sauna to the water, we were completely relaxed and ready for dinner. After a wonderful day and fabulous dinner, Curt guided us back to our hotel, as we would never have been able to find the way on our own with all the lakes, bridges, and winding roads. It was a great finale to our trip to Scandinavia.

Alaska

In early June 1997, our good friends Lee and Dee Lindberg accompanied Marg and me on a two-week trip to Alaska. Our flight arrived in Fairbanks where we spent a couple of days looking around before boarding a train to Anchorage. It was a strange sight to see the sun set around midnight and rise at 3 a.m. Halfway to Anchorage the train stopped at the foot of Mt. Denali (summit 20,320 feet) where we spent two days of fantastic sightseeing then continued on the trip to Anchorage. The train averaged about thirty or thirty-five miles per hour, which allowed us to enjoy the scenery and the wild life. This was a beautiful trip and we saw every kind of wildlife imaginable right out of our window.

The parking lots and grocery stores in Alaska all had what looked like parking meters in several locations. We learned that they were actually electrical outlets. All the cars in Alaska had an electrical plug hanging out of their grill, which were hooked to head bolt heaters on their engines. People plugged their cars in to the outlets to keep their car engine warm in the frigid winters.

After spending two days in Anchorage, a bus took us to Stewart, Alaska where we boarded our cruise ship headed to

HELICOPTER SETTING DOWN ON
TOP OF A GLACIER IN ALASKA

VACATIONING TOGETHER, DEE LINDBERG, MARG, AND MARLIN ON TOP OF A GLACIER IN ALASKA

Vancouver, Canada, just north of Seattle, Washington. The cruise ship traveled at night and then pulled into a new port each day where we were able to go ashore and visit the local sights. On one excursion we took a helicopter to the top of a glacier. What a wonderful site! I have included a picture of Marg, Dee, and me on top of the glacier.

Marg says that of all the vacations trips we have taken, both here and abroad, the Alaska trip was the best. She would go again in a heartbeat.

Lake of the Ozarks

One year we went to Lake of the Ozarks in Missouri for a week. Grandpa and Grandma Olson (Earl and Helen) met us there. Our daughter Kathy took her friend, Ann Striker along. Kathy and Ann were in eighth or ninth grade, and they literally lived at the pool. Paul was only about three and was not the least bit afraid of the water. We had to constantly be on watch as he would run and jump in the water whenever he got close to the pool. Of course at that age he couldn't swim, but he had no fear. He knew someone would be there to rescue him. One day we rented a boat and navigated around the lake for several hours. It was truly a very memorable vacation. One of the things that made this vacation so memorable was that we had Marg's parents with us for that whole week.

Israel and the Greek Isles

We went on this vacation with our church group. There were about twenty-five people in our group led by Pastor Jack Nieme and his wife Ruth. The trip started with a few days in Greece, followed by a cruise where we stopped at many of the Greek Islands. After touring the Greek Isles for several days and purchasing plenty of souvenirs, we disembarked at Tel Aviv, Israel. We spent the next week touring Israel. One day we were going to visit the Golan Heights when Israeli fighter-bombers were bombing along the Jordanian border, right where we were headed. Our travel plans for that day were changed. Another day we were in a line of about six tour busses when gunfire broke

MARLIN FLOATING IN THE DEAD SEA, ISRAEL. IT IS IMPOSSIBLE TO SINK BECAUSE OF THE HIGH CONTENT OF SALT.

out ahead of us. Fortunately, we were the last bus, and the driver was able to back up and turn around. We got out of there fast. All in all it was a fantastic two weeks, but until the fighting stops for good, I think tourism in Israel will suffer.

Lake Kagianagami

One of our most memorable vacations was a trip to Canada. We started driving north 430 miles to Sault Ste. Marie, on the Michigan, Canada border. From there we went almost straight north another 430 miles to the end of the road. My brother-in-law Greg had made all the arrangements to rent a remote cabin on Lake Kagianagami through a friend of his named Dan Gapen. Dan was a fishing expert that had a syndicated radio program on fishing. After we arrived we met Marg's sister Ann and her husband Greg and their two boys Geoff and Peter. Within minutes, Marg's parents Helen and Earl joined the group. The next leg of the trip was by seaplane. The pilot had to be sure we weren't over the weight limit, so we gathered our gear and took it down

ONE OF THE TWO PONTOON PLANES THAT TOOK US TO LAKE KAGIANAGAMI. THIS WAS A WONDERFUL FAMILY VACATION IN THE WILDERNESS. WE REALLY HAD TO ROUGH IT.

CHAPTER 23 / *Vacations*

ONE OF THE SEA PLANES THAT TOOK US TO LAKE KAGIANAGAMI. THEY WEIGHED EVERYTHING BEFORE WE BOARDED THE PLANE TO MAKE SURE WE WEREN'T TOO HEAVY TO LIFT OFF THE WATER.

to the docks to be weighed. We had clothes, fishing gear, eleven sleeping bags, and food for eleven people to last for a week. We had a lot of stuff, including a big LP gas tank for the gas stove and gas refrigerator at the cabin. We hired two seaplanes to haul all that gear and the eleven people plus two pilots. The seaplanes had extra powerful engines to overcome the drag caused by the floats. There were no wheels on these babies. It seemed like it took a long time to get up enough speed to lift us off the water, but then it was smooth sailing.

About forty-five minutes north of the base camp we set down to what would be our home for the next week. The two cabins sat close together. They were really basic and very rustic. One cabin served as the kitchen and dining area. The other, a much larger cabin, had bunk beds all around the perimeter of the single room. The bunk beds were simply plywood with a piece of four-inch foam rubber for the mattress. We brought our own

OUR SON PAUL AT LAKE KAGIANAGAMI SHOWING OFF THE CATCH OF THE DAY

sleeping bags, and that was it. We had no electricity or any of the other finer things in life. There was a "John" out back, and we had to take a branch with us when we went to the "biff," as everyone called it. We were instructed to slap at the underbrush so as to make noises in case there might be a bear nearby, which oftentimes there was. On several occasions we caught a glimpse of a small cub and knew Momma Bear wasn't far away. On our first night at the cabin, bears got into the garbage that we had put outside. After that lesson we stored it inside.

We had use of a motorboat, so we could fish whenever we wanted. We even had an Indian guide who assisted us whenever we needed anything, which was seldom. Basically, we were on our own.

Every campsite had a flagpole at the edge of the lake. The flagpole's purpose was to alert the outfitters' planes if there was

PLENTY FOR DINNER AND EVEN
BROUGHT SOME HOME

an emergency. All the pilots knew who was using the campsite and would radio for a plane to come check it out if the flag was up. If anyone ever put the flag up it better be a true emergency, not a call for more beer. We didn't bring any beer or soft drinks, as they were too heavy. Our drinking water came right out of the clear blue lake.

OUR CABIN AT LAKE KAGIANAGAMI. NOTHING
FANCY, BUT WE HAD A GREAT TIME.

PAUL WITH A MESS OF FISH, GEOFF BERGERON AND ERIC IN THE BACKGROUND

We caught a lot of walleye fish that we ate for dinner every night. Everyone caught fish, except Marg and Ann who didn't go fishing. Helen, Marg's mom, was always the first one in the boat; she loved fishing and would go at the drop of a hat. We were eating walleyes about as fast as we were catching them. The day before we were to leave, our Indian guide came with a whole bunch of walleyes. He wanted to make sure we had our limit when we left for home. He also showed us the best part of the fish was the walleye cheeks, which are about the size of a half dollar and about a quarter of an inch thick. But the walleye has to be four pounds or more, or the cheeks are too small. Those walleye cheeks are a true delicacy. Almost all the walleyes we caught weighed about five or six pounds.

The day we were to head for home, we took all our gear down to the lakeshore to have it ready to load when the seaplanes arrived for our return trip. It was a fantastic vacation, and though we saw the bear cub several times, we never did see Momma Bear. Good thing!

Vacationing in Our Motor Home

We had three different motor homes over a period of eleven years. The last one was a 37-foot long, 102-inch wide Vogue with a big diesel pusher engine. It was a fantastic coach with all the bells and whistles. Soon after we got our new Vogue, we went on a trek with the Vogue Country Club where we were members. The Vogue Country Club is made up of members who own a Vogue motor home. It doesn't matter if it is brand new and cost a gazillion dollars or if it's twenty-some years old and on its last legs, or rather, "wheels." As long as the coach is a Vogue, the owners are welcome to join the club. We were a country club without a building or a golf course. Our club house was wherever we stopped for the night.

This particular trek started in Prior, Oklahoma where the factory that made Vogues was located. We had one hundred and twenty coaches on this particular trek as we headed for Independence, Missouri, hometown of President Truman. From there we went up the Oregon Trail, stopping at a predetermined place every night. Since the campground where we would stay each night was well documented, people who couldn't go on the entire trek could pop in or out as they pleased. When we broke camp we would break up in groups of five to eight coaches, and each group would leave about five or ten minutes apart so we wouldn't tie up traffic with a long string of coaches. At the end of each day every coach would end up at the same park, and the party would begin. Vogue members from the area where we stopped planned our stay and scheduled things for us to see. The vast majority of our stops were two or three days, allowing us enough time to enjoy the sites and surrounding area.

It was great driving that diesel pusher because it had so much power. The previous year we were with a group of Vogues heading to the world's largest Balloon Festival in Albuquerque, New Mexico. I couldn't keep up in my gas buggy. In the mountains the diesel powered motor home made all the difference in the world.

We drove from Seattle, Washington down to Los Angeles, California stopping to see Hearst Castle, then over to Las Vegas, and down to the Grand Canyon. Then we drove up through Texas and back to Prior, Oklahoma. We stayed in Prior for four days then headed to Branson, Missouri where we stayed several days. The trek ended in Branson, and everyone headed in different directions. We headed for Marco Island. That total trip was 10,500 miles long and took three months.

Over a period of years, we joined the Vogue Club on a Midwest trek, a Southern trek, and a Northeastern trek. It was a fantastic club.

MY 1992 VOGUE MOTOR HOME WITH TOW CAR. WE PUT A FEW THOUSAND MILES ON IT WHILE TRAVELING AROUND THE COUNTRY WITH OTHER VOGUE OWNERS. GREAT MEMORIES!

THE VOGUE MOTOR HOME FACTORY IN PRIOR, OK, WHERE WE PURCHASED OUR MOTOR HOME

24

KATHERINE ANN (KATHY) ELVIN

Everyone has a photographic memory. Some don't have film.
—AUTHOR UNKNOWN

ON NOVEMBER 9, 1954 WE had been married almost two years when our first child Katherine Ann was born. Marg and I were both twenty-four at the time. I was six weeks into my freshman year at the University of Minnesota and her birth allowed us to move into the married students' housing. The housing was located at University Grove East, on the edge of the St. Paul Campus. The housing apartments were converted Army surplus buildings, with corrugated metal roofs and corrugated metal siding and when it rained, it sounded like hail. Our apartment had a small front yard of about ten feet by twenty-eight feet that was bordered by the sidewalk on the front, and the road on the short side. Since we were on a corner, the road came up to within one foot of the side of our house. Our yard was extremely small and was the only place outside for the kids to play. I made a picket fence for our yard in the wood shop in the Student Union. The fence was only two feet high except for the gate, and for safety reasons, I made the tops of the pickets round rather than pointed. It kept the kids fenced in and looked quite nice. Oftentimes, our daughter Kathy would play with Brian, who was about the same age and lived in the other end of our duplex. His dad was in a PhD program at the university. When our other children were born, Kathy became a real mother's helper to Marg.

As Kathy got a bit older, we let her walk up and down the sidewalk, but she wasn't allowed to cross any streets. That worked for a while, until one day Kathy and Brian crossed the street at the end of the long block and wandered on to the university golf course. I found them about 150 yards down the fairway, on their way back home. I guess they decided they had gone far enough. The punishment was quite severe, and Kathy still has vivid memories of her exploration, or rather the punishment she received because of her unauthorized venture. She didn't do it again.

Because of all my job related moves, Kathy attended several schools over the course of her K-12 school years. She started kindergarten in Wadsworth, Ohio. We moved in the middle of her first grade year and enrolled her in L.O. Jacob Elementary School in Coon Rapids, Minnesota. She attended schools in Minnetonka, Minnesota, Des Moines, Iowa, and Davenport, Iowa before our move to Naperville, Illinois where she was in the sixth grade.

On her first day of school in Naperville, the class she was in was given a math test, which she failed. The F bothered her a great deal since she had always been an A student up until then. Kathy brought the test home, and I went over it with her. Every math problem that didn't involve fractions was correct, and every problem that involved fractions, she got wrong. As it turned out, the sixth grade class in Naperville had just finished their math section on fractions, while her class in Davenport was about to begin fractions. She didn't know anything about fractions. Her teacher didn't recognize the fact that all her fractions questions were wrong and all others correct. I taught Kathy how to do fractions as we sat at our kitchen table, and by the end of the year the teacher understood very well that she didn't have a dummy from Iowa. Kathy got an A in her math class, same as she did for all of her classes. Our moves didn't hinder any of our kids, as they all excelled academically.

Kathy was always busy doing things she enjoyed. She was

involved in Girl Scouts, volunteered as a candy striper at Edward Hospital, and sang in the high school chorus under the direction of Mr. Pierce.

One Saturday morning shortly after her sixteenth birthday, and in possession of her new driver's license, she somehow managed to get my new Oldsmobile Tornado wedged against the side of the garage door opening. I couldn't get it out without doing some serious damage to the rear fender. I drove our other car to the Phillips 66 station and borrowed their hydraulic jack. I jacked the rear of the car and then slid the car sideways on the jack's rollers to ease it out. She still remembers that rather traumatic experience, more so than the rest of us. No punishment necessary. The trauma was punishment enough. During the summer after completing her junior year at Naperville Central, Kathy realized that she had enough credits to graduate at the end of her junior year. She wanted to go to college and not wait for another year. When we learned about the possibility of an early graduation, it was too late to enroll in college for the fall semester. She applied and was accepted to Gustavus Adolphus College in St. Peter, Minnesota where she started college in the middle of what would have been her senior year of high school.

Marg and I took Kathy to Gustavus to get her settled into her dorm room in Wahlstrom Hall. We discovered that she was assigned the same dorm room that Marg had occupied some twenty-five years earlier when she was enrolled at G. A. That discovery was a pleasant surprise to all of us.

On June 29, 1974, after attending Gustavus Adolphus College for a year and a half, Kathy married Phil Richardson, a fellow Gustie and her boyfriend from Naperville. Our permission for the marriage was given under the condition that she continued in college full time. After the wedding they moved to Wheaton, Illinois, and she transferred to Elmhurst College. Two years later, after three and one half years of college, Kathy graduated with high honors, the same distinction she received from high school three years earlier.

Two years after graduating from college she blessed us with our first grandchild. After Jennifer was born, Kathy made the decision to be a stay-at-home mom. Kristin was born three years later, and we now had two beautiful grandchildren.

But after thirteen years, the marriage sadly ended. Kathy, who had been a stay-at-home mom for nine years, began working to support herself and two daughters, Kristin, six, and Jennifer, nine. She also began graduate college courses in Business, which opened more opportunity for her in the job market.

On January 5, 1991, after being on her own for three years, Kathy married Doug Elvin. Doug has turned out to be a great guy. One couldn't ask for a nicer son-in-law.

After she and Doug were married, Kathy continued working at Euclid Beverage in administration. During that seven-year period she received several promotions, but came to the conclusion that as a woman she was at the end of the line at Euclid. Only men were promoted to the higher positions. When she saw she wouldn't advance any farther, Kathy decided to move on.

SON-IN-LAW
DOUG ELVIN

CHAPTER 24 / *Katherine Ann (Kathy) Elvin*

DOUG ELVIN AND OUR DAUGHTER KATHY

Around the same time, Eric and I were looking for a professional to head up our administration and accounting department for our expanding Burger King businesses. We were in the process of interviews when we learned that Kathy was available and wanted to be considered for the position. Kathy had all the skills we needed and joined Reishus Management Inc. Hiring Kathy turned out to be one of the best moves we ever made, as she proved to be a fantastic addition.

Later when we formed Viking Development LLC, an architectural and construction firm, my youngest son Paul, who was a Registered Architect, joined us. Kathy supervised our administrative people for both businesses.

When the economy turned down a few years later, Paul decided to move to Dallas. Kathy bought his interest in Viking and has been the owner of Viking Development LLC ever since. The construction firm built the Burger King restaurants as well as those for several other Burger King franchisees. In addition to building our Burger Kings, Viking also built some high-end homes, a group of town houses, office buildings, and gas stations.

25

REFLECTIONS BY KATHY

Under Promise, Over Deliver
—ANONYMOUS

AS THE FIRST-BORN CHILD OF the family I was the first to learn the many lessons that Mom and Dad had for the four of us kids. One of my earliest memories is when my friend, Brian, and I decided to explore our neighborhood. We were both about three years old at the time. I don't remember trying to break a rule, but I sure remember what happened when I did break that rule. I did not want do something like that again.

I learned another lesson when we lived in Wadsworth, Ohio. I was about five years old, and Eric was four when Dad took us to the gas station to fill up the car with gas. There was no paying with a credit card at the pump back then, so Dad had to go inside to pay. I had the bright idea to do something nice for Dad and asked Eric to help me wash the car when we got home. I saw the paper towels that the gas station had on hand for window washing, and I got out of the car and took several of the paper towels for Eric and me to wash the car when we got home as a surprise for Dad. Of course, when we started the project, Dad caught on fast and asked where we got the paper towels. I admitted that I took them from the gas station and told why I took them. Dad explained that taking the towels without permission was stealing. It would have been a lot easier for Dad to look the other way or just explain that this was wrong, but instead he took us to the gas station and made us apologize to the owner.

CHAPTER 25 / *Reflections by Kathy*

As the eldest sibling in the family I learned responsibility at a young age when I began babysitting my siblings, and at age twelve, I began babysitting for other families. We lived in a neighborhood with lots of kids, so I was busy most weekends making fifty cents an hour.

At age fourteen, Dad decided that I should go out and get a real job. He did not believe me when I told him that no one would hire me at that age. I had to apply at several places before he understood. When I turned sixteen, I got a job at Dunkin Donuts. My job was to finish, frost, and sell the donuts and to waitress. I wore a cute pink dress with an apron and hat and made $1.25 an hour working after school and during the summer.

After Dunkin Donuts I applied for a job at Fabric Inn, which was a dream job because I was working with fabric and making samples. I made most of my own clothes. Mom taught me to sew and knit, and I loved to work with a needle. I worked as a clerk until the manager fell ill, and the owner asked me to become the manager. I was attending Elmhurst College full time, but I accepted the promotion and worked at Fabric Inn full time until I graduated.

After graduation I found a job as a computer operator. The computer back then was the size of a large desk. I ran the computer and did some programming for the company.

In 1979, when Jenny was born, I quit my job to stay at home with Jenny. Almost three years later our daughter Kristin was born, and our family of four was complete. We lived on Nordic Court in Batavia where there were many other stay at home mothers with children the same age as Jenny and Kristy. When Kristin was in kindergarten, and Jenny was in second grade Phil and I divorced. The girls and I stayed in the house.

I returned to the working world. I was hired by Euclid Beverage and worked in the accounting department. In addition to my accounting job, I attended Illinois Benedictine College taking Masters in Business Management. Mom and Dad were very active in Jenny and Kristy's lives and really helped me out a lot.

In January of 1991, three years after my divorce, I remarried. My husband Doug was a long time postal letter carrier in St. Charles, and he fit right into our lives. Doug and I lived on Nordic Court for three years before moving across town. Jenny and Kristy stayed in the same schools, because there is only one junior high and one high school in Batavia. Both girls graduated from Batavia High School.

After seven years working at Euclid, I was ready for a different challenge. I learned that Eric and Dad were expanding their Burger King business and wanted to add an office/accounting manager. I applied for the job, was hired, and began working daily with my other family members. At one time Dad, Mom, Eric, Jean, Paul, and I were all working at some aspect of the company.

Our daughter Jenny graduated Illinois State University with honors, and later married Kyle Hohmann, her high school sweetheart. They have given us our two grandchildren, Jacob and William, who are identical twins. Jenny and Kyle live close to us in Batavia. In addition to taking care of the twins, Jenny uses her business degree to manage a Salon and Day Spa. She also enjoys quilting and knitting. Kyle does lots of traveling in his salesman job and enjoys Batavia history.

Kristy married early and our first grandchild Connor was born. The marriage didn't work out and she was divorced when Connor was still a baby. Kristy and Connor came back home to live with Doug and me. During this time, Kristy went to beauty school where she graduated and got her license. She also worked for me in the office at Reishus Management. During the time she was working at Reishus Management she met Jason Roy who was a project manager for Viking Development. Jason has a degree in construction management. Kristy and Jason were married and have blessed us with two more grandchildren, Coda and Tegan. Kristy and Jason live close to us in Batavia where Kristy is a stay-at-home mom, and Jason continues to work for Viking Development. My leisure time is spent with the grandchildren and quilting. We all enjoy family trips to our Galena house and weekly Sunday night dinners.

CONNOR, JASON ROY, TEGAN, KRISTIN, AND CODA

26

ERIC MARLYN REISHUS

*Work as if you were to live a hundred years. Pray
as if you were to die tomorrow.*
—BENJAMIN FRANKLIN

SIXTEEN MONTHS AFTER OUR DAUGHTER Kathy was born, our son Eric arrived on March 5, 1956. I was a sophomore at the "U." Marg woke me at two-thirty in the morning and said it's time to go. I was a bit groggy and said, "Go where?" She said, "To the hospital, and we have to go now!" I called Marg's mother to come to look after Kathy, and we flew out of there, knowing that her mom would be there shortly.

We didn't like leaving Kathy, but it was 2:30 in the morning, she was fast asleep, and Marg's mom was on the way over. There was no traffic on the road at 2:30 a.m. I drove 60 miles per hour through the Minneapolis city streets headed to Swedish Hospital. For the whole drive I only saw one car, crossing the road a couple of blocks in front of us. No police cars around, thank God. We got to Swedish Hospital six miles away in less than six minutes. We were flying.

Marg pointed to her left and said, "Go check in," as she rushed to the elevator. At the admissions desk the attendant said, "Where is your wife?" I replied, "She is on the way to the sixth floor." "She can't do that," he told me. "Well, she just did," I told him. I told the guy, "She is a graduate nurse from this hospital and knows her way around." He kept repeating over and over, "She can't do that, she has to register here first."

We both heard a scream coming from the elevator.

Finally he said, "Go up and check on your wife, and then come back to fill out the admission papers." He was fully expecting that I would bring Marg back to get properly admitted. But there are two words that would describe that ever happening... and they were Slim and None. *None* fit our situation the best.

I took the elevator to the sixth floor where Dr. Wykoko, a Hawaiian intern, met me coming down the hall and immediately announced, "Congratulations, you have a baby boy." This was less than three minutes after we had left our car parked in front of the entrance to the emergency room.

Dr. Wykoko told me, "I have delivered babies a lot of ways, but this is the first time I have done it barefoot. He had been asleep in the doctor's lounge when they sent for him, and there was no time for such things as shoes and socks, or latex gloves for that matter. Marg never made it to the delivery room. Eric arrived, and there was no stopping him. She was lucky to get on a gurney before Eric made his grand entrance.

KATHY AND ERIC SAYING THEIR PRAYERS

I went back to admissions, and I finally got the admissions papers completed. Later, when Marg and Eric were released from the hospital, it was discovered that the papers stated that Eric was born before Marg had been admitted. Could that be? No! It couldn't. The admission papers had to be changed. We heard another one of those, "We can't do that," from the admissions guy.

Marg's mother arrived to take care of Kathy, and I didn't even miss a class, and we had a healthy new son.

Because of their closeness in age, Eric and Kathy became good buddies and playmates.

We were living on Grandview Avenue in Wadsworth, Ohio, when Eric fell down a full flight of stairs. One of his front upper teeth turned black and was dead. All of this happened when I was home on a Saturday morning with the kids. Marg was out shopping and returned home to some excitement. In spite of our fears of future problems with his permanent tooth, they didn't materialize. The permanent tooth came in fine, which was a pleasant surprise to our dentist and us.

MARLIN GIVING ERIC A HAIRCUT WHEN WE LIVED IN OHIO. LOOK AT THAT TELEPHONE ON THE WALL.

One day while we were living in Wadsworth, Ohio, Eric found a shiny copper penny. Some kids are tempted to put things in their mouth, and that is where this penny ended up and was accidentally swallowed, which is nothing serious. This happened the same day that we brought a new puppy home. Everyone agreed that the puppy's name should be "Penny," and so it was.

Eric enjoyed sports, and we enjoyed watching him play. He was in Little League Baseball and on the Naperville Youth Football team and quite good at both, but excelled in football. He was selected to play on the varsity football team both his junior and senior years in high school, which was quite an honor in such a large school. Many really talented athletes didn't make the team. His class of over 900 was the largest graduation class the city had ever had.

ERIC, 17, VARSITY FOOTBALL AT CENTRAL HIGH IN NAPERVILLE. BOTH OUR BOYS WERE OUTSTANDING ATHLETES.

When we moved into our house on Huntington Court in Naperville, I thought there was something wrong with the paint job. I talked to Jerry Gerten, our builder about it. I said, "Jerry, I presume that it is just a primer coat on the house. When are you going to paint the finish coat?" Jerry said, "No, that is the finish coat, but it isn't right." He went on to say, "The siding was supposed to be pre-painted with no additional paint required. But I knew it just wasn't right, so I called the factory rep and had him come to take a look at it. The factory rep agreed that the siding pieces had many shades. They aren't all the same color." Then he told me, "The factory rep agreed to pay for a finish paint job." I was happy.

A few days later I called Jerry and proposed that he hire Eric to paint the finish coat. Jerry agreed and told me that he would pay Eric the amount he was authorized by the factory rep to paint the house, which, I might add, was a nice sum. Eric was home for the summer after his freshman year in college and was working at McDonald's as an hourly manager. He went to see Jerry, and Jerry hired Eric to paint our house. It was a good deal for Eric, as he would have all summer to finish the job, and Jerry knew he wouldn't get any complaints from us about the quality of his work. It was a good deal for us in that Eric would earn some good money that summer. We also knew Eric would be particular, and we would most likely get a better paint job with him holding the brush than we would a professional painter who would be under the gun to get the job done in the shortest time possible. He did a great job, and Jerry didn't get any complaints from us. In fact Jerry complimented Eric on a great paint job.

Eric was an excellent student and made A's without really trying. He graduated in the top two or three percent of his Naperville Central High School class. When he started college at Northwestern University in Evanston, Illinois, virtually everyone at Northwestern had graduated in the top four or five percent of their high school class. In college he really had to study, which was something new for him.

ERIC IN HIGH SCHOOL

Once when Eric was home on break from Northwestern he made a surprising comment during a family discussion. "I am just an average student," he told us. "My classmates at Northwestern are highly competitive honor students, and I have to really work hard to maintain my high grade point average." We knew that Eric was far from average.

After two years in a pre-med program at Northwestern, Eric decided he did not want to be a doctor. His grades were very good and his advisor urged him to continue with medical school, but Eric considered Northwestern a "city school" and decided he wanted to transfer to a school located in mountain country. He applied to the University of Colorado in Boulder and was accepted. Two years later he graduated with high honors and a double major in Biology and Psychology.

Eric was offered a teaching assistantship (T. A.) at Southern

Illinois University in Edwardsville, Illinois where he was responsible for teaching undergraduates. During that time he completed the graduate course work and wrote his thesis for his master's degree and graduated with high honors.

At the time Eric was completing his thesis for his graduate degree, Jayne Blanchard, the girl who lived next door to us in Naperville, Illinois was attending graduate school at the University of Illinois majoring in German. Jayne and Eric met while working part time at McDonald's. They began dating and decided to get married.

DAUGHTER-IN-LAW JAYNE REISHUS, MARRIED TO OUR SON ERIC

After graduate school, Eric was hired as a biologist with Union Electric, a large public utility in St. Louis, Missouri. After five years working at Union Electric he decided to join me in the Burger King business. As we continued to build or buy more stores every year, I had pretty much turned over the day-today operation to Eric. Eric the biologist was now successfully running a multi-million dollar Burger King business.

While living in Edwardsville, Illinois, a suburb of St. Louis, Eric and Jayne had their first child, a baby girl they named Kimberly. Marg and I always enjoyed watching our grandchildren grow up. In June 2008, Kim graduated from the University of Missouri with high honors and a degree in Journalism. She works for the *Chicago Tribune* in their magazine section.

KIM'S GRADUATION. WE WERE SO PROUD OF HER.

GRANDDAUGHTER KIM ON THE TENNIS TEAM

FLAG GIRL JULIE LOOKING VERY COMPETENT

GRANDSON DANIEL WITH HIS KEYCHAIN COLLECTION

Two years after Kim was born, Julie arrived. Julie attended Hope College in Holland, Michigan where she graduated as an honor student in May 2010.

After his two sisters, their son Daniel was born. He graduated Naperville Central High School in May 2010, where both sisters and his mom and dad graduated. He is also an honor student. Daniel is an Eagle Scout, just like his dad and his Uncle Paul. Eric now serves as an assistant Scout master in that same troop. This picture of the Eagle Scout badge appears twice in the pages of my book, as it is such a great achievement for all who wear it proudly.

Our Savior's is the largest Lutheran Church in metropolitan Chicago, with some 4700 members. It is also the largest Protestant church in Naperville. Eric served six years on the Our Savior's Lutheran Church council. Five of those years he served as president of the council, which was longer than any other council president. His wife Jayne served on the same church council before Eric was elected, just as I had many years earlier.

EAGLE SCOUT BADGE

ERIC AND JAYNE WITH THEIR THREE CHILDREN, JULIE, DAN, AND KIM

OUR GRANDSON
DANIEL—
ERIC AND JAYNE'S
YOUNGEST AND
ONLY BOY

KIM, JULIE, AND
DAN ABOUT 1997

27

REFLECTIONS BY ERIC

A Scout is never taken by surprise; he knows exactly what to do when anything unexpected happens.
—ROBERT BADEN-POWELL

MY MEMORIES OF GROWING UP include the fact that we moved around quite a bit. Our family lived in several states during my early years, including Minnesota, Ohio, Iowa, and Illinois. In some states we lived in multiple locations, so by the time I finished fifth grade, I had attended seven different grade schools. We finally settled in Naperville, and I was able to stay in the same school district, changing schools only as I moved on to junior high and high school. However, when I was a senior at Naperville Central, our family moved again, this time back to Ohio, and I spent the last month of my senior year living with a friend and his family to finish up the semester. As it was, I graduated a semester early and then followed my family to Ohio.

When we lived in Des Moines, Iowa, I was a nine-year-old fourth grader, and Mom was pregnant. I remember getting a call as we were staying at a neighbor's house when the baby was delivered and getting the news that I had a new baby brother. I was so happy that Paul was a boy that I thanked Mom for that gift; I thought I already had enough sisters.

I remember visiting my grandparents frequently, and when I was old enough, I visited them alone during the summer months. Those were special times when I didn't have to share them with anyone else and had some truly memorable experiences with them.

When visiting my Reishus grandparents, I had the bonus of visiting my cousin David and his family and hanging out with his friends in the small town Cottonwood, where my parents grew up. I didn't know very many people there, but everyone seemed to know me as "Marlin and Margaret's boy."

I remember some truly great family vacations to places like the Black Hills and Mt. Rushmore in South Dakota and a visit to the East Coast that included stops at Annapolis, Plymouth, Niagara Falls, and New York City. For these trips we pulled either a pop-up or regular camping trailer, and it was always an adventure. The best vacation, in my memory, was a family fly-in trip to Lake Kagianagami, Ontario. We were with my Olson grandparents, the Bergeron family, and our entire family except for Kathy, who could not make the trip. We stayed in an unimproved camp and fished and played cards and generally had a hilarious time in the remote north woods.

Another memory that is clear in my mind is a time we went to Christmas Lake, Minnesota, the lake house of my dad's boss. I was in first or second grade. We kids were fooling around with some rowboats near shore, and Kathy and I got into one that started drifting out to the middle of the lake. When Mom noticed our predicament, she yelled for us to stay in the boat. I got scared as the water got deeper and decided I would swim back to shore and jumped out of the boat. Not being a strong swimmer, I was soon in trouble and started to sink like a stone. I did hold my breath, however, and just as I thought I was a goner, Mom arrived at the scene, dove down, grabbed me, and brought me up to the surface. I survived that episode only because Mom was such a strong swimmer.

The childhood activities that were important to me in my early years were Y-Indian Guides with Dad, Cub Scouts, sports, including baseball and football, and eventually Boy Scouts. Soon after we moved to Naperville in 1967, I joined Boy Scout Troop 505 as an eleven-year-old Tenderfoot. Scouting was very important to me, and as I got to be an older Scout (age 13), I went on high adventure trips to the Namekogin River in northern Wisconsin, the Boundary Waters Canoe Area of northern Minnesota, and Philmont Scout Ranch near Cimarron, New Mexico. The adult leaders of Troop 505 had a profound influence on my development, as I stayed active all the way through high school, earning my Eagle award along the way in 1972. Scouting was no doubt a big influence on my love of nature and eventual study of biology in college and graduate school.

Scouting came full circle for me in 2003 when I rejoined Troop 505 as an adult leader with my son Daniel. As Daniel progressed up the ranks of scouting, I got to share his scouting experience with him, including summer camp twice and four high adventure trips. Daniel earned his Eagle award in 2009, and we became the first father-son Eagles from the troop in its 44-year history.

DAN EARNS EAGLE SCOUT. HIS FATHER ERIC IS ASSISTANT SCOUT MASTER.

Some of my best memories are of the times we spent at our family cabin at Nest Lake near Wilmar, Minnesota. Our cabin wasn't big or fancy, but it was a place where I could fish and catch snakes and frogs and take boat rides on the lake. We shared many special times at Nest Lake with many family members, and it was heaven on earth for me as a young boy growing up.

The other constant in our lives growing up was church. Wherever we lived, we soon found and got involved as a family with a nearby Lutheran church. My clearest memory of church is Our Savior's Lutheran. I was a fifth grader when we moved to Naperville and joined that church. I was confirmed at Our Savior's, and Jayne and I had the privilege of having our own children baptized (Julie and Daniel) and confirmed (all three children) there as well. A strong Lutheran faith was the heritage I enjoyed from both sides of my family as I grew up, and it is important to me that Jayne and I were able to pass that heritage on to our own children.

I started my first real job at age sixteen at the local McDonald's in Naperville, starting as a kitchen worker and eventually working my way up to an assistant manager. Working at McDonald's was a big part of my life as a high school student growing up in Naperville. Little did I know then that my experience at McDonald's would be the foundation of my later career at Burger King. Fast food was, and still is, a challenging job where every day is a new and different adventure.

∼ 28 ∼

JEAN SUSAN REISHUS (MARTIN)

No one is as deaf as the man who will not listen.
—JEWISH FOLK SAYING

DR. ZITTO DELIVERED OUR DAUGHTER Jean on September 11, 1958 at the Wadsworth-Rittman Hospital just a short time after we had moved from the upper to the lower level of a split-level duplex on Grandview Avenue in Wadsworth, Ohio. Our son Eric was two and one half, and Kathy was three years, ten months. Three weeks after Jean was born, Marg had surgery to remove one half of her thyroid. When she came home from the hospital after her surgery her doctor came to our house to check up on Marg. Dr. Zitto was a family practice MD when doctors still made house calls. Marg continued to nurse baby Jean, even with a sore neck from the recent surgery.

The first house we owned was in Wadsworth on Wolf Avenue. Jean became good friends with the lady next door and called her "Cookie Grandma." It got so that whenever Jean wanted a snack she would simply knock on "Cookie Grandma's" door, and she would get a cookie.

In 1961, we moved to Coon Rapids, Minnesota. A few weeks after we had moved into the neighborhood, three-year-old Jean was across the street playing in the snow with some neighbor kids. She had to use the bathroom and attempted to walk to our house at the dead end of the dead end street about one hundred and fifty feet away. Somehow Jean went the wrong direction. She walked over one half mile up the street, crossed a four lane very busy highway, and went up to a house and knocked on the door. A lady answered the door, and after realizing Jean was lost, brought Jean in and called the police. She informed them she had a little lost girl named Jean who had just knocked on her door.

Marg was outside checking on the kids when she realized that Jean was nowhere to be found. After rushing in all directions, including the creek next to our house, she called the police. They were happy to inform her where she could find the little lost girl who told the lady that her name was Jean. Marg drove over immediately to pick Jean up. When she asked Jean what happened she replied, "The nice lady gave me two cookies and a milk." Jean wasn't the least bit concerned, but her mother was a basket case.

We lived in Davenport, Iowa when Jean entered kindergarten. Her teacher, Mrs. Husher, was the nicest person and a wonderful teacher. I remember Mrs. Husher inviting all her students' fathers to visit her kindergarten class one morning. Every dad except one came to the classroom and was sitting in a circle cross-legged on the floor in business suits. We were all so proud of our little kindergartners. It was a neat experience.

When we moved from Des Moines, Iowa, to Davenport, Iowa, Mrs. Husher's class gave Jean a little canvas octopus. The body of the octopus was about the size of a volleyball and was signed by Mrs. Husher and all Jean's classmates. She kept that toy octopus for years.

During her school years Jean was very active in Girl Scouts, earning lots of badges and eventually assuming leadership positions.

Naperville North High School was a brand new school in our district. Jean was in their first graduating class. After graduation, Jean enrolled at Illinois State University (ISU) in Normal, Illinois.

After one year at ISU, Jean married Cliff Martin and looked lovely wearing her mother's wedding dress. She still has that wedding dress, and years later, her daughter Lindy used parts of it when she married on May 29, 2010.

Jean and Cliff moved to Atlanta and both enrolled at Georgia State. They worked part-time jobs as they continued their college studies. During the years they lived in Georgia, Jean and Cliff had two daughters, Jessica (Jessy) and Melinda (Lindy).

SISTERS, JESSY AND LINDY AS CHILDREN

LINDY AND JESSY AS YOUNG LADIES

DAUGHTER JEAN ABOUT 1998

OUR GRANDDAUGHTER
LINDY

OUR GRANDDAUGHTER
JESSY

The girls are now grown. Jessy and Elliot Henry have two sons. Dakota was born February 9, 2007 and Rylee was born May 26, 2009. Their family lives in San Antonio, Texas where they bought a house in the spring of 2009.

GREAT GRANDSON DAKOTA

GREAT GRANDSON RYLEY

JESSY AND ELLIOT HENRY WITH CHILDREN
RYLEE AND DAKOTA AT LINDY AND ADAM'S
WEDDING IN FT. WAYNE, INDIANA

Lindy graduated from Indiana University with a degree in Business. She not only graduated with high honors, but also graduated number one in her class. She was a straight A student during her four years of college with a 4.0 **GPA**. She also worked

LINDY'S GRADUATION

thirty to thirty-five hours per week. It's obvious that she must have more of her Grandma Marg's genes than her Grandpa Marlin's. Lindy currently works as an account executive for a marketing firm in Fort Wayne. In the spring of 2009 she bought a new house. On May 29, 2010 Lindy and Adam Connley were married.

BRIDE AND GROOM, LINDY AND ADAM CONNLEY WITH REISHUS WEDDING PARTY. THE COUPLE MARRIED AT SAINT JOSEPH UNITED METHODIST CHURCH IN FT. WAYNE, INDIANA.

JEAN AND CLIFF MARTIN, PARENTS OF THE BRIDE

CHAPTER 28 / *Jean Susan Reishus (Martin)*

ADAM AND LINDY'S ENGAGEMENT PICTURE

In 1976, when Jean learned that Eric and I were going to buy two Burger King restaurants, she called and said she would like to be considered for a management position in one of the stores. She already had some experience as an assistant manager at a fast food place in Atlanta.

Jean and Cliff moved back to Naperville and eventually bought a house in Aurora, the town next to Naperville where we had lived for many years. Jean became an assistant manager in our Lockport, Illinois store. Later, she became the store manager and served as store manager in several of our B.K. restaurants.

In 2003, Jean and Cliff moved to Fort Wayne, Indiana where she now works as a supervisor at Walmart.

~ 29 ~

REFLECTIONS BY JEAN

When a woman tells you her age, it's all right to look surprised, but don't scowl.
—WILSON MIZNER

MOST OF MY CHILDHOOD MEMORIES are when we lived at 429 Aspen Court in Naperville, Illinois. That was the place where we lived the longest. On the court we all had friends and played outside much of the time. Each summer we would have "the court picnic" where all the families got together for fun and games. The softball game in the Koller's back yard was an annual hit.

Each summer we went on a vacation, and sometimes we kids were able to help choose our destinations. A lot of times we went camping. The pop-up trailer was exciting, especially in the pouring rain! One year we went to the Black Hills in South Dakota and saw a lot of interesting and new things. All of our vacations included new places and educational experiences. Mom and Dad gave us each a certain amount of spending money to use as we chose throughout the trip. On one trip we found a place that sold homemade jewelry. The man explained how they spun the silver and added the stones. Mom and I bought identical silver band rings. Well, they weren't identical because each was spun individually, but they were very similar.

About forty or so years later Mom and Dad's condo in Florida was broken into. The thieves took all of Mom's jewelry, even the small trinkets and mementos, including her silver ring. She did have a lot of valuable pieces, but some things can't be replaced.

Mom felt a loss of the special items like her college pin and her original wedding ring. I knew those things were gone forever, but I still had my silver ring. I gave it to her so that she would remember those special times on our family vacations. Mom said how much she treasures that silver ring as well as all the memories.

When we lived on Aspen Court, Dad got into a creative landscaping kick. His first project was a pretty garden with a retaining wall. The flowers were great. He took pride in his odd shaped trees, yucca plants and the water fountain addition. When it was completed, the whole thing was quite beautiful. The next year had a bit of a different result. His aim was another flower garden in the front yard. He dug up the grass and brought in additional dirt. He planted and weeded and watered. The garden was about ten feet long and four feet wide. It looked like a grave! The neighbors asked if he buried someone or if it was an old Indian mound!

I helped Dad build a deck in back of our North Canton, Ohio house. Eric, Paul, and I were his free labor. He taught us about decks and teamwork. This is the first time that I remember Dad using the term "wood butcher" versus "carpenter." After all, his brother Dale was a carpenter. Dad wasn't skilled enough to be called a carpenter, so he called himself a wood butcher.

I can remember singing the popular song "Ragg Mop" with Eric as we mixed the concrete to set the posts. I think Paul absorbed all the carpenter theories since he grew up to become an architect. Mom was in charge of lemonade, sandwiches, and of course, our new puppy Archie. Mom and Dad taught us a lot growing up. Most was about life lessons, and all of it was out of love.

One of my favorite memories is when we visited Grandma and Grandpa Olson each Thanksgiving, and Grandpa played banjo. Grandma was in the kitchen making cookies and all sorts of wonderful treats.

I have wonderful memories of playing the card game Pit with cousins and all of us laughing!

I'll never forget Sunday mornings with Mom motivating us sleepy heads to get ready for church as she played the German Army Chorus record with the volume on high. Girl Scout camp, piano lessons, and Vacation Bible School all play a special part when I remember my years growing up.

One time my cousin David and I took off in a canoe on Cottonwood Lake. Before we returned to the dock, it got dark, and everyone was worried. The whole town was in an uproar and looking for us. Another time was when Eric fell in a hole at the cabin, and Mom was so upset.

My respect and adoration grew greatly for Mom when our neighbor Reverend Tourney fell off his roof, and Mom took him to the emergency room. My good friend Susan ran to get Mom to come and help. Reverend Tourney was bleeding from his head and confused. With her background in nursing, Mom took charge. When Mom got home from the hospital that afternoon, she went right back to the task of recycling the soup cans. What a woman! What a Mom!

Dad, as you know, I'm not much for writing, but my heart is in these stories and I remember them all. You gave me a great beginning. I love you. . . . Jean.

30

PAUL BRIAN REISHUS

Asking a working writer what he thinks about critics is like asking a lamppost how it feels about dogs.
—CHRISTOPHER HAMPTON/JOHN OSBORNE

November 2, 1965

THREE MONTHS AFTER THE ARRIVAL of our fourth child we moved to Davenport, Iowa on the coldest day in Davenport's history. We lived in Des Moines, Iowa when Paul was born. The day we moved, the temperature dipped to twenty-five below zero. With the doors of our house constantly open, the furnace couldn't keep up. We put several blankets and some pillows in the bathroom tub for a makeshift bed for Paul, who slept through the day in the only warm room in the house.

Meanwhile, I had been promoted to Branch Manager and was responsible for sales in much of the state of Illinois, Eastern Iowa, and Northwestern Indiana. I had branch sales offices, a sales manager, a sales team, and a systems manager with a system team in Davenport, Iowa, and Peoria, Rockford, Lansing, and Oakbrook, Illinois. We were having great success in replacing IBM equipment in our territory. Things were good at work and at home too.

On a lighter note, when Paul was about two years old, his mother was attempting to get him potty trained. Paul was sitting on the seat, and each time Marg went past the open bathroom door, she would say, "You go B M!" This happened several times, and each time as she passed the doorway, she repeated, "You go B M!" Finally after she had repeated those directions several times, she found Paul standing and pointing into the seat while he proudly exclaimed, "Look Mommy, IBM, IBM." Of course, Marg was hysterical with laughter. When I came home from work that afternoon, Marg told me of her experience with Paul regarding his potty training. I said, "The kid is only two years old, and he already knows the competition when he sees it."

Paul was a gifted athlete like his big brother Eric. He played Naperville Youth football and was one of the best players in the league.

PAUL IN NAPERVILLE YOUTH FOOTBALL LEAGUE

Though he was good at all sports, baseball was Paul's game. He starred in Little League, Pony League, and Colt League where he was a star player from the beginning and made the Varsity team as a junior in high school. That was quite an accomplishment considering he was enrolled in a school of over eight hundred in his class alone. Many really good players didn't make the team.

Paul was very active in Boy Scouts and earned his Eagle Scout award as his older brother Eric had done some ten years earlier. Only two percent of boys who join Boy Scouts earn the rank of

PAUL IN HIGH SCHOOL

Eagle. Both Eric and Paul hold the proud distinction of Eagle Scout, as does Eric's son Dan. Paul's son Adam is a Life Scout and is on a pace to earn his Eagle in a few months.

Early in his senior year, Paul decided he wanted to be an architect. While he was very good in all his studies, he didn't really like math and hadn't taken enough math to successfully enter the architecture field.

After having a discussion with his mother and me about a possible solution, Paul decided on his own that he should enroll at College of DuPage to take some additional math classes while he was still in high school. College of DuPage is a two-year community college located in Glen Ellyn, Illinois. The college also owns and operates facilities in the Illinois communities of Addison, Bloomingdale, Carol Stream, Lombard, Naperville, and West Chicago.

Paul took an entire year of math at COD so he would be up to speed when he started college in the fall. To accomplish this, he had to drop his one true love, which was baseball. When Paul said he was going to drop varsity baseball his senior year of high school, so he could complete his math courses at COD, we knew he was serious about architecture. It paid off, as he worked hard and got straight A's in all his college math courses.

Paul applied at a half dozen Midwest schools of architecture and was accepted by all. He chose the five-year professional program at the University of Arkansas because of the School of Architecture's extraordinary reputation. The University of Arkansas is well known for football, basketball, and architecture.

Among the reasons the University of Arkansas School of Architecture is rated so high, is the student teacher ratio is seven to one, and the percentage of the graduates who pass the test on their first try is high. Their percentage was higher than any other school of architecture in the country. Virtually all of the University of Arkansas graduates eventually pass. At some schools, a large percentage of students never pass the exam to become a Licensed Architect, also called a Registered Architect.

Three major awards were given at Paul's graduation ceremony. The first award was for valedictorian. The second award was for the number one student in design. And the third major award was given to the number one student in all the technical architectural courses, except design. Paul was awarded the third honor for getting straight A's in all his classes and graduating number three overall in his class.

Paul and Jana Latshaw were married after Paul graduated from the University of Arkansas. Jana, a native of Dallas, also attended the University of Arkansas where she and Paul met. After the wedding, Paul and Jana moved to Naperville and over the next two years, Jana finished her last two years at North Central College in Naperville, Illinois where she received her degree. Paul finished his first two years of architecture apprenticeship while they still lived in Illinois.

PAUL IN COLLEGE

PAUL AND JANA'S ENGAGEMENT PICTURE

CHAPTER 30 / *Paul Brian Reishus*

JANA GRADUATES FROM NORTH CENTRAL COLLEGE, NAPERVILLE, ILLINOIS.

After their move to Dallas, Paul found a job working for an international architecture firm headquartered in Dallas, Texas. HKS, Inc. is the third largest architectural firm in the country with over 1700 employees of which half are architects, and the other half support staff. After Paul completed his third year apprenticeship, he was eligible to take the architecture test, which he passed. Paul was now a registered and licensed architect. HKS assigned Paul to work on the team that exclusively designed hospitals and hospital additions. Every project was big. The smallest project was a $30,000,000, and many cost over $100,000,000.

After working for five years in Dallas, Paul and Jana made the decision to move back to Naperville where Paul used his architectural skills to form Viking Development, Inc. Viking Development designed and built primarily for the commercial market, but also designed and built a few high-end houses, ($600,000 to $850,000), including a group of town houses.

Paul and Jana moved their family back to Dallas where they currently live. They have raised three children. Katelin, who we all call Kate, is a junior in high school, Adam is in the eighth grade, and Leah is in the third grade as of 2010–11.

Paul volunteers as an assistant scoutmaster in a Scout troop in Dallas. His son Adam is a Scout and is following in his father's footsteps. He is a Life Scout on his way to earning Eagle Scout within the next year.

EAGLE SCOUT BADGE

GRANDDAUGHTER LEAH
(PAUL AND JANA'S DAUGHTER)

GRANDSON ADAM
(PAUL AND JANA'S SON)

JANA AND PAUL WITH THEIR THREE
CHILDREN: KATE, LEAH, AND ADAM

KATELIN
(PAUL AND JANA'S DAUGHTER)

31

REFLECTIONS BY PAUL
PAUL BRIAN REISHUS

The most important object in Boy Scout training is to educate, not instruct.
—SIR ROBERT BADEN-POWELL

ALTHOUGH I WAS BORN IN Des Moines, Iowa, the family moved to Davenport, Iowa a few months later. About a year after that, we ended up in Naperville, Illinois where I grew up, the town I consider my hometown. I have fond memories of playing baseball in the Naperville Little League through my junior year at Naperville North High School. I was very involved in two other activities: my youth group at church and Boy Scouts. As a Scout, I advanced through the ranks, ultimately achieving the highest rank of Eagle in 1982.

My senior year I chose not to play baseball in order to take some college level math courses at the local community college. I felt this was necessary in my pursuit to be an architect. My high school was fortunate to have drafting and architecture courses and I attended classes on those subjects for three years. My search for a college began during my junior year in high school and I ended up as a Razorback at the University of Arkansas. I chose this school of architecture for several reasons. Faye Jones, who had been a student of the great architect Frank Lloyd Wright, was a design studio instructor at the university. I took advantage of learning from such a master and studied under Jones in my third year. I also attended a program that was offered during the summer at the Harvard Graduate School of Design.

I spent the summer of 1987 in Boston at Cambridge Design Studio under the leadership of the Harvard design staff. The University of Arkansas is the only school of architecture in the entire country to be invited to study under the Harvard Graduate School of Design. Twelve classmates and I had the opportunity to experience Cambridge in Boston, and life on the East Coast. One unique experience was buying lobsters right off the boat from the fisherman who caught them. I showed some of my friends from Arkansas who had never had lobster before how to cook and eat them.

There were numerous opportunities to get involved in clubs and organizations in college. I became a member of Alpha Rho Chi, which is a professional fraternity for architecture students, and also joined a social fraternity known as Phi Kappa Psi.

The most significant thing that happened at Phi Kappa Psi is that I met my wife Jana who is my best friend. A mutual friend introduced us at a Phi Kappa Psi fraternity party. Jana Latshaw and I were married on August 13, 1988. Jana worked as a flight attendant for American Airlines from 1992 until 2007, when she made an important decision to quit her job and stay at home with our growing children. Before that occurred, I was the laundryman and chauffeur for all the kids' activities as Jana worked a lot of weekends so that we didn't need to have the kids in daycare.

I continue to enjoy many of my friends that I met at Phi Kappa Psi and Alpha Rho Chi. Last summer, Jana and I traveled to Cabo San Lucas, Mexico to meet up with some fraternity brothers that I hadn't seen in years.

Our twenty-two years of marriage has given us three incredible children. Katelin, sixteen, is our intuitive, perceptive, and selective daughter. She is a varsity softball player and loves playing her clarinet in the marching band during football season. Kate and I share many memories of being in the Indian Princess program together. I think this is where she acquired her love for the outdoors.

Adam, thirteen, is also very intuitive, but is very laid-back and easygoing, most of the time. Adam is a very musically talented kid that plays percussion in the school band and acoustic and electric guitar. Adam and I were also involved in the Indian Guides program. He is currently a Life Scout (just one rank from Eagle) in a troop where I am one of the adult leaders.

Leah, nine, is our little socialite and full of energy. She enjoys playing piano and attending Girl Scouts, but one of her favorite things is when we have Daddy/Leah time. The Indian Princess program in our area is weak, so we oftentimes spend the day together doing fun things like ice skating and Paint-your-Pottery. It doesn't really matter to me what we do, I just like to have special time with her. The kids are growing too fast and continue to challenge us, but I am so very proud of each of them.

My career as an architect has included a rich variety of projects in both size and scope. After college I began working for Eichstaedt Architects, a small firm in Roselle, Illinois. This only lasted about two years, as my boss was out in Santa Barbara, California much of the time where he owned a house. I needed mentorship and guidance during my internship, so I looked elsewhere and ended up at HKS, Inc. in Dallas, which was Jana's hometown. While at HKS I finished my required three-year internship, and in 1992 passed the architect registration exam. For close to five years I worked primarily on healthcare projects before deciding it was time for another change. We ended up moving back to Naperville, and I started a new firm with my siblings, known as Viking Development. I designed and built a number of restaurants, single-family homes, and designed a couple of small church projects. After working at Viking for nearly ten years, the folks at HKS in Dallas invited me back. I accepted and was with HKS for five and one-half years until June of 2009 when they let me go in their fifth round of lay-offs.

I have now been with Camp Dresser and McKee for six months. I mostly work on mid-sized projects that are municipal in nature. They are not as high profile as other projects, but good people who are also working on the same kind of projects surround me. I have been blessed to work on a wide variety of project types and sizes throughout my career, including healthcare, hospitality, mixed-use, commercial, religious, and residential, ranging from $500,000 to over $250 million in construction costs.

As for the future, I am anticipating that I will "retire" in Missouri, with my bride Jana at the Latshaw family farm, the place she calls home. It is 376 acres of gorgeous land in the southwestern corner of Missouri. Jana and her sister inherited the farm from their grandfather upon his death in 2007 at the age of eighty-nine. There is an old farmhouse on the land that Jana is going to update with my assistance. We plan to rent it out as a vacation home and enjoy our own vacations there as well. We look forward to the farm as a beautiful place to go when I retire from architecture.

Growing up, my parents have always been there to support my activities—Mom attended my baseball games, Dad coached baseball, and encouraged me to get over the last few humps to achieve my Eagle rank in Boy Scouts. They faithfully came to the University of Arkansas every parents' weekend while I was in architecture school and continue to love and give support to me, my wife, and even more importantly, our children. Recently they came to visit us in Dallas and had the opportunity to experience some of the kids' activities with us. Just like when we were growing up, they attended a softball tournament that Kate played in and Adam's basketball games.

32

W. (WALLACE) DALE REISHUS

It has been said that there is no fool like an old fool, except a young fool. But a young fool has first to grow up to be an old fool to realize what a damn fool he was when he was a young fool.
—HAROLD MACMILLAN

June 25, 1924

ALTHOUGH MY OLDER BROTHER'S FIRST name was Wallace, we always called him Dale. Dale was a guy with a mechanical eye for everything. He could do most everything he set his mind to. Just to name a few of his many talents, he was a carpenter, a cabinet maker, built houses, remodeled houses, and repaired farm buildings. In the Navy he had trained as an electrician, so having that skill enabled him to also do the electrical work when he remodeled houses. The closest plumber was in the next town, so he learned plumbing too. Dale could do it all.

His skills as a carpenter kept him busy, but especially after the frequent storms that came though our area raised havoc leaving debris in their wake with heavy damage to property and buildings. Dale's skills as a carpenter were always in demand.

One job he was called on to do was moving and erecting metal grain bins. The farmers bought surplus government grain bins, but needed someone to move and erect them on their farms. Dale designed and built a special trailer to haul those huge bins. He moved hundreds and hundreds of them over a period of several years.

CHAPTER 32 / *W. (Wallace) Dale Reishus*

DALE'S HIGH SCHOOL
GRADUATION PICTURE, 1942

Dale graduated from Cottonwood High School in May of 1942, about six months after the beginning of WWII. Right after graduating high school, he tried to join the Navy, but the Lyon County Draft Board would not release him, so he could enlist. About one year later, he was drafted. After Dale and the 200-plus men drafted at the same time had completed their physicals and other processing, they were about ready to be sworn in when they heard a voice say, "I need six guys for the Navy." He pointed at the group and said, "You, you, you, you, you and you." One of the guys he pointed to was Dale. The remaining 200-plus guys were sworn into the Army. Dale had originally tried to join the Navy and now was being drafted into the Navy, where he had wanted to serve. Dale was one happy guy. He went to Farragut, Idaho for boot camp, and on to the Iowa State University in Ames, Iowa where he studied to become an electrician.

After his electrician training, Dale was assigned to the destroyer *USS Dale*. The ship's name was the same as his, but had been named after Admiral Dale of many years past. But the coincidences didn't end there. We picked our mail up at the post office because there was no mail delivery at our house. Our post office box in Cottonwood was number 353, exactly the same as the 353 numbers painted on the side of the *USS Dale*.

Dale served for about two years aboard the *USS Dale* and was involved in many naval battles in the Pacific and South Pacific. He told me they should have received submarine pay as the *Dale* was a small destroyer and was under water as much as it was above the water. In rough seas no one could be on deck for fear of being swept overboard.

Dale continued his service in the Navy after the war ended. He married one of his former classmates and high school sweetheart, Donna Mae Larson. For the next few months, until he was discharged, they lived in Orange, Texas while Dale assisted the Navy in the decommissioning of another ship.

After leaving the Navy, Dale went back to school at Dunwoody in Minneapolis, Minnesota where he studied drafting, estimating, and construction. After completing his courses, he started his own carpentry business in Cottonwood.

Dale and Donna Mae have three children. Their son Allan became a medical doctor and has a practice in Craig, Colorado. Allan's son, Dustin, earned his PhD in May of 2009, and his daughter, Anna Lisa, became a schoolteacher and is married to Nick Som who also earned his PhD in May 2009.

Rebecca, or Becky, as everyone calls her, became a schoolteacher and married Tim Johnson who is a dentist. After their children arrived, Becky quit teaching to become a stay-at-home mom living in Coon Rapids, Minnesota, northwest of Minneapolis. Their kids are Katy and Sarah. Katy graduated from Gustavus Adolphus College in St. Peter, Minnesota and currently works for the federal government in Washington, D. C. Her younger sister Sarah graduated in May 2009 from Wartburg College in Waverly, Iowa with a degree in education.

CHAPTER 32 / *W. (Wallace) Dale Reishus*

THE USS DALE

DONNA MAE AND DALE WITH
ALLAN, BECKY, AND DAVID

David Reishus, Dale and Donna Mae's third child, is a captain with the Minnesota Correctional System and is married to Sheryl. David graduated from Concordia College in Moorehead, Minnesota. They also have two children: Kyle, who graduated from high school in 2009 and is a sophomore at the University of North Dakota majoring in Engineering. In 2009/10, Alec attended the eighth grade.

In 1986, Dale and Donna Mae moved to Naperville, Illinois where Dale found more work than he could handle. I don't know how many basements he remodeled, but there were a lot. When he got to his mid-seventies he began to do less and less. After working all his life, he deserved to slow down a bit.

He was head usher at his church for twelve years. When he retired from that position, they had a special day in his honor.

December 18, 2002, Dale had open heart surgery and surgery on his curetted arteries. Unfortunately, he suffered a stroke during the operation. He died December 30. His grandchildren called him "Grandpa Fix It," but because the doctors could not fix "Grandpa Fix It," he has gone to a better place. We all miss him.

DONNA MAE AND DALE

33

GENE ORVILLE REISHUS
BORN NOVEMBER 29, 1937

The future ain't what it used to be.
—YOGI BERRA

MY YOUNGER BROTHER GENE WAS born as the economy was starting to recover from the Great Depression. Things were still difficult, and money was scarce. The unemployment in the country was about twenty-five percent, but the unemployment in small towns like Cottonwood, where we lived, was closer to forty or fifty percent. Unemployment was even higher in some other towns in the area.

The WPA (Works Progress Administration) was in full swing. There were many more acronyms for those letters, some were pretty funny, but none of them true. Cottonwood took advantage of the federally funded WPA as a new sewer system was put in place for the entire town. I can still picture a hundred men digging ditches, one shovel of dirt at a time. They were just earning a few cents an hour, but it was a job, and better than no job. People weren't just hurting; they were desperate. None were starving, but a lot of people, including children, went to bed hungry.

The men earning a few cents an hour were often seen leaning on their shovel half the time because once the sewer project was complete, they didn't know if another paycheck would come. The theme of the WPA workers was, "Let's make it last as long as we can." Some of the men were admonished by their peers for working too fast, while other workers wanted to stretch the job out for as long as possible.

On December 7, 1941, Japan awoke a "Sleeping Giant." Our country and world would never be the same again. A full recovery from the Great Depression wasn't achieved until WWII, as the country came together in an unbelievable cooperative effort to stimulate the war machine. It was guns or butter as Americans got by on less butter (food) in order to produce more guns (all war machinery). Almost everyone had a "Victory Garden," making more commercial food available for the troops.

Like most kids his age, Gene didn't realize what it meant to be in a Depression. He attended first grade through high school in Cottonwood Public School District 15, with the exception of missing the second semester of his freshman year due to the fact that he contracted polio and was in the hospital. Sister Kenny Hospital had tutors at the hospital for the school age kids that could not attend school. Gene earned three credits while at Sister Kenny Hospital and was able to make up the difference before graduation in 1956.

GENE'S HIGH SCHOOL GRADUATION PICTURE, 1956

GENE AND KAY

One winter day while our parents were visiting some of our country relatives, Gene and I stayed home. They would be back in a couple of hours, and I was given the assignment of shoveling the snow off the sidewalk. Gene was about seven or eight, and I was thirteen or fourteen. I convinced Gene that the job was for the both of us, not just me. I was shoveling the sidewalk, and Gene was shoveling the snow off the front steps. Well, Gene slipped and the shovel hit him on the bridge of his nose. Because he was bleeding profusely, I took him downtown to the drug store. There was no doctor in town, but Mrs. Seitz, the pharmacist's wife, was a registered nurse and would know what to do. We didn't see her husband George Seitz, who was the town pharmacist. He was probably in their apartment above the store either drunk or recovering from a drunk and most likely had a big hangover. It was best that we saw Mrs. Seitz, who was much better at these things, and also was always sober, I might add. I felt really bad that Gene had this accident, and felt it was my fault for asking him to help me do what was really my job.

Gene was an outstanding basketball player and in eighth grade was the team's high scorer by a wide margin, and led the "B-Team" to an undefeated season. He was the only player in the entire school who could touch the rim. I never could touch the rim. In the first game of his freshman year, Gene outscored the entire competing team.

Mrs. (Mary) Hatlestad, Gene's math teacher, taught general math to the eighth graders, elementary algebra to the freshmen, geometry to the sophomores, and advanced algebra to the juniors. She taught Dale, Gene, and me and was Mother's teacher when she was in school. She had been teaching for so long, she actually taught three generations in some families. We all hated to see her go when she said, "It's time for me to retire." She was undoubtedly the best teacher I had in high school, and just a wonderful person.

On Christmas morning 1952, Gene came down with polio. I was home on military leave for the Christmas holidays. Fortunately, he was full-grown, and though one leg is much smaller than the other, both legs are the same length. Gene wears a brace and walks with a short crutch, but he is able to do most everything.

In 1954, Dad built a cabin on Nest Lake. Maybe I should say we all built that cabin, but Dad paid for it. It was near Willmar, between Spicer and New London, Minnesota. Gene, who doesn't like heights, was up on the roof shingling. Like I said, "The brace didn't stop Gene, it may have slowed him down a bit, but it sure didn't stop him."

Cottonwood was in the middle of pheasant country, and on opening day the population swelled to twice its normal size. Friends and relatives from the Twin Cities took over the town. Dad's Coast-to-Coast store would sell an enormous number of shotgun shells over the three-week season. The restaurants were busy, and the town was buzzing. People would hunt during the day and party at night. During World War II pheasant hunting season was canceled and ammunition production went toward the war effort. After the war the sloughs were drained, which allowed the farmer to farm more land. Draining the sloughs also took much of the coverage away for the pheasant population, and pheasant hunting declined around Cottonwood. The ring neck pheasants were not a native bird to these parts, or anywhere in the United States for that matter. They were brought here from China over a hundred years ago.

After graduating high school, Gene attended St. Olaf College in Northfield, Minnesota where he earned a degree in Business in 1960.

Gene worked for several years at both G. C. Electronics and Liberty Mutual before joining Xerox where he started as assistant credit manager and worked his way up the corporate ladder. He had a big job. Gene was with Xerox for twenty-nine years. His last position was corporate credit manager. When he retired, Gene was head of administration for one-third of the company. While climbing the corporate ladder, like our family, Gene moved a lot. He had offices in Boston, New York, Lansing, Michigan, and lived in Naperville when he retired.

Gene tried his hand at the Burger King business and was an owner operator of two Burger King restaurants for about five years. He was recruited out of retirement by Danka, a competitor of Xerox, where he headed up administration for most of the country. He retired from Danka in 2003 at age sixty-six. This time he retired for good.

Gene and Kay have three adult children. Scott is a vascular

surgeon. He and his wife Carolyn have two children. Matthew was born in 2001 and Jake in 2004. Gene and Kay's second son Jeff is an airline pilot flying for Sky West (United Express) and is married to Terri. Their third son Craig sells telephone systems to large corporations. He is married to Kati, and they have three boys, Graham born in 2001 and twin boys, Will and Drew, born in 2005.

34

MIGRATING TO MARCO ISLAND

> *Government is not the solution to our economic problems; government is the problem.*
> —MILTON FRIEDMAN

MY BUSINESS PARTNER FROM BURGER KING, Chuck Cerniglia, owned a condo in Marco Island and offered to let Marg and me stay for a few days. At the time, we didn't even know where Marco Island was located. (Marco is as far south as one can go on the Gulf of Mexico side of the peninsula, directly across from Miami). There is nothing south of Marco Island but alligators and everglades.

We liked Marco Island so much, that I wanted to buy a condo right then. However, Marg convinced me that we should wait and see if we still had that "urge" a year later.

The following spring Marg and I drove our motor home down to Marco and stayed in Chuck's condo again for a few days. We enjoyed it even more this time. After spending three days the previous spring and three days again, it was enough to convince us that Marco was the place to be.

Marg and I were confident. "Where could we find a better place to have our own condo than on the island everyone called Paradise?" We were convinced we couldn't. We learned about a condo for sale in the Riverside Club, which was in the same complex as Chuck and Cathie.

The condo we purchased was located on the bay side of the island. It needed some work to bring it up to date, but that was one of the challenges that appealed to us. We were able to remodel and replace the furnishings with furniture to our liking.

We enjoyed that condo immensely. In the beginning we only spent three or four weeks a year on Marco because I was still working.

For the first four years, to help pay the bills, we rented the condo when we were not there. After those first four years, we began to extend our stay in "Paradise." We remodeled, bought new furniture, and no longer rented it. We didn't want to chance it with all our new furnishings.

Marco Island is about three miles wide and five miles long with a total area of 17.1 square miles. It is the largest barrier island within Southwest Florida's Ten Thousand Islands. We lived in the land of ten thousand lakes in Minnesota and now lived in the 10,000 islands of Florida. The climate is subtropical, and the island is surrounded by water. However, because of the tides and the ever flowing current, the Indians called the backside of the island a river. That is how the Riverside Club got its name. We have about 15,000 permanent residents, which grows to 45,000 in "Season," as it is called here on the island.

There are 275 condos located in a total of six buildings at the Riverside Club. It is a rather large complex. Our condo was on the fifth floor of a six-story complex where the vast majority of the condo owners were snowbirds. We are called snowbirds because we live up north in the summer and migrate south in the winter. We loved the Riverside Club. We had great times and made many new friends.

However, after living in the Riverside Club condo for eleven years we wanted more space, and the lure of the Gulf of Mexico on the other side of the island was beckoning. We began to look for a condo directly on the beach. After searching for about three months, we found a unit in the Princess del Mar. It was a three bedroom, three bath unit on the sixth floor of a thirteen-floor building with a total of seventy-two units. It was perfect. The new condo needed a lot of remodeling and new furniture, but that appealed to us, as we could fix it up the way we wanted.

We have been wintering in Marco for twenty-four years.

OUR CONDO ON MARCO ISLAND

VIEW FROM OUR CONDO
ON MARCO ISLAND

CHAPTER 34 / *Migrating to Marco Island*

THE ARROW POINTS TO OUR MARCO ISLAND CONDO.

That includes our eleven years at the Riverside Club and thirteen years at the Princess del Mar.

For several years we spent about six months in Naperville and six months on Marco Island. We came to the island for October and November and returned to Naperville for the holidays. Then we returned to Marco the first of January and stayed until the end of April or early May.

We have our friends Chuck and Cathie Cerniglia to thank for introducing us to "Paradise." Buying a condo on Marco was truly one of the best decisions we made.

During the time we are on Marco, we are very active in the Marco Lutheran Church where Marg and I both have enjoyed singing in the choir for the past twenty-plus years.

In 2000, I started the "Artist Series" at Marco Lutheran with the help of the director of music, Craig Greusel. During the winter, which is high season on Marco, we bring professional entertainers to our church to give concerts as a part of our outreach program. The first year we started with three concerts, but quickly expanded. For the past several years we have contracted to have five or six concerts during "season." The program has been unbelievably successful. Three years ago, I started a similar series at Monarch Landing, the retirement community in Naperville that we now call home.

I joined the Marco Island noontime Rotary Club several years ago, and have made a couple of international trips for Rotary and intend to make more. We currently spend only January through April in Marco, which means more time in Naperville. Because of our extended time up north, I have transferred my Rotary membership to Naperville.

MARLIN AND MARG

~ 35 ~

RETIREMENT AND ONE LAST MOVE

On Retirement:
When I get up in the morning, I don't have anything to do, and when I go to bed at night, I'm only half done.
—MARLIN REISHUS

LOOKING BACK OVER THE YEARS, there is one thing certain . . . we have made a lot of moves and lived in a lot of different houses. Now, with a contented sigh of relief, I would like to tell you about our last . . . yes, our last move!

On December 30, 2004 we signed up at Monarch Landing, a retirement community in Naperville, Illinois. On August 11, 2006, with the new construction complete, we made the big

MONARCH LANDING RETIREMENT COMMUNITY

move. We are living on the third level of a six-story building. We grew up in Cottonwood, Minnesota and ironically, now live in a building called Cottonwood Court. Like the old saying goes, "What goes around comes around."

We looked around at other communities locally, and in Florida, and couldn't find anything that compares to Monarch Landing. It was almost in our back yard, right here in Naperville. Well, not quite in our back yard, we had to move six miles.

Monarch Landing is one of nineteen continuum care residences spread across the East Coast and Midwest. They are operated by Erickson Retirement Communities. One such facility was scheduled for the Minneapolis, St. Paul area, but is on hold because of the economy.

Most of the Erickson Communities are rather large. Some have over 3,000 residents. Ours is a new community that was started when the economy began to go south. We currently have

CLUBHOUSE AT MONARCH LANDING

CHAPTER 35 / *Retirement and One Last Move*

COURTYARD AT MONARCH LANDING

about 385 residents with future growth to include 1,497 apartments and approximately 2,300 residents. Many future residents are still on hold with their houses for sale and waiting for an upturn in the housing market.

To qualify for the Monarch Landing Retirement Community one must be sixty-two. Couples buying must both be sixty-two and healthy, as we do not have an assisted living facility or a skilled nursing home at this time. Both of those facilities will be added to Monarch Landing in the near future.

When it was announced that Erickson was going to build in Naperville, we were among the first to sign up. Signing early meant we could choose the floor plan we wanted, the location we wanted, and the floor we wanted to live on. We had twenty-five floor plans to choose from. We decided on the Wilmington, a two-bedroom, two-bath unit with a den and a sunroom off the kitchen. We had our choice of appliances, hardwood floors, ceramic tile or carpet and chose some of each. It was almost like building a custom home, with granite counter tops, all new appliances and the whole nine yards. We have two indoor parking places. One parking spot is reserved, right outside our door on the same level as our apartment.

The standard Erickson plan allows us to pick one meal for the day, which can be breakfast, lunch, or dinner, and we normally choose dinner, or supper (for you dyed-in-the-wool Minnesotans). That way Marg doesn't need to cook. We can purchase other meals as well, but for the most part, we simply go for the dinner meal as our meal of the day and fix our breakfast and lunch in our own complete kitchen. Some of our friends ask about the meals after one has been here for an extended period of time. Well, it's been four years, and we still say the food is great. It has met the test of time.

There is so much activity going on that you really need to pick and choose. It is impossible to partake of everything. Some of the facilities include an indoor-outdoor pool that is open twenty-four hours a day, seven days a week, a large fitness center with the latest exercise machines open 24-7, a computer lab with free Internet access open 24/7, and I could go on and on.

I started an artist series at Monarch Landing, just as I did on Marco Island. We have six or seven professional artists perform in the February through November time frame, and have been doing this for three-plus years now. It has been a complete success.

This summer, Marg and I became octogenarians and feel maybe, just maybe, it is time to slow down a bit. With the good Lord willing, Monarch Landing is where Marg and I intend to live the rest of our lives here on earth.

We both accept that there will be one last permanent move, and that will be when they carry us to our heavenly home. But Lord, if you don't mind, we can wait a little longer for that move.

∽ 36 ∽

FAMILY, TRAVEL, AND MORE

Government is like a baby. An alimentary canal with a big appetite at one end and no sense of responsibility on the other.
—RONALD REAGAN

MARLIN, GENE, AND DALE (2000)

KRIS WITH HER NEW SON. THE BAPTISMAL DRESS WAS MADE BY GRANDMA ANNETTA IN 1895 AND WORN BY ABOUT FORTY-FIVE OF HER DESCENDENTS, INCLUDING ALL OF OUR IMMEDIATE FAMILY.

MARGARET AND ANN

MARLIN AND MARG, ANN, MARG'S SISTER,
AND GREG, MARG'S BROTHER-IN-LAW

EARL AND HELEN
OLSON WITH
MARG AND ANN

JENNY,
KATHY'S
DAUGHTER

IDENTICAL TWINS,
WILL AND JACOB

JENN AND
HUSBAND
KYLE

KRISTY

KRIS AND HUSBAND JASON AND SONS

MARLIN AND MARG, GENE AND KAY, DALE AND DONNA MAE

PRESENTED MISS WILLIS WITH A GOLDEN APPLE ENGRAVED "TEACHER OF THE CENTURY"

CHAPTER 36 / *Family, Travel, and More*

REISHUS REUNION AT JERRY REISHUS'S FARM JUST OUTSIDE OF COTTONWOOD. ONE HUNDRED SEVENTY-FIVE REISHUSES ATTENDED THE REUNION.

ERIC AND MARLIN PLAYING BALL AT FIELD OF DREAMS WITH THE ORIGINAL CAST OF THE MOVIE *FIELD OF DREAMS*

OUR FAMILY
DOG ARCHIE

OUR CAT
TAFFY

JENNY, KATHY, KRIS, AND MARG

CHAPTER 36 / *Family, Travel, and More*

OUR VACATION HOME IN GALENA, IL.
PRESIDENT GRANT'S HOMETOWN

JEAN, MARG, HELEN OLSON, MARG'S MOTHER, ANN, MARG'S SISTER AND KATHY AND OUR DOG ARCHIE

EARL OLSON, MARG'S DAD, WAS THE SCHOOL SUPERINTENDENT IN COTTONWOOD.

MARLIN AND MARG, GENE AND KAY, DALE AND DONNA MAE

KATHY, PAUL, MARG, ERIC, JEAN, AND MARLIN

Part 4

The Reishus Genealogy

My first advice on how to grow old would be to choose your ancestors carefully.
—BERTRAND RUSSELL

THE REISHUS
COAT OF ARMS

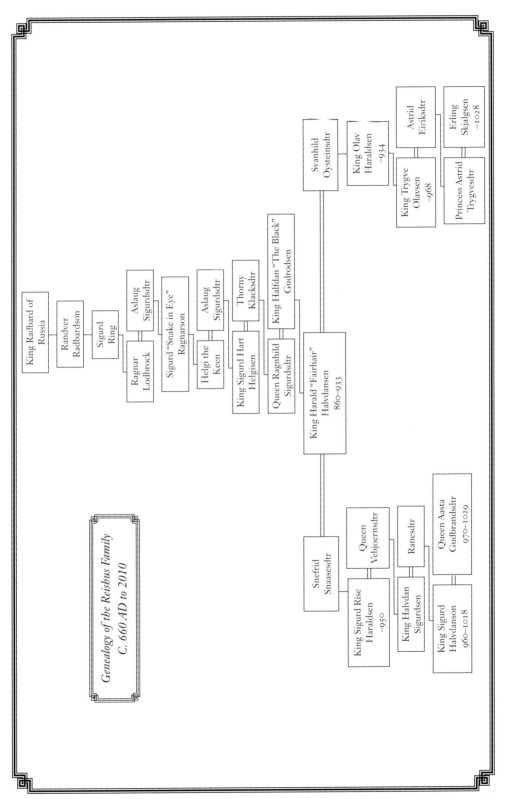

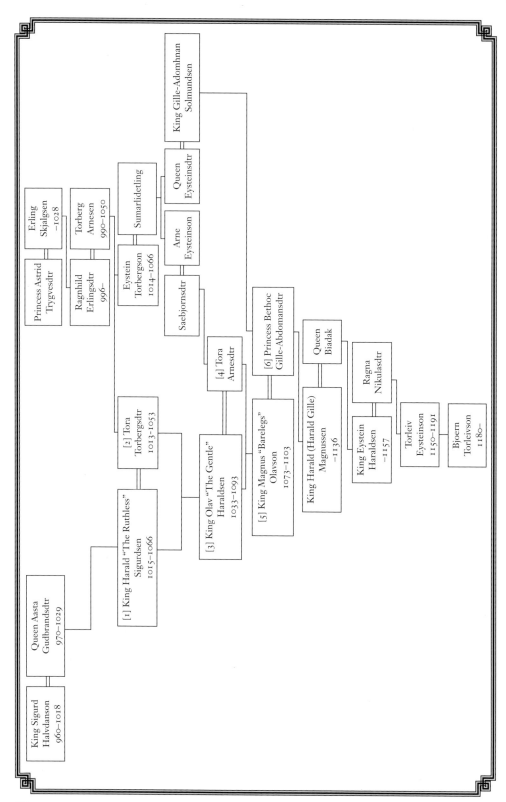

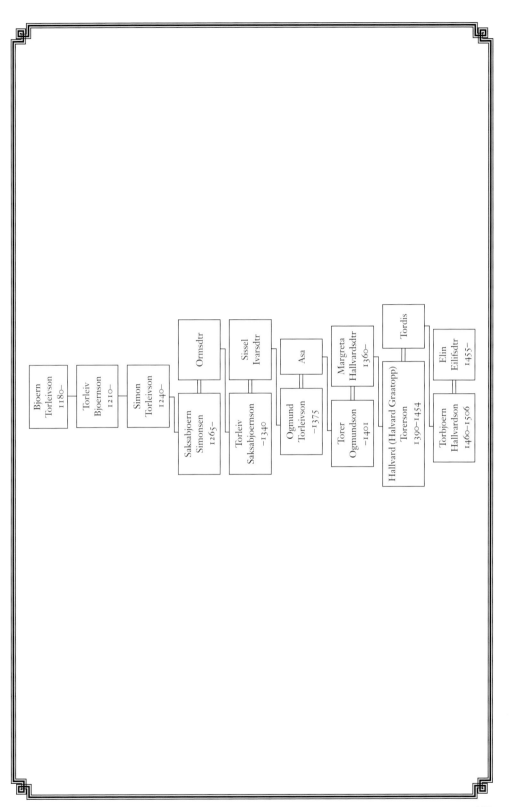

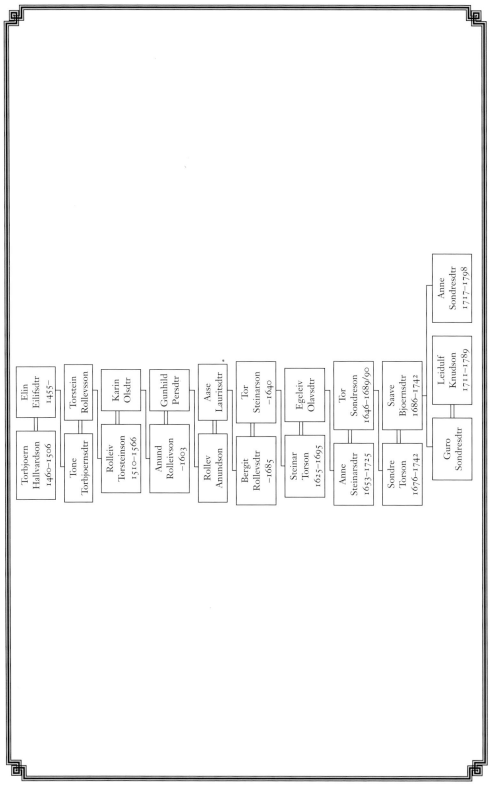

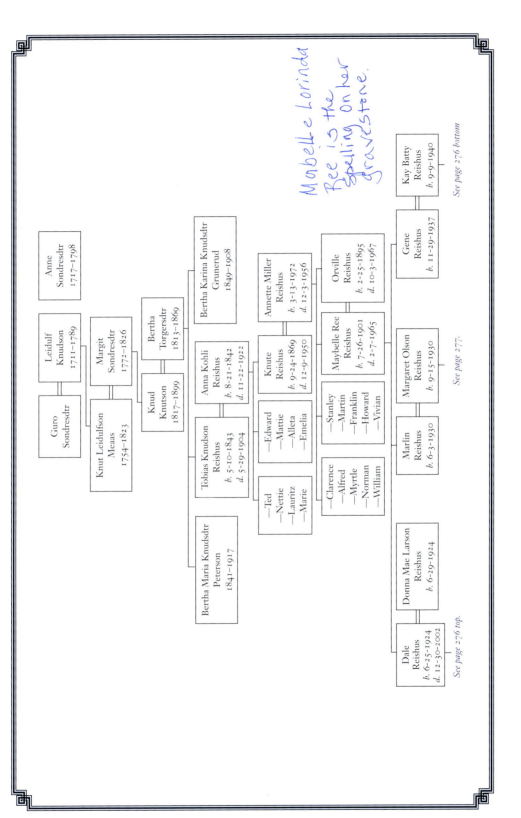

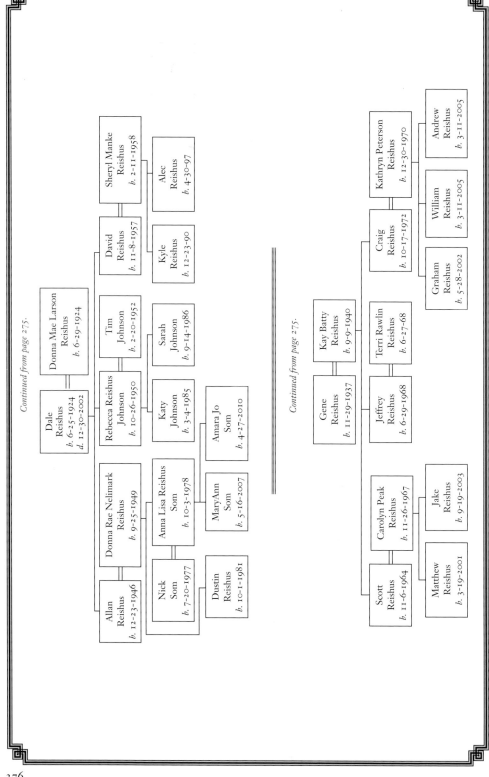

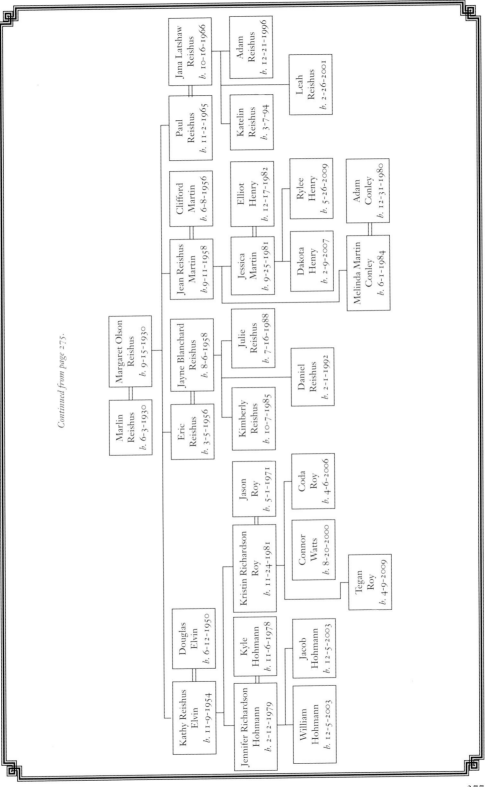

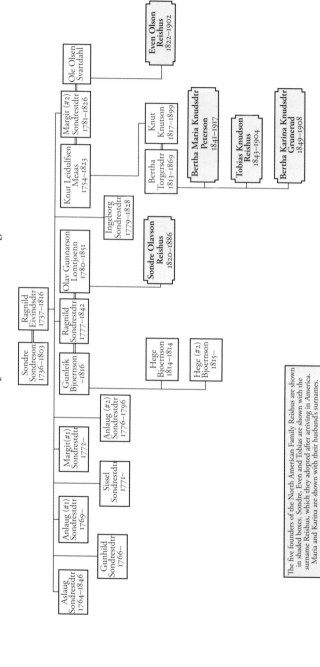

Descendants of Sondre Sondreson and Ragnild Eivinsdtr

The five founders of the North American Family Reishus are shown in shaded boxes. Sondre, Even and Tobias are shown with the surname Reishus, which they adopted after arriving in America. Maria and Karina are shown with their husbands' surnames.

~ 37 ~

EXCERPTS FROM *SLÆGTEN REISHUS* BY JAMES T. ENGH

*People will not look forward to posterity, who
never look backward to their ancestors.*
—EDMUND BURKE

James T. Engh, great-grandson of Tobias Reishus, wrote this account. He has done a great deal of research on Slægten Reishus, which means the "Family Reishus" and has utilized many sources, including assistance from Norway. For a more detailed synopsis of the "Family Reishus" see the book Slægten Reishus Family Reishus: *third edition by James T. Engh.*

The word *Reishus* is used in this title to describe where the family came from. It was the name of the place where the original family lived. It also became the name of some of our ancestors. But the scope is not limited to only those persons who used Reishus as a surname. It focuses on Sondre Olavson, Even Olson, Bertha Maria Knudsdtr, Tobias Knudson, and Bertha Karina Knudsdtr, all related, who came to America from Norway in the middle 1800s. See the chart for these family relationships.

Sondre and Ragnild lived in what is now known as Telemark County, but was then known as Bratsberg or Bratsberg County in southern Norway. According to the Norwegian census of 1801, the parish was known as Silljord and the sub parish was Fladdahls Annex. Today the communities are known as Seljord and Flatdal. They are located about 85 miles southwest of Oslo.

When Marg and I were in Norway, I had the opportunity to visit the place where the Norwegians organized and declared their independence from Sweden. They declared their independence, and voted to pay no more taxes to Sweden. An emissary was sent to the King of Sweden where he announced Norway's independence, and that there would be no more taxes collected for the benefit of Sweden. Much to their surprise, the King of Sweden did not object. I guess he thought the wilderness of Norway wasn't worth fighting for. It was truly a "velvet revolution."

The Norwegian Language

Before we go any further, it may be helpful to understand some background information about the language of Norway. Over the centuries the Norwegian language has undergone a number of changes, the most recent in the twentieth century. The predominant written and spoken language used prior to the 14th century has been called Old Norwegian. In 1397, the Union of Calmar united Sweden, Norway, and Denmark in a kingdom, and the Danish Queen Margaret was ruler. Soon Danish was used for the official written language, and it also influenced the spoken language.

Sweden revolted in 1521 and then fought and won a war with Denmark in 1814. Their prize was control of Norway. Although Norway was now ruled by Sweden, she was given some political independence and efforts were begun to establish a New Norwegian written language. This was a gradual change and was not uniform across the country. Sometime around 1864 a Norwegian National Language or Landsmål emerged. Norway gained its complete independence from Sweden on May 17, 1905 (syttende mai, Norwegian Independence Day). The name of the language was changed by the Norwegian Storting (Parliament) in 1929 to New Norwegian or Nynorsk.

In the late 1890s, another language called Official Language or Riksmål began to develop in some places. That name too was changed by the parliament, in 1929, to Book Language or Bokmål. Both languages were in use in the early 1900s, and two forms of Norwegian language persisted through the 20th century. Because of these variations over the centuries, genealogists (and some Norwegians) sometimes struggle to translate Norwegian documents written before 1900.

The Norwegian alphabet today includes three letters that are not found in the English alphabet. They are æ, ø, å. These letters are regularly found in earlier writings and in names, and if you look carefully in early Norwegian writings, you may find other letters derived from the Danish and Swedish influence.

This evolution of the Norwegian language has resulted in several spellings of some words and names. What was customary at one time might be different at a later time. Regional dialects still exist today in the spoken language. Writers used different spellings depending on where they lived or when they lived. Recent dictionaries may not have the earlier spellings. Modern day translators may produce different translations of a document.

Norwegian Names

In the old days, their Christian name and their father's name identified Norwegians: Olav Håkonsen (or Håkonsson,—søn), ie [Olav] the son of Håkon, Sigird Håkonsdatter (or—dotter) [ie Sigird] the daughter of Håkon. [This system of using the father's name is called a patronymic name].

In addition, a third name was very often used, usually a farm name. This 'surname' does not necessarily identify a family or relationship; it signified the dwelling place. When farmer Ole Olsen Li moved from Li to another farm, e.g., Dal, he was called Ole Olsen Dal. A farm laborer could be named in the same way without being kin of the farmer.

Sometimes, however, the preposition på (at) could be placed between the patronymic and the farm name, indicating that the person concerned had his occupation at that particular farm [Jens Nilsson på Luten].

It is also noted that a woman did not change her name after marriage but continued to use the name she had before marriage.

The bygdeboks offer many examples of these naming practices and confirm that often the name of the farm was added as another surname. You may see several different spellings of an individual's name in this writing, depending on the source that is then being used. These naming practices continued well into the 1800s and remained in use longer in the rural areas than in the cities.

Sondre Sondreson and Ragnild Eivindsdtr

Sondre Sondreson was born in 1736, the son of Sondre Nalvorson Bakkén and Aslaug Halvorsdtr Einar-Gjuve. Ragnild Eivindsdtr was born in 1737, the daughter of Eivind Olavson and Aslaug Jesperdtr. Ragnild has also been spelled Ragnhild and Ragna and Ragne, and Eivindsdtr has been spelled Evensdtr. They were married in 1762. Sondre died in 1803, and Ragnild died in 1816.

The Name Reishus

The book *Rag Rug* authorized by Martha Reishus and other family history that has been handed down reports that "Sondre...came from 'the easterly'...and that he...found no difficulty in obtaining work, going from gaard (farm) to gaard whenever the need for an extra hand existed." This seems to imply that he was itinerant. According to the book, he met Ragnild while working on a church building, and before they were married in 1762, he built a house for his bride using a rock precipice as one wall of the house, and he constructed the other walls by raising timbers against the rock. In this way he raised a house (reis hus), and according to the book, those two words became the single word reishus that was associated with the place and became the family name.

That story of Sondre and where he came from and the origin of the name have long been accepted, but the bygdebok history and recently found church records show a different version of the facts.

CHAPTER 37 / *Excerpts From Slægten Reishus by James T. Engh*

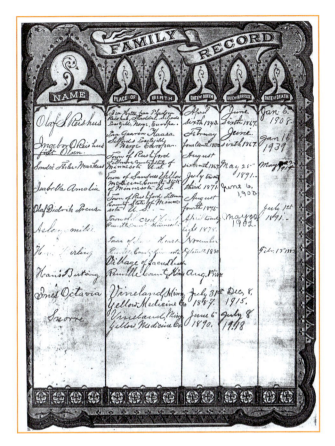

PAGE FROM FAMILY BIBLE OF
OLAF SONDRE REISHUS

The Seljord bygdebok shows that Sondre Sondreson was born to a Seljord parish family, and he bought the Bakkemoen farm from his father-in-law Eivind Olavson in 1764 for 604 dalar and sold it in 1773 for 661 dalar. A dalar is an obsolete unit of Norwegian currency. This confirms that he was a resident of the community area and had his own farm.

Copies of church records obtained by Ida Bell record the birth and baptism of Knud Knutsen and Even Olsen. The record for Knud in 1817 lists his mother as Margit Sondresdattor Röyshûûs and Ragnild Sondresdattor Röyshûûs as a witness.

The record for Even Olsen in 1822 lists Margit Sondresdattor Röÿshûûs as mother. The handwriting is not easy to read, but I think I have correctly read the letters used in the spelling of the names. These are the earliest known records of the name.

On a later page, which records the death of Margit on September 1, 1826, her last name is again written Röÿshûûs. Her age was recorded as 44.

Still another page records the confirmation of Knud on June 26, 1832, and his surname appears to be spelled Reishus. The writing is difficult to decipher.

The surname that was written for Knud in 1817 and Even in 1822 and Margit in 1826 was probably some mixture of Danish and Old Norwegian alphabets and included characters not used today. The characters ö, ÿ, and û shown above are not used in Norway today.

My understanding is that ö and ø were used interchangeably for a while in Norway. My guess is that Röÿshûûs at some time evolved into Røyshus as the alphabet changed. The family story dictated by Ingeborg, wife of Sondre Olavson Reishus, to her son Gunder, included a family tree and the name is spelled both Reishus and Røyshus. The change to Reishus in 1832 may have been another evolution. Although a person's name might have been well known in those days, the way a name was recorded at any time was probably whatever that scribe at that time thought was the correct spelling.

Because there was no address system of rural road names and numbers, farms were known by a name. The Norwegian word røys means a heap of stones. It could be a big heap, like a hill. Since farm and dwelling names were sometimes related to some feature of the land, the name Röÿshûûs/ Røyshus may refer to a heap or hill of stones (røys) found near the house (hus) and was first used as a farm name. Families living on a farm often used the farm name as a surname, and thus the name Röÿshûûs/ Røyshus may have come into use as a surname.

CHAPTER 37 / *Excerpts From Slægten Reishus by James T. Engh*

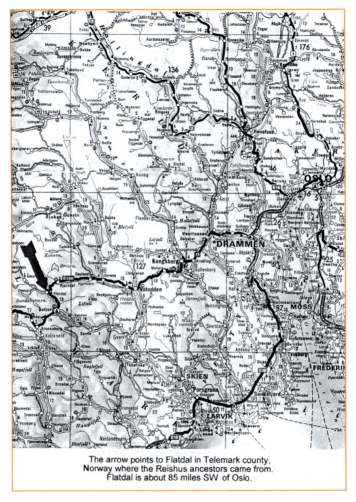

The arrow points to Flatdal in Telemark county, Norway where the Reishus ancestors came from. Flatdal is about 85 miles SW of Oslo.

MAP LOCATION OF REISHUS ANCESTORS FAMILY FARM

Olav Veka who lives in Norway researches Scandinavian names. He has characterized the name Reishus as "unique" and advised that there are no persons in Norway today who use that surname. He, too, suggested that it might be related to a heap of stones. He directed me to the *Dictionary of American Family Names*, a three-volume set published in 2003 that offers explanations for 70,000 of the most frequent names in the United States. There is an entry for Reishus that reads, "Norwegian:

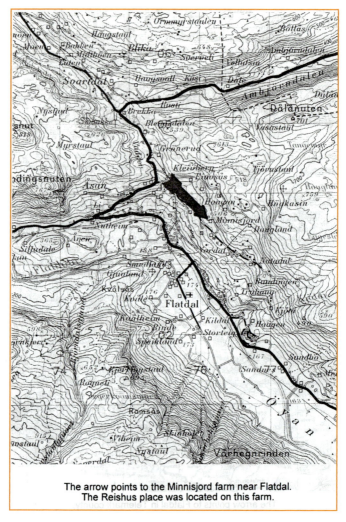

The arrow points to the Minnisjord farm near Flatdal. The Reishus place was located on this farm.

REISHUS FARM LOCATION

habitational name from the name of an abandoned tenant farm called Reishus in Flatdal, Telemark. The first element is probably røys, Old Norse hreysi 'heal of stones,' the second is hus 'house,' 'small farm.'"

All of this seems to deal a blow to the story that the name Reishus evolved from building a house for his bride by raising timbers up against a rock wall, but it is still an entertaining story.

When Sondre Olavson, Even Olson, and Tobias Knudson decided to adopt the name in America, they had to use the spelling Reishus, regardless of what spelling they knew from Norway because the letter ø was not used in America.

Where was the Reishus (or Röyshûûs or Røyshus) Place?

During this period in Norway, it was common for owners of large farms to lease a small piece of land to a tenant farmer who was known as a husmann, or cotter, or crofter. These sites were known as husmannsplas, or cottars places, and the tenant farmer usually had lifelong tenure. Records would describe the husmannsplas as "under" the farm where the word "under" was used to associate the place with a farm, as in Reishus under Minnisjord.

The land Register Draft of 1950 (Matrikkelutkastet av 1950) is a list of real estate in Norway. In the section for Telemark/Seljord/73 Minnisjord are found the places located on the Minnisjord farm, and number 14 is Reishus. The location of the Minnisjord farm is shown on area maps today.

The family history dictated by Ingeborg says that, "Ragnild, as the oldest, inherited the Reishus home." And goes on to say that "Reishus (the cottars home) belonged to Minsjord. Old Ragnhild paid taxes to Minsjord in the form of 2 bismerpund [an obsolete weight measure of about 12 pounds . . . of butter per year."

Use of Reishus (or Röyshûûs or Røyshus) as a Surname

This leads to a question about when use of Reishus (or Röyshûûs or Røyshus) as a surname started. Remember that people sometimes (but not always) added the name of the place where they were then living as a surname. The 1801 Norway Census for the Minnisjord farm did not show it being used. Among the names and descriptions shown in that census were Sondre Sondresen (head of household), Ragnild Eivindsdtr (wife), Ragnild Sondresdtr, (grown child of head). Asloug Sondresdtr (hired help or servant) is included in a different household on that farm. That same census shows Margit Sondresdtr, age 20, living on the Sundboe farm, also in the Flatdal area.

CHURCH IN NORWAY WHERE SONDRE
AND RAGNILD WERE MARRIED

The earliest known use of the name was as noted earlier when Margit Sondresdtr and Ragnild Sondresdtr were recorded with the surname Röÿshûûs in 1817 and 1822. It may be that a name was not attributed to the place and then used as a surname until sometime after the 1801 census.

The passenger list for the ship *Lorena*, arriving in New York on July 17, 1843 includes Sunder Olsen, Ingeber Olsen, and Ola Olsen (whom we know today as Sondre, Ingeborg, and Olav), so Sondre Olavson was not using the name Reishus when he arrived in America. The first known use by Sondre of the name is found in Fillmore County, Minnesota records where a deed was recorded for Sundry Oleson Rishus on June 22, 1857. The US Census for 1870 includes S O (Sondre O) Reishus. Sondre's son Olav enlisted in the Union Army in 1864 as Ole S Reishus.

A deed was recorded in Fillmore County, Minnesota for Even Oleson on January 17, 1855 and in the Census of 1870 he is listed as Even Oleson, so Even was not using Reishus at that time.

Pay records and other military papers show that Tobias Knudson did not use the surname Reishus during his military service in the Union Army from August 1862 to August 1865.

However, the US Census of 1880 for Minnesota lists Olson E [Even Olson] Reishus and Tobias Reishus along with thirty-one other family members with that surname, so by 1880 all three

Digitalarkivet: Norwegians living in Minnesota according to 1880 Census.
All rights: Vesterheim Genealogical Center, Madison, Wisconsin.

HOME HELP ANALYSIS ALL [ ] NEXT

Find records where [Surname] [er lik] [ ] [Search]

Given name	Surname	Sex	Age	Occupation	Birthplace	Father's birthplace	Mother's birthplace	Page	Township	County
20465 T S	Reishus	m	32	lumber agent	W	N	N	159	Rushford	Fillm-
20466 Ellen P	Reishus	f	20		W	N	N	159	Rushford	Fillm-
20467 Lysander T	Reishus	m	10/1 Sept		Mn	W	N	159	Rushford	Fillm-
20468 Gunder	Reishus	m	20		Mn	N	N	159	Rushford	Fillm-
23906 Olson E	Reishus	m	58	f	N	N	N	205	Arendahl	Fillm-
23907 Anna	Reishus	f	44		N	N	N	205	Arendahl	Fillm-
23908 Gunnild	Reishus	f	20		Mn	N	N	205	Arendahl	Fillm-
23909 Ole	Reishus	m	17	lab	Mn	N	N	205	Arendahl	Fillm-
23910 Aletha	Reishus	f	15	dom	Mn	N	N	205	Arendahl	Fillm-
23911 Edward	Reishus	m	13		Mn	N	N	205	Arendahl	Fillm-
23912 John A	Reishus	m	11		Mn	N	N	205	Arendahl	Fillm
23913 Stefen M	Reishus	m	9		Mn	N	N	205	Arendahl	Fillm
23914 Anna	Reishus	f	7		Mn	N	N	205	Arendahl	Fillm
23915 Emma	Reishus	f	5		Mn	N	N	205	Arendahl	Fillm
23916 Edeline	Reishus	f	3		Mn	N	N	205	Arendahl	Fillm-
48410 Edwin	Reishus	m	28	f	N	N	N	558	Sannes	Yello Medi
48411 Carrie	Reishus	f	26		Con	Con	Con	558	Sannes	Yello Medi
48412 Walter	Reishus	m	10/1 Aug		Mn	Mn	Con	558	Sannes	Yello Medi
48413 Julia	Reishus	f	18	dom	Mn	N	N	558	Sannes	Yello Medi
48824 Tobias	Reishus	m	37		N	N	N	568	Normania	Yello Medi

NORWEGIANS LIVING IN MN, ACCORDING TO 1880 CENSUS

\multicolumn{7}{l}{Digitalarkivet: 1801-telling for 0828 Sillejord. [8837/56]}
\multicolumn{7}{l}{Post 94 av 172/2420 totalt i databasen}
Amt	Prestegjeld	Sokn	Gard			
\multicolumn{3}{l}{94 Bradsberg Sillejord}	\multicolumn{4}{l}{Fladdahls Annex Minnesjord Søndre}

	Førenamn	Etternamn	Hushaldstatus	Alder	Sivilstand	Yrke	Kjønn
1519	Søren	Guttormsen	Huusbonde	43	2det ægteskab	Gaardbruger	M
1520	Birgit	Tollefsdtr	Hans kone	30	2det ægteskab		K
1521	Guttorm	Sørenssønner	Deres børn	11	Ugivt		M
1522	Gregar	Sørenssønner	Deres børn	9			M
1523	Leuf	Sørenssønner	Deres børn	2			M
1524	Anne	Sørensdøttre	Deres børn	15			K
1525	Ingeborg	Sørensdøttre	Deres børn	13			K
1526	Gudnild	Sørensdøttre	Deres børn	7			K
1527	Gudve	Leufsdtr	Konens datter i 1 ægteskab	7			K
1528	Johans	Johansen	Tieneste folk	18	Ugivt		M
1529	Halvor	Halvorsen	Tieneste folk	18			M
1530	Tone	Asbjørnsdtr	Tieneste folk	29			K
1531	Asloug	Sondresdtr	Tieneste folk	38			K
1532	Torkild	Halvorsen	Mand	63	1 ægteskab	Huusmand med jord - faaer almisse	M
1533	Anne	Olsdtr	Hans kone	63	1 ægteskab		K
1534	Sondre	Sondresen	Mand	63	1 ægteskab	Huusmand med jord - faaer almisse	M
1535	Ragnild	Evensdtr	Hans kone	63	1 ægteskab		K
1536	Ragnild	Sondresdtr	Deres barn	24	Ugivt		K
1537	Gunvor	Jacobsdtr	Enke	43	Enke 1 ægteskab	Huuskone med jord fattig	K
1538	Ole	Evensen	Hendes søn	10	Ugivt		M
1539	Halvor	Olsen	Mand	60	1 ægteskab	Huusmand med jord	M
1540	Ragnild	Heljesdtr	Hans kone	66	1 ægteskab		K
1541	Helje	Heljesen	Konens broder	71	Enkemand 1 ægteskab	Inderste	M
1542	Halvor	Torkildsen	Tieneste karl	30	Ugivt		M
	Førenamn	Etternamn	Hushaldstatus	Alder	Sivilstand	Yrke	Kjønn

Norway census of 1801 showing inhabitants of the farm Minnesjord South. At that time it was typical for a person to have a "husmannsplas" or "cottars place" which was a house was built on land leased from the farm owner. Thus multiple families are shown on one farm.

NORWAY CENSUS, 1801

men and their families had adopted the name. Other places where the name Reishus was found include the *History of the Minnesota Valley*, published in 1882, which recognizes Tobias K Reishus, and that same book includes notes about S O Reishus,

CHAPTER 37 / *Excerpts From Slægten Reishus by James T. Engh*

O S Reishus, and G S Reishus. A similar *History of Fillmore County* published in 1882 recognizes Even O Reishus.

This adoption of a single surname by the three of them seems to show a desire to maintain their family connection in this new country and to retain a reminder of the place they came from.

The Journey to America

The journey to America could not have been an easy one. In May of 1843 Sondre Olavson and Ingeborg Torjusdtr Speikland and their two-week old son Olav sailed first from Skein, Norway to Le Havre, France, a journey of two weeks. After several weeks in France they spent another six weeks on the ocean en route to America. Ships in use at that time were sailing vessels that were very small by today's ocean-going vessel standards and were usually built to haul cargo. The journey from Norway direct to America typically took two months. Today you can fly in six hours.

Although some sailing vessels had a very small amount of cabin space, most accommodations were no more than space on a lower deck, called steerage, and passengers usually brought their own food. Cooking facilities were limited or non-existent, and food sometimes spoiled. The weather was always a potential danger, drinking water was in limited supply, and illness sometimes broke out. A study of passenger lists shows that both births and deaths occurred on these voyages. This was not a journey for pleasure, and those who undertook it had to have a determination to seek a new life.

People had not been leaving Norway in great numbers prior to 1843 when Sondre and Ingeborg left. According to records, a total of only 2,300 people left Norway in the six years from 1836 through 1841, and only 1,600 more left during the year 1843. They were among the very early emigrants. The peak Norwegian emigration years were from 1866 to 1893 when emigration averaged more than 14,000 people per year. The *Dictionary of American Family Names* reports that the US Census of 1900 showed that Minnesota alone had 105,000 people who had been born in Norway together with 115,000 Swedes and 16,300 Danes.

The passenger list for the Norwegian brig *Favoriten*, which arrived in New York on November 6, 1850, shows Bertta Torgerdotter age 38, Bertta age 10, and Tobias age 8. Bertta age 10 was the person we know as Bertha Maria. Bertha Karina is not shown on the passenger list. However, she was included on the Norwegian passport list on September 3, 1850 for those departing for "Nord Amerika" and Ingeborg to have arrived with her mother Bertha Maria and Tobias at their home in First Lake, Wisconsin. So her arrival was confirmed. Sometimes passenger lists did not name infants, only reporting them as infants. Bertha Karina was 1 ½ years old at this time, and I don't know how she was accounted for.

Getting Started in America

Sondre and Ingeborg and their infant son reached Milwaukee in southeastern Wisconsin 13 weeks after they left Norway in the spring of 1843. They first settled in Muskego, about 15 miles southwest of Milwaukee. They moved several times before settling near First Lake, Wisconsin in the spring of 1848. First Lake is believed to have been located south and east of Madison, Wisconsin near Koshkonong. This was an area of Norwegian settlers. It was here that they were living when Bertha and her children arrived at their door.

To put the five family founders in proper perspective, in 1850 Sondre would have been 30 years old, Even 28, Bertha Maria 10, Tobias 7, and Bertha Karina 1.

CHAPTER 37 / *Excerpts From Slægten Reishus by James T. Engh* 293

Letter from Sondre Olavson Reishus to Knut Thorsen Minesgard,
Fladdal, Siljords Prestegjeld, Norway, January 28, 1879

LETTER FROM SONDRE TO KNUT, JANUARY 28, 1879

i god Økonomisk Stilling, heller ikke Du
saa Gammel, Du kan endnu leve til at
se en opblomstret Slægt og ikke lade Din
vakre Gaard komme i fremmede Hænder.
Du vil maaske synes dette er noget Tøv
som er bare at lee af, det kan gjerne være
men det skulde da heller ikke være til at
græde over, men det er mit ramme Alvor
Jeg vil da gaa over til at fortælle lidt om
om forholdene her i dette fjerne Westen
Jeg tror Vinterkulden er noget barskere
her end i Norge især er dette tilfælde naa
disse nordvestens Storme kommer strygende
over de endeløse Prairier (Sletter) men disse
3 Vintre jeg har været her har vi ikke
haft noget af disse Storme, her var temmelig koldt ved Jule Tider men nu er her
meget Mildt og Marken er ganske bar
saa vi er nød til at bruge Vognen Ifjor
gjorde vi Vaaraannen i Marts men det
bliver vel ikke noget rigtig godt Aar thi
den stærke Varmde i Juni drev Hveden for
fort til Modenhed saa den ikke blev saa
god som den pleier. Dette i forening
med de lave Priser gjør at Tiderne er
temmelig Flove og stor Pengemangel. Prisen
paa Hvede er fra 45 @ 53 cent pr Bushel

LETTER FROM SONDRE TO KNUT,
JANUARY 28, 1879 (CONTINUED)

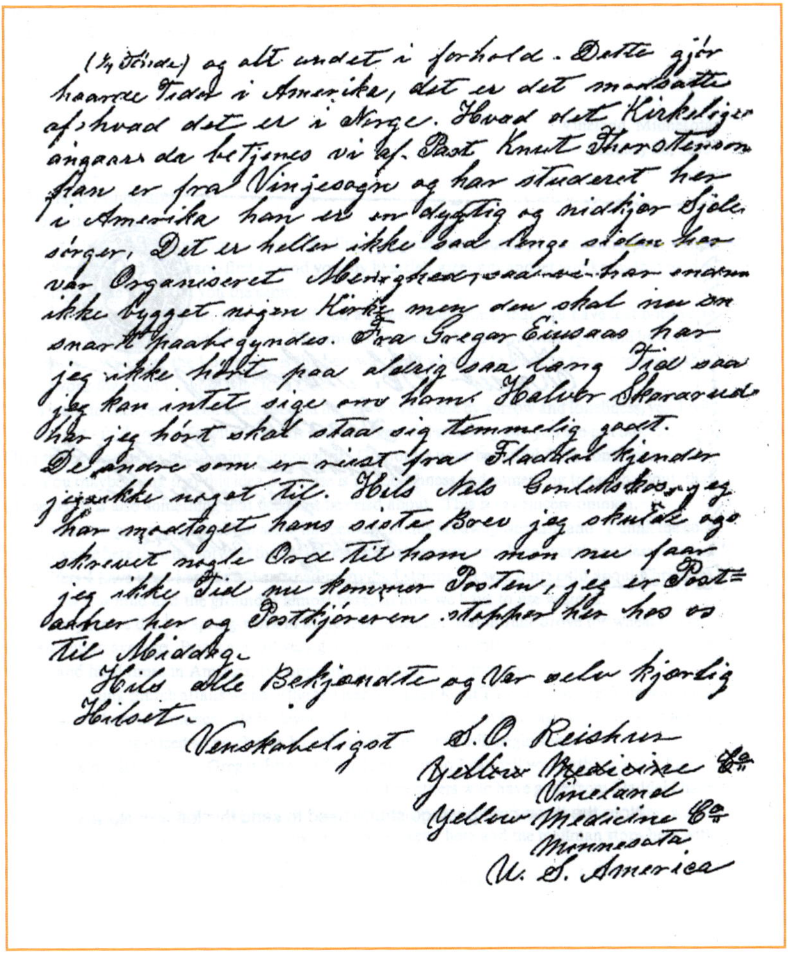

CHAPTER 37 / *Excerpts From Slægten Reishus by James T. Engh*   295

[handwritten letter in Norwegian]

LETTER FROM SONDRE TO KNUT,
JANUARY 28, 1879 (CONTINUED)

Translation of letter from Sondre Olavson Reishus to Knut Thorson Minesgard. Letter is in the possession of Knut H Minnesjord, Flatdal, Norway.

-- o --

Vineland, Minnesota
January 28, 1879

Knut Thorson Minesgard
An Unforgettable friend!

    For a long time I have thought about sending you some lines, but as you see I am a poor writer and it has been put aside. I want, first to send you my heartfelt greetings and let you know that we are fine and hope these lines find you the same.

    I see by Nel's letter that you have suffered a severe misfortune, that you have lost both your children and your dear wife and are alone. This must have been a hard blow which you will have to try to understand. We know the Lords way is the best way, and we have to learn to trust and know that all things work for good to those who love God.

    I want to then, as a friend to advise you not to be overcome by sorrow and loneliness, yes, I will say it right out - find yourself a wife! You are in good financial standing and you are not old. You can still live to see a growing blossoming relationship. Do not let your beautiful farm come into strange hands. You maybe think that this idea or advise is all foolishness and something to laugh about, that might be but it is also something that need not be cried about. This is my sincere opinion.

    I will now go on and tell about some happenings in this far away western land. I think the cold weather is worse here than in Norway, the northwestern storms come streaking over the endless prairies. The 3 winters I have been here we haven't had many bad storms. It was quite cold about Christmas time but now it is mild and the ground is almost bare, so now we have to use wagons.

    Last year we did our spring-work in March, but the high heat in June drove the wheat too fast so it wasn't up to average. Prices are not very good, from 45 to 55 cents a bushel. There is a shortage of money and hard times in America, the opposite of what is in Norway now.

    Concerning church affairs we have the services of Pastor Knut Thorstenson he is from Vinesogn and has studied here in America. He is clever and ambitious. It is not long ago since the soul seeker congregation was organized so no church has been built, but they will begin soon.

    I have not heard from Gregar Einsaas for a long time so I can tell you nothing about him. I have heard that Halvor Skararust is financially well of. The others who have gone from Fladdal I have heard nothing about. Greet Nels Gonlickos, I received his last letter and should write him a few words but now there isn't time as the mail is coming. I am postmaster here and the mailman stops here with us for dinner.

    Greet all the people we know and to yourself our best wishes.

Your Friend S O Reishus
Vineland
Yellow Medicine County
Minnesota
U S America

TRANSLATION OF LETTER FROM SONDRE TO KNUT

Even

Even's mother Margit died when Even was four years old. He was living at Bekkhus (probably part of Seljord) when he was confirmed on March 18, 1838, just short of age 16. He was "unmerket godt," very, very good. He went to Stavanger on the west coast of Norway and apprenticed as a blacksmith. In 1848, when he was 26 years old, he arrived in America. He went to Wisconsin where he was in contact with Sondre, and he worked in logging. In 1854 Even moved to Fillmore County in southeast Minnesota along with Sondre and Tobias, and he established a farm near the village of Rushford.

Even married Anna Teigen in 1855. According to the US Census in 1870, at that time they had six children. Even's real estate was valued at $4,000 and his personal estate at $850. He had 310 acres (140 improved), 4 horses, 6 "milch cows," 1 other cattle, 3 sheep, and 9 swine. The livestock were valued at $700. He had grown 1400 bushels of spring wheat, 175 bushels of Indian corn, 750 bushels of oats, and 150 bushels of barley in the past year.

EVEN OLSON REISHUS AND ANNA TEIGEN REISHUS

Even and his family stayed in the Rushford area, and he was a well-known farmer. He and Anna ultimately had 12 children, and they also raised Tobias. Even died in 1902, and Anna died in 1913. They are buried at North Prairie Lutheran Church Cemetery, located on highway 30 about 10 miles west of Rushford, Minnesota.

Tobias

Tobias came to America in 1850 when he was seven years old. He and his mother and two sisters crossed the Atlantic in a small sailing vessel in October and November, which was certainly not a pleasant time to be on the North Atlantic.

His mother took the children to Wisconsin, and it is not clear where, or how, they lived at this time. They were in contact with Sondre and Ingeborg and Even. In 1854 at age 11, Tobias went with his Uncle Even when his uncle moved to Minnesota. Even married Anna Teigen after arriving in Minnesota, and Tobias was raised by Even and Anna.

In 1862 Tobias enlisted in Company D, 8th Infantry of the Union Army and served until 1865. In 1866 he returned to Minnesota and on February 5, 1867 married Anna Kohlei in Forest City, Iowa. In the spring of 1867 they moved to Yellow Medicine County in southwestern Minnesota. They lived on several different farms in the area before settling on a place in Normania Township in Yellow Medicine County, west of the village of Cottonwood. They had nine children. One of those nine was my grandmother.

Tobias was the first sheriff of Yellow Medicine County and was also a self-taught veterinarian. He was a successful farmer and well known for helping neighbors.

In 1902 he went to Canada and applied for a homestead in what was then the Northwest Territory, near what is now the town of Hawarden, Saskatchewan. That location was about 25 miles from what would later be the home of his sister Bertha

CHAPTER 37 / *Excerpts From Slægten Reishus by James T. Engh*

Karina Grunerud. He came home that fall and returned to the homestead in 1903. That year he broke 35 acres of prairie sod while his son Theodore took care of the farm near Cottonwood. When he returned to Cottonwood in the fall of 1903, he

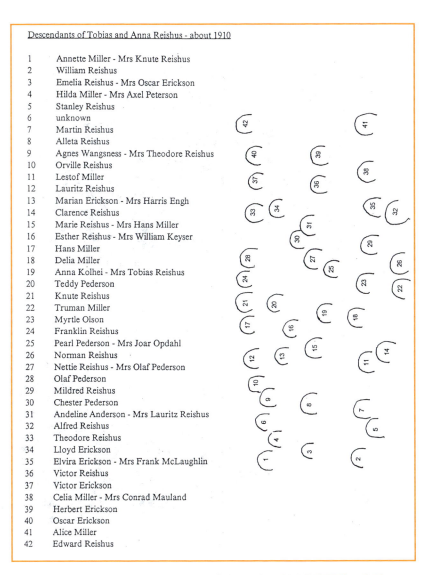

Descendants of Tobias and Anna Reishus - about 1910

1. Annette Miller - Mrs Knute Reishus
2. William Reishus
3. Emelia Reishus - Mrs Oscar Erickson
4. Hilda Miller - Mrs Axel Peterson
5. Stanley Reishus
6. unknown
7. Martin Reishus
8. Alleta Reishus
9. Agnes Wangsness - Mrs Theodore Reishus
10. Orville Reishus
11. Lestof Miller
12. Lauritz Reishus
13. Marian Erickson - Mrs Harris Engh
14. Clarence Reishus
15. Marie Reishus - Mrs Hans Miller
16. Esther Reishus - Mrs William Keyser
17. Hans Miller
18. Delia Miller
19. Anna Kolhei - Mrs Tobias Reishus
20. Teddy Pederson
21. Knute Reishus
22. Truman Miller
23. Myrtle Olson
24. Franklin Reishus
25. Pearl Pederson - Mrs Joar Opdahl
26. Norman Reishus
27. Nettie Reishus - Mrs Olaf Pederson
28. Olaf Pederson
29. Mildred Reishus
30. Chester Pederson
31. Andeline Anderson - Mrs Lauritz Reishus
32. Alfred Reishus
33. Theodore Reishus
34. Lloyd Erickson
35. Elvira Erickson - Mrs Frank McLaughlin
36. Victor Reishus
37. Victor Erickson
38. Celia Miller - Mrs Conrad Mauland
39. Herbert Erickson
40. Oscar Erickson
41. Alice Miller
42. Edward Reishus

DESCENDANTS OF TOBIAS AND ANNA REISHUS, 1910

proposed moving to Canada, but his wife Anna said she did not want to homestead again, so they stayed in Minnesota.

The next year, on May 29, 1904, Tobias died, and his daughter Antonette and son-in-law Oluf Pedersen took over the homestead land in Canada. Anna died in 1922. Tobias and Anna are buried in St. Lucas cemetery in Normania Township, about six miles west of Cottonwood, Minnesota.

Desendants of Tobias and Anna Reishus, about 1910

PICTURE OF DESCENDANTS

38

EXCERPTS FROM SONDRE REISHBY INGEBOR, WIFE OF SONDRE

The lives of great men all remind us we can make our lives sublime and departing leave behind us footprints on the sands of time.
—THOREAU

THE HISTORY OF THE REISHUS family is typical of other immigrating Norwegians who journeyed from their homes in various parts of Norway to seek fortune in a promised land. The experience of this well known family as they moved westward, finally locating in Minnesota, make interesting reading, which they have kindly offered to share with our readers. The article is in narrative form related by the wife of the first immigrant, Sondre Reishus to her son Gunder, who put her words down as she dictated. It reads as follows.

Deep in the heart of Telemark, encircled by jagged rock covered mountains, lays Flatdal, one of the loveliest and most fruitful valleys in Norway with its neat little homesteads scattered over the lowlands.

The steep and jagged mountains known as the Skorvefjield rear its majestic height like a wall to the west, its rock scarred sides covered with green and brown moss. Only in a few clefts and crevices are green leaves and brush visible, but here and there small waterfalls shine like ribbons against the dark and rocky background.

On the west side of the valley lays the Reishus homestead with its small huts clustered about the mountainside.

The place is small but beautiful as it lies between the mountain and a little mountain stream called Vasjaa.

The first Sondre (father of immigrating Sondre) had cleared the place and built his first house by raising huge timbers up against the mountainside. This place got its name from this method of house building, and the name Reishus or Raise-house originated from this procedure.

Sondre (the elder) had come to the valley from the east in the 1700s. He had served in the war against Sweden. He fell in love with a farmer's daughter, but she refused to marry him until he could provide a home for her.

In due time he was able to buy a piece of uncleared land, which looked rather unpretentious, being covered with brush and stone, but with labor and perseverance, he succeeded in clearing the land and built a home to which he brought his bride, whose name was Ragna.

They became parents of seven children, all girls, the oldest Ragnhild inheriting the homestead as was customary in Norway. The oldest son customarily inherits the homestead, but being no son, the inheritance went to the oldest daughter. She married Olaf Aamodt, and they had one son, whom they named Sondre after his grandfather.

When Sondre was 22 years old he married Ingebor, a daughter of Jarjus and Gra, from Flatbyden in Siljord, who is the narrator of this family history.

She goes on to say, "We were married by Pastor Tonneson in the fall of 1842 in Seljord's ancient stone church from where one could look up the mountain side and see the three statues of rock resembling two girls with a ram beside them which were called 'Knile Moer.'"

Folklore has it that one Sunday while a minister was preaching, a beautiful melody floated up the mountain, and the churchgoers left one by one to follow the music.

The minister, irked by the disturbance of the singing of the fairies, became very angry and invoking the sign of the cross turned them to stone. This myth is that the old church was built by Hellig Olaf (Holy Olaf) and had the help of trolls.

Because he was the only child, Sondre had expected to take over the homestead on the death of his mother, as his father was old and lame; but he refused to give it up to his son and soon after we left Norway, he remarried.

Our decision to go to America was prompted by his father's action. Many of our friends had already immigrated there, and although high officials tried to dissuade us, saying we did not have the necessary amount of money to undertake the journey, we were determined to go. Sondre said times were now so hard and wages so low, he saw no chance of getting ahead in Norway.

Sondre and I each owned two head of cattle when we married. I also owned a roll of homespun cloth and a silver broach, all of which we sold to finance our trip to America. We bought only the barest of necessities and had $50 left over to take us on the long journey.

We left Flatdal the latter part of May in 1843 with our son Ole, two weeks old. We took with us on the long journey, a chest full of cloth and food, consisting of flatbread, butter, cheese, a small amount of coffee, and some flour.

We hired the chest hauled to Seljord Bay, a distance of about seven American miles, while we walked, and I carried the baby. From Lomadden we took a boat to Boherred where Sondre turned in the military equipment, which had been issued to him as he was now of military age and was soon to report for training.

The next day we walked to Norsho, thence by boat a 35-mile stretch, and finishing the trip on foot to Skein.

At Skein we engaged passage on the sail ship, *Nora*, with accommodations for 200 passengers.

Our problems now were to procure our visas or passports, which Sondre had been refused because he was eligible for military duty. We were in a quandary as to what to do when help came from an unexpected quarter. The interpreter on the boat came to our aid by smuggling us aboard that night, saying that once the ship got underway we would be safe.

The *Nora* lifted anchor and the journey was begun, but our troubles were not over yet. The next morning all passengers were ordered on deck to be counted, and there was great excitement when the passenger list numbered 202. The result of the irregularity was that two young single men were taken in a small boat back to land. They were obliged to wait for the next boat, but eventually reached their destination, and we met them in New York several weeks later.

We reached Havre, France after two weeks of sailing, where we waited another two weeks for a larger ship to take us over the ocean. We spent six weeks on the ocean and encountered at least one bad storm when the ship listed badly, and passengers and their possessions were thrown hither and yon.

When we had disembarked at New York, I sat down on a pile of timber with my child in my arms while Sondre went up town to arrange for our journey inland.

During his absence I accompanied a group of ladies in our group a short distance to see the town, and when he returned and found me missing, he was frantic with anxiety and searched for me up and down the dock. We soon returned, and he was both angry and glad to see me.

Our destination inland was Milwaukee, Wisconsin, where we had friends living about 15 miles west, who had located in the Norwegian Muskego settlement, but here we were stranded in New York almost penniless. Fortunately, old Margit, with whom I had made friends on the ship, tucked five dollars in my hand, admonishing me not to mention it to her husband.

The husband, by the way, was out to celebrate their arrival in the new country, which he did so thoroughly that he was not responsible for his actions. If at some future time we wished to repay the loan she hinted we could simply say with all innocence, "Here is the money you loaned me." He would be none the wiser.

CHAPTER 38 / *Excerpts From Sondre Reishby Ingebor, Wife of Sondre*

We now started up the Hudson River, passing Albany, Buffalo, and Niagara, moving slowly, sometimes by sail or rowboat and sometimes by horse drawn canal boats, reaching Milwaukee after a three week journey.

In order to meet expenses on this last lap of our journey, we were forced to sell some of our homespun and later even our chest bartered for bread. We had no milk, but I bought a twenty-cent prime roast, which I shaved up and mixed with water. With that and the barley flour we still had, I made porridge, which kept us alive.

Thirteen weeks had now passed since we left our home in Norway.

One day in September we again resumed our journey westward going by foot, as we did not have the means to hire a livery as some of our more fortunate friends had. Besides the baby we also carried a heavy sack of food and clothing and a spinning wheel. We were obliged to sell the latter because it became too heavy to carry, and we received the huge sum of twenty-five cents.

In our group of traveling companions were a man and his wife and their large family of children. We trudged along carrying our burdens on our backs. The weather was extremely warm, and our heavy wool homespun clothing became almost unbearable. Sondre had an extra coat, vest, and pants, which he was forced to give away. At one point in our travels we were beset by hunger, and Sondre said for a joke to our companions, "Torkel, you are such a fluent talker, why don't you go up to the farm house and ask the lady if she can spare us a bite to eat?" Torkel did so and returned with the food saying, "The Yankee woman understood my language very well."

As we neared the log house in the woods where our friends lived, we were very happy. They owned 40 acres of land and two cows. The men had secured work in the neighborhood and lived there with them throughout the winter.

In the late fall another family arrived from Norway, and they also joined our group, but sad to say, during the winter the wife and baby died.

Later on Knute Tusberg, his wife and three sons and a daughter, also arrived at the log hut, but it was already filled to overflowing, and the Tusbergs had to dig a sod cellar. They lived there throughout the winter. The Tusberg boys made good in the new world. One of them, Aslak, served at one time on the faculty of the St. Olaf Academy at Northfield.

Sondre had worked out for three weeks when he came home with what was then called cold fever, or as some others called it "Ague." The rest of the household came down with the same illness, and all through the winter we had sickness and poverty to contend with.

The Muskego settlement lay in an unhealthy location with woods and swamp. Hardly a home escaped having Ague or jaundice, and many died. As for Sondre, the baby, and me, we were all sick at the same time. Our comforts were few, which did not help conditions any. We slept on the floor and had only a couple of robes for covers. We often slept with our clothing on in order to keep warm.

When Sondre's health was somewhat improved, he went into partnership with Tusberg, and together they made ax handles, wooden spoons, and bowls. Tusberg did the chopping in the woods, mostly hickory, and when he trimmed the wood to the desired length and shape, Sondre did the finishing with plane and knife. They were then peddled around in the settlement or traded for pork or flour.

In the spring of 1844 we, together with two other families, again took to the road. This time our objective was Koshkonong, some 60 miles to the southwest. We carried a large bundle of food and clothing besides our one-year-old son, which were all our possessions.

On the way I played out, and we were forced to lay over a day while the rest of the company continued on their way. After a night's rest I was able to continue the journey. The first man we met when we reached out destination kindly invited us to remain with his family until we became established.

Sondre took a job about 20 miles away but was unable to continue working as he again came down with the "ague." We then moved to another place where I worked doing chores and milking cows, but we did not thrive there.

Sondre had made some improvements on a piece of government land, which he sold for $12.00 and then bought 40 acres of timber land on which he dug and built a sod house. From stones he fashioned a stove, or fireplace, but as we owned neither kettle nor spider, I was forced to borrow these from some kind neighbors on special occasions. Otherwise I would lay the bread dough and potatoes in the ashes over coals and bake.

Sondre had his workbench in the hut and made pails, pans, and other receptacles of wood, which he sold.

I bought calico and made a quilt, but was offered $3.00 for it, so I sold it.

Now that we had a little money we bought half interest in a cow, and every other day I walked morning and evening three quarters of a mile to milk the cow, carrying my child with me besides the milk on the return trip. Sometime later we sold our half interest in the cow and bought one of our own for $10.00, which was the first cow we owned in America.

One day while Sondre was working in a little town called Codfish, he found a pocket book that had money and valuable papers for which he received a reward of $5.00. He bought a team of oxen for $30.00, part of which he went into debt for. Half a year later, one of the oxen died from lung fever, which placed us in difficult circumstances. Luckily, we were able to sell the remaining ox for $23.00.

In March 1846, our second child, Ragnhild, was born. She died at the age of two months from smallpox. Ole, who was now three and one-half years old, also contacted the disease but survived.

Reverend L. C. Clausen who came to Muskego from Norway in 1843, the same year we did, had accepted a call there and was perhaps the first ordained Lutheran pastor in America. He baptized Ragnhild.

Reverend Diedrieksen came over from Norway in 1844 and was called to the Koshkonong congregation. He was ambitious and evangelic, and it was during his stay, the East and West Koshkonong churches were built. Sondre was employed for a time in splitting fence rails in the tamarack forest east of the East Church near a little town of Clinton. He was considered a better than average rail-splitter, his usual output being about 300 rails a day. One day he was unfortunate in chopping a deep gash in his foot. He started limping home, but was unable to go much further when he came to an Indian tent where a squaw bandaged his foot, and he was able to reach the next neighbor, where he borrowed a horse to ride home. The next day he rode the horse back two miles where he had borrowed it and returned on foot.

Sondre sold his improved 40 acres for $75.00 and together with a neighbor took another piece of land. That was 40 acres each and a little later another 40 together, which cost them $50.00. The latter they went into debt for, and Sondre was able to borrow the money from Reverend Diedrieksen with whom he was well acquainted from the time the East Church was built. Sondre was on the building committee and was chosen supervisor so went on inspection trips several times a week and also supervised the building of the parsonage.

Reverend Diedrieksen was a strong man mentally and physically but was often discouraged and disheartened over criticism and opposition he received from various sources.

One day at work a man came to him and began berating and abusing him. He stood up under it for a while, but finally lost patience and asked Sondre to throw him out. Sondre, being a stranger and not acquainted with the circumstances hesitated, so the pastor grabbed the man by the collar and threw him out bodily. In his fall, the man claimed to have sprained his ankle and had the pastor arrested for assault. This experience and others prompted him to return to Norway, which he did in 1850.

CHAPTER 38 / Excerpts From Sondre Reishby Ingebor, Wife of Sondre

While living at Vraas, Sondre's partner Torjus and the second Ragnhild were born, and Reverend Diedrieksen baptized both.

In the spring of 1849, we sold our farm and moved six miles out to near First Lake. This time we drove with a team of oxen and a "kubbe-rulle" (the latter is a wagon on which run long wheels around slices of log having bored in the middle installed on axles).

We had bought 80 acres near this place, and later we added another 40. While we were living there, Sondre's cousin, Evan Olson, arrived from Norway. With him came his sister-in-law, Bertha Knutsen, with her two daughters, Karina and Marie, and her little son Tobias, who made their home with us for a time. It was about this time we bought our first cook stove for which we paid $15.00. It lasted 23 years.

We lived on the farm near First Lake for five years; among other things we raised wheat, which we sold in Milwaukee at 25 cents a bushel. But the distance being so great (80 miles), there was very little profit. Once we hired a man to haul a load there and had scarcely enough after paying him for his work to buy a barrel of sale.

In 1853, the railroad came through, and it was routed across a corner of our land. The highway also cut into our land, so we sold out for $600.00.

That same summer began a new influx of settlers to southeastern Minnesota along the Root River. The state was still a territory. The Indians were moving westward and giving up their land. Sondre and his cousin Evan took a trip out to look over this new territory and were so well impressed that the next spring, 1854, we again started moving west.

Reverend A. C. Preus, who had come from Norway in 1840 and had accepted the call left vacant by Reverend Diedrieksen, gave Sondre a letter of transfer, which helped us to become properly established in our new surroundings.

This time we traveled in style as we now had a buggy, together with a white mare we called "fly" which I drove with the children beside me. Ole was now eleven years old and big and strong for his age. Sondre drove an ox team and wagon and Evan who had bought a wagon in Milwaukee drove another.

It was a hazardous trip, poor trails, steep hills, and lots of rain. We crossed the Mississippi river on the ferry at McGregor, Iowa, thence north past Decorah and into Minnesota to Fillmore County near where the town of Rushford now stands. We were on the road three weeks.

The farm at Rushford proved to be a good investment, and we prospered.

Sondre and Evan were inseparable during these years, but as time went on, Evan moved six miles west, where he acquired a 300-acre tract of timber and prairie land. He married, and some of his descendents still live in Rushford.

When Sondre and Evan came to Minnesota, they took young Tobias, then seven years old, with them, and he made his home with his uncle Evan Reishus until he was a young man of 19.

Tobias Reishus joined Company D, 8th Minnesota Volunteers during the Civil War and saw much service. When called to Minnesota to help quell the Indian uprising, his company was in Tennessee and because of poor railroad facilities, they marched on foot a quarter part of the way. The young soldier had a good opportunity to observe the various parts of the country in those years of fighting, and at the end of the war he decided to move west to live.

In 1867 he led a covered wagon train to what is now the Yellow Medicine River, west and north where they took homestead and settled down with their families.

Older residents will remember Tobias Reishus as a kind and rather old looking man who was never too busy to help his neighbors or anyone who called on him in time of need. He wore a long beard, which made him look older than his years for when he passed away, he was but 61 years of age.

His had been an exciting life, which very few men have experienced.

CHAPTER 38 / *Excerpts From Sondre Reishby Ingebor, Wife of Sondre*

Letter from Sondre Olavson Reishus to Knut Thorson Minesgard:

Vineland, Minnesota January 28, 1879

Knut Thorson Minesgard An Unforgettable friend!

For a long time I have thought about sending you some lines, but as you see I am a poor writer and it has been put aside. I want first to send you my heartfelt greetings and let you know that we are fine and hope these lines find you the same.

I see by Nel's letter that you have suffered a severe misfortune in that you have lost both your children and your dear wife and are alone. This must have been a hard blow, which you will have to try to understand. We know the Lord's ways are best, and we have to learn to trust and know that all things work for good to those who love God.

I want to then, as a friend to advise you not to be overcome by sorrow and loneliness, yes, I will say it right out—find yourself a wife! You are in good financial standing and you are not old. You can still live to see a growing blossoming relationship. Do not let your beautiful farm come into strange hands. You maybe think that this idea or advice is all foolishness and something to laugh about, that might be, but it is also something that need not be cried about. This is my sincere opinion.

I will now go on and tell about some happenings in this far away western land. I think the cold weather is worse here than in Norway, the northwestern storms come streaking over the endless prairies. The three winters I have been here we haven't had many bad storms. It was quite cold about Christmas time, but now it is mild and the ground is almost bare, so now we have to use wagons.

Last year we did our spring-work in March, but the high heat in June drove the wheat too fast so it wasn't up to average. Prices are not very good, from 45 to 55 cents a bushel. There is a shortage of money and hard times in America, the opposite of what is in Norway now.

Concerning church affairs we have the services of Pastor Knut Thorstenson he is from Vinesogn and has studied here in America. He is clever and ambitious. It is not long ago since the soul seeker congregation was organized so no church has been built, but they will begin soon.

I have not heard from Gregar Einsaas for a long time so I can tell you nothing about him. I have heard that Halvor Skararust is financially well off. The others who have gone from Fladdal I have heard nothing about. Greet Nels Gonlickos, I received his last letter and should write him a few words but now there isn't time as the mail is coming. I am postmaster here and the mailman stops here with us for dinner.

Greet all the people we know and to yourself our best wishes.
    Your Friend so Reishus
    Vineland
    Yellow Medicine County Minnesota us America

39

EXCERPTS FROM *SLÆGTEN REISHUS*

Tobias—Written by Agnes Reishus (Mrs. Ted Reishus)

> *There is no king who has not had a slave among his ancestors, and no slave who has not had a king among his.*
> —HELEN KELLER

THE REISHUS FAMILY HAD ITS origin in the lovely little valley of Flatdal—deep in the heart of Telemark. The first Sondre we have a record of bought a small piece of stony ground near the mountains. It didn't look very promising as it lay there all covered with stones, brush and trees, but Sondre was stout and strong and after a time succeeded in clearing the land and building his house there. This he did by raising huge timbers up against the mountainside in lean-to fashion. His home got its name from this method of house building—namely "raise house," or Reishus. He brought his bride, Ragna, home to this little "gaard."

Sondre and Ragna had seven children, all girls. In Norway the eldest son always inherits the homestead, but as they had no sons the oldest daughter, Ragnhild, inherited the place. The second daughter, Mary, married Knut Vold and moved to his home for a time, but Vold died soon after their son Knud was born, so Mary returned to her old home. She married a few years later a man named Ole Langemo, or Langeman. They had one son, Even, who became the forefather of the Rushford Reishuses.

Ole Langemo died young, and shortly after that his wife Mary also died. This left two half-brothers, Knud and Even, orphans at an early age. Knud was six years older than Even, and he went to sea, while Even was put out "paa legd" (to work for his board) somewhere in the district. Knud continued his work on the sea, and in spite of the hardships and hard work he had to do, he became an accomplished sea man and very strong. He could lift a 400 pound barrel of fish.

He married a red haired girl named Bertha. They had three children—Mary, Karina, and Tobias. Knud went to sea and was often gone for many months, sometimes years, and as times were hard in Norway at this time, I imagine Bertha had a hard time making the money reach from one sea voyage to another. Even said she, Bertha, was very quick tempered too, and she nagged him a lot when he was home about getting another job and staying at home and taking care of his family. But jobs were scarce, and Knud loved the sea as all sailors do and he continued to sail, even around the Horn to the East Indies and China. These sail ships were very slow, and it often took four to five months to get to America and several years to get to China and back.

After Tobias, the third child, was a little over a year old, Knud went on a long journey to Asia. The winds blew them far off their course, and the ship was badly damaged. There was no Panama Canal at that time, and they had to sail way around Cape Horn, the south tip of South America. After many months and probably years of travel, they finally reached China. Their ship was laid up for repairs, and rather than wait months on land, Knud shipped out on a boat bound for another port. This went on and on, and it was quite a few years before he returned.

People from Norway had begun emigrating to America before this time, and now in 1848, Knud's brother Even, who had served his apprenticeship and was now a full-fledged blacksmith, decided to go to America. Many others, among them Sondre and Ingebor, Even's cousins, had gone to Wisconsin back in 1843, and Even decided to go to their home near Muskego in Wisconsin.

All this time Bertha had been waiting for Knud to come home, but months and years passed, and she heard nothing from him. (To me this seems very cruel as Knud could write, but in those days of slow travel, I suppose he thought he could get home as soon as a letter). She often thought he must be dead. Then she thought he might have gone to America. When she heard her brother-in-law Even was going to America, she made up her mind to go too. She sold her home and the few belongings she had and with a little help and loans from friends and relatives, she was able to buy tickets for herself and the children. Mary was now eleven years old, Karina was nine, and Tobias was five. They were on the Atlantic for 14 weeks and encountered bad storms and gales, which made the sea so rough that they were not only seasick but also feared for their lives.

After reaching New York they traveled up the Hudson by sailboat, sometimes by canal rowboat and sometimes by rail, and eventually reached Milwaukee on the west coast of Lake Michigan. From there they reached First Lake near where Sondre and family lived at this time. I'm sure Sondre enjoyed Even's visit as he could tell him of old friends and relatives back home in Flatdal. Sondre's family came over in 1843, and it was now 1848, so much must have happened in the interim.

Even worked on farms during the summer, but in winter he worked in the pineries as they were then called—logging camps. Even was a good swimmer, so in the spring he also helped take the logs down the Wisconsin River, a thrilling though dangerous occupation.

Bertha, Knud's wife, worked on farms too, doing housework, of course. The girls, Mary and Karina, soon got places as nursemaids, and so she had only Tobias with her. She drifted northwest to Madison and finally settled near Menomonie, Wisconsin. When Even moved to the Rushford vicinity in 1854, he took Tobias with him, and from that time on until he went into the Army, he made his home with his Uncle Even.

Mary married a farmer named Nels Peterson and became the mother of a large family. They had 14 children, and their names are Gurine, Bertha, Tilda, Anna, Emma, Johanna, Elias, Syvert, Knute, Tom, Andrew, Johnny, and Martin. Poor Bertha (Karina, Mary, and Tobias's mother) was not happy. She didn't find Knud in America, so decided he must have died. She worked out for some years, but after Mary's children began coming, she was needed there. Nels Peterson's mother died, and his father came to live with him. I imagine the house was pretty noisy with so many children, so the two old folks, his father, and her mother, married and moved into a little house by themselves. Mary said her mother always worried if she should have married. She died in 1869 before the news came that Knud was alive.

In the meantime Knud had finally returned to Norway and found his family had gone to America. He still went to sea for some years, but when at home, he stayed with Bertha's sister-in-law, Anna. In Norway in those days, weddings were occasions of great celebration, with plenty of food and strong drinks, which often brought on fights and bickering. Bertha's brother had been in such a fight and used his knife on an opponent who later died of the wounds. He was, therefore, sent to prison and his wife, Anna, took in roomers and boarders to make her living.

In 1854 when Even and Tobias came to Fillmore County, they settled on a farm in the valley near the bluffs, where they had shelter from the cold blasts of the winter. However, the Root River flowed by the farm, and in the spring when Chinook winds melted the snow in the hills, flash floods came up in no time to inundate the land. Only four miles west of there you came out of the hills and on to fine rolling prairie land, and Even decided this had its advantages.

He sold the farm in the valley and bought 300 acres on the prairies, although at that time much of it was covered with timber, such as oak, elm, ash, walnut, butternut, and hickory nut trees. Much hard work and elbow grease were expended to clear this land. Sixty years ago when this writer was a child, there was still much timber in the pasture especially, but now the trees have all disappeared. The log house that Grandpa Even built has stood until just a few years ago, proving that he built well to make it last 100 years. Here Tobias spent his boyhood in a beautiful environment.

But our country was coming into a difficult period. The Civil War broke out and in 1862; Tobias then 19 years old, volunteered for service and joined Company D, the 8th Minnesota Volunteers. He was tall, broad shouldered, and very strong like his father before him.

Tobias saw much service in the South, as well as fighting the Indians here in the Northwest. The soldiers in those days suffered much, having inadequate weapons, clothing, and food. He wrote Grandpa Even that he often wished himself back near their garbage pail as Even's hogs fared better than they did. They poached corn as they marched along, and ate raw meat when too hungry to wait for it to fry or cook.

When called to this portion of the country to quell an Indian uprising, his company was way down in Tennessee, and with such poor railroad facilities, the poor soldiers had to walk much of the way. This war was no snap either as the Indians were formidable foes, never fighting in the open, but in sneak attacks on small groups, perhaps hauling freight or coming up as reinforcements.

In the old records, I read of the commander of the forces here writing to Alex Ramsey, then Governor of Minnesota, pleading for more guns and ammunition. They had no guns to spare, but sent ammunition, which turned out to be the wrong gauge or caliber for the guns they did have.

As I mentioned before, Tobias was a strong man and absolutely fearless. His captain liked to drink and carouse, and usually got into arguments ending in fights. He appointed Tobias as his orderly and always had him go with him to bring him home after such a fracas. Being drunk, he would get flying mad at Tobias and threaten him with all sorts of dire reprisals, but Tobias just picked him up and carried him back to his tent. By the time he sobered up again, he had forgotten all about his threats. Perhaps it is this captain's sword Tobias brought back from the Army.

A Reverend Peterson, a missionary from India, who was raised in the Hanley Falls area, told another story of his fearlessness. He said there was a group of Indians firing on the Whites from a bunch of trees where they were all well protected. Tobias, Knud Kjemhus, and Jens Stevens went in there after them and routed them out. Reverend Peterson said he would like to write about those men and call it, "When Men Were Men." He told several stories of their bravery and brawn, but I've forgotten so much I could not repeat it.

In a record book, *Minnesota in the Civil War*, I find the 8th Minnesota Volunteers had been relieved from duty by the Northwestern Indian Expedition and were ordered to go south and west to the Missouri, still fighting Indians. From July until October, four months, Colonel Thomas says they marched and fought 1625 miles, much of the time on short rations, and on one day of their worst battles, without water, and the thermometer 110 in the shade. No wonder he writes, "Their patient endurance, their bravery, and fighting qualities have stamped them as true and disciplined soldiers."

After Tobias was mustered out, and the war was over, Tobias had his narrowest escape. They were traveling home on freight, and as he was walking on top of boxcars, they came to a bridge. It was low, and he was hit in the back of his head and knocked unconscious. Luckily his pal was able to hold him prostrate until he came to a station where he was given first aid.

Tobias was very favorably impressed with the farming country he had seen out here in his fighting with the Sioux Indians. In the fall of 1866, he with Garmon and a couple of other men came up here again to look it over.

That winter he married Anna Kolhei, and in the spring of 1867 they traveled in covered wagons with Anna's parents and brothers. Knute, Mary, and Lettie were born, then Lauritz, Nettie, Emelia, Theodore, and Edward. Tobias was away from home a great deal after his boys were able to help. He was a self-educated veterinarian and drove around the country a great deal doctoring horses and cows. He was kind and helpful, and often left his own work to go and administer aid to someone else's sick animals.

He was Yellow Medicine's first sheriff and no doubt had many interesting experiences during his term of office. Later he worked with J S Johnson in the machinery business in Granite Fall and only came home on weekends.

At one time Knute was horseback riding after cattle, and very likely on a wild bronco that crowded him into the fence and cut a deep gash in his leg. Later it festered, and the doctor thought it had to be amputated. However, Tobias refused to allow this, and used remedies he knew were good for blood poisoning or infections. Knute recovered.

Everyone knew that Tobias was a strong man. One day at services a drunk man was causing a disturbance and old Pastor Thorstenson lost patience and called, "Tobias, tak han ud." Which Tobias did.

In the early 1880s Grandpa Knud got in touch with his brother Even at Rushford and also his son, Tobias. He was born in 1817, so was now in his late 60s and no longer following the sea. He wanted to come to America, which he did in 1884 or 1885. He stayed at the home farm for a time but later had a little home built down in that part of the woods, which we still call "bestefar skogen." He was still strong and would carry a sack full of feed for his cows and chickens on his shoulder from the granary at home way down to his home.

My Ted got in trouble down there one day. He and Eddie had been fishing in the river and went up to Grandpa Knud's for lunch or a drink. Anyway he had left his pole on the ground, and a big rooster swallowed both bait and hook. Result was that Grandpa had to take the head off his rooster.

Another time Grandpa Knud came up to the farmhouse while the family was still at the table. Not seeing Theodore, he asked where he was. When told he hadn't come back from the field where he was plowing, Grandpa started right out to look for him. He found him with the horses and lines all tangled. He had started to unhitch to go home when a wild bronco had swung around and got the lines all tangled. Ted was only a little fellow and was unable to get them straightened out. Grandpa couldn't either, so he took his knife and cut the lines. He was mad to think they would send a little kid out plowing with such an outlaw horse.

One time Nettie was stretching to take a hunk of dried beef off the wall. They had just hauled chunks of ice and partly filled the cistern. The cover was open yet, and Nettie fell in. No one else happened to be in, and when someone did come, she sat on the ice chunk saying, "Can you help me out?"

Emelia nearly drowned one time. On the way to school they crossed the river on a log, and when she got half way over, their dog tried to pass her and pushed her off. Lauritz saved her by hanging on to the branch of a tree, and she came up close to where he was, so he was able to grab her.

Ted fell in the river once too, and Nettie Lende, who was teaching him, made him undress and sit with a girl's coat on by the stove until his clothes got dry.

Millers and Reishuses owned a buck together. Lauritz and Magnus teased him so much that he got pretty ugly. They would stand by the barn wall, and when he lowered his head and came toward them, they would jump to the side, and he would hit the wall. When at the Millers, they would stand on the riverbank, and when they dodged, he would fall in the river. Mr. Miller thought he would try that trick too sometime, but he was not quick enough, and the buck butted him into the river.

CHAPTER 39 / Excerpts from *Slægten Reishus*

Pioneer life agreed with Tobias, and as this country settled, he probably wished for new lands to conquer. Around the turn of this century, new lands in Canada were opened for settlement. John Lines, George Anderson, Ing. Kolhei, Peter Eliason, and Tobias went to Hanley, Saskatchewan to give the country the once over. They were all pleased with the prospects there, and all invested in land. I guess Peter Eliason benefitted the most on this land venture. At one time it was said that he owned nearly the equivalent of a township, which is 36 sections, or about 2400 acres.

Tobias bought land west of Hanley and also one half section near Kenaston. For two summers he lived there while Theodore took charge of the farming at home. In 1904 Netty was married to Oluf Pederson, and they immigrated to Canada, taking over the farm and buildings, which Tobias had built.

For several years Tobias had been bothered with asthma, and on May 29, 1904, for this reason and other complications, he died. The funeral was held on Memorial Day, which seemed very appropriate since he was a Civil War Veteran. He was a comparatively young man, only 61, at the time of his death. Some of you—his grandchildren—still remember him as a tall, broad shouldered, distinguished man, with a bald head and a long white beard. He and his old bay team, Sam and Charley, were often seen on the roads around Normania.

His wife, Anna, lived on the old home place after his death with Theodore running the farm. Later after Theodore was married and on his own place, Eddie took over. Grandma Anna died in 1922.

Much more could have been written of this interesting couple, of their early hardships in pioneer days, their kindness and helpfulness to anyone in need, their hospitality to kindred and strangers alike, their honesty and respect for God and man. However, I have brought this history up to the time, which many of you remember. Let someone more competent than I write the history of the future.

Tobias Knudson Reishus and Anna Kolhei Reishus and family
Rear: Emelia, Antonette, Marie, Knute, Lauritz
Front: Alletta, Theodore, Anna, Tobias, Edward

TOBIAS KNUDSON REISHUS AND ANNA KOLHEI REISHUS

BACK ROW, Left to right; 1. Theodore (6-2-1882, 7-13-1956); 2. Nettie (Mrs. Oluf Pederson) (11-1-1877, 1-29-1954); 3. Lauritz (3-23-1875, 1-16-1953); 4. Knute (9-24-1869, 12-9-1950); 5. Marie (Mrs. Hans Miller) (2-22-1872, 1-22-1944); 6. Edward (3-21-1885, 1-5-1948).
FRONT ROW, Left to right, 7. Mattie (Mrs. Andrew Michalson) (1-19-1867, 5-8-1950); 8. Tobias Reishus (5-10-1843, 5-29-1904); 9. Anna Kolhei Reishus (8-21-1842, 11-22-1922); 10. Alleta (7-23-1867, 9-27-1937); 11. Emelia (Mrs. Oscar Erickson) (12-17-1879, 2-11-1959).

REISHUS DESCENDANTS

CHAPTER 39 / Excerpts from Slægten Reisbus   323

First page of the two-page passenger list for the Brig Favoriten arriving in New York Harbor on November 6, 1850. Passenger 17 is Bertte Torgersdotter, 18 is Bertte [Maria] and 19 is Tobias

40

THE FAMILY OF KNUTE T. REISHUS
(9/24/1869–12/9/1950)

AND ANNETTE MILLER
(3/13/1872–12/3/1956)

By Norma Reishus Dovre

Every man is his own ancestor, and every man his own heir. He devises his own fortune, and he inherits his own past.
—FRANCIS HERBERT HEDGE

KNUTE WAS BORN SEPTEMBER 24, 1869 in Dakota Territory, later organized in 1871 as Sannes Township, Yellow Medicine County. He was the oldest son of Tobias and Anna (Kolhei) Reishus. Knute's brothers and sisters included the following:

Mattie (Mrs. Andrew Michaelson) lived on Tobias' tree claim near Porter, Minnesota. The family moved to Voltaire, North Dakota after Andrew died.

Alleta had polio while young and used crutches.

Marie's (Mrs. Hans Miller) family ended up buying Tobias' home farm. Bob Benson, 5th generation (from Tobias), started farming this land in 1983.

Lauritz moved to Cottonwood and was in banking.

Nettie (Mrs. Olaf Pederson) settled on Tobias' Canada claim and expanded near Hanley, Saskatchewan, Canada.

Emelia (Mrs. Oscar Erickson) lived on a farm. Alfred Reishus bought that farm, and his son Jerry Reishus was still there in 1983.

Theodore was a farmer. His daughter Myrna and Henry Broughton, 3rd generation, now live on the farm.

Edward, who with Tobias proved the Canadian land, then settled on part of Tobias' land here. John Reishus, 4th generation, lives on this farm as of 1983. Eddie later ran pool halls in Cottonwood and sold many handyman jacks, which were a new device that everyone wanted.

Knute was two years old when he moved with his parents into Normania Township, Section 25, Yellow Medicine County, which was to be their homestead. He grew into manhood and helped with farming and livestock until 1894 when he married Annetta Miller. Annetta was the daughter of Ole and Mathia (Amundsdatter) Miller who were pioneers in Normania Township. The Millers came in 1868 with Lara Hansons and Ole Brusvens. The only white families there previously were the Halver Gullicksons who settled by the lake named for him, Spillman (Fiddler in Norwegian). Annetta's brothers and sisters included the following:

Andrew farmed south of the Miller place (Darris Kompelien in 1983).

Hans was the second white child born in the area to be called Normania. Hans married Mary Reishus; so Knute and Annetta were doubly related to them.

Magnus bought land in Lyon County south of the Miller homestead (his grandson Lee Miller was there in 1983).

Olaus lived on the home place, Section 32, and bought land north of the river.

Martin lived on the Miller homestead until his death.

After Knute and Annetta's marriage, they farmed in Lyon County until 1901 when Knute bought land in Section 35, Normania Township, YMC and built their home there. This home had three bedrooms upstairs with the girls sharing a single room. The southeast bedroom had two double beds, and the west bedroom, three double beds. Downstairs the bedroom sometimes had two double beds.

The north kitchen was not used in the winter. The pantry had a trap door with barrels of apples that Knute would bring home and roll down the steps. The big enameled coffee pot was usually half full of grounds. You just added a little more for each batch of stout coffee. Lump sugar and white cookies were always on hand. Milk was kept in running well water in the summer.

Their bills and correspondence lay on the south windowsill. Upstairs there was an old pump organ that Annetta used to play. When granddaughter Norma Dovre visited, she enjoyed pumping it too.

The Reishus family always had oyster stew on Christmas Eve. The presents were in the parlor where a big issenglas stove had been filled with a big bucket of coal.

Family of Knute and Annetta Reishus, 1944.
Rear row, L to R, Orville, Norman, Stanley, Franklin, Alfred, Howard, William, Clarence, Martin. Front row, Myrtle, Annetta, Knute, Vivian

FAMILY OF KNUTE AND ANNETTA REISHUS, 1944

CHAPTER 40 / *The Family of Knute T. Reishus and Annette Miller*

Knute and Annetta had a large family of 11 children: Orville, Clarence, Alfred, Myrtle (Mrs. Nuel Olson), Norman, William, Stanley, Martin, Franklin, Howard, and Vivian (Mrs. Kurt Wendshuh).

Knute and his family farmed a lot of land for that day. They owned 680 acres at one time and raised many cattle, hogs, and also some sheep. Norman remembers when they had as many as 19 horses in harness at one time.

Knute built one of the first hip roofed barns in 1911. It still stands. The barns were painted red, and the house was always white.

Norman hadn't started school when one day Knute was sawing wood with a big 30˝ circle saw powered by horses walking in a circle. One horse slipped, and Knute reached out and cut four fingers off his hand. The older kids tried to find the fingers in the sawdust, but Knute had taken them along to the doctor where he insisted they be sewn back on. Knute did have stiff fingers, and they pained him in later years.

Knute bought a lot of green and wild broncos that no one else wanted at livestock sales. They were broke and harnessed for work or riding, but not without difficulties. Vivian remembers once when cousin Barbara Miller was visiting. They saw a bronco rear up, hit Alfred in the head, and knock him out.

Knute was also a self-made veterinarian like his father. He would travel over the countryside tending to the ills of horses and other livestock. In the spring Knute would castrate all the colts in the area from Monte to Canby. Alfred usually went along to help.

Knute was a co-op man and helped organize a Farmers Co-op Elevator in Cottonwood. He served on the Co-op Creamery Board several years, helping in its organization, and he managed the Livestock Shipping Association for several years.

He would take livestock from an area into a holding stockyard, then sort, and ship them by railroad to South St. Paul or Sioux City, Iowa. Some weeks he would have many carloads to get out. Some winter mornings he would start out the door in a snowstorm with a team of horses pulling a bobsled full of straw and feed to go to town to tend the livestock and get them loaded by train time.

When Norman was a teenager, he worked for his Uncle Martin Miller. They had been cultivating, and as they were coming home from the field, they saw some supposed strangers picking gooseberries by the river. Martin said, "Let's sneak up on them for some fun." So they crawled up, stole the flour sack full of gooseberries, and forded the river. Norman took off his trousers. Martin didn't. They hid the berries back of the barn. Anyone who has ever picked gooseberries knows that a sack full represents a lot of scratchy, tedious work.

Later, cousins Truman and Lestof Miller and the Pederson boys stopped by saying, "Boy, our mothers are really mad." Mary complained about the theft on the telephone party line, although she blamed Amanda Brusven. It was many years later before Norman dared confess this deed to his Aunt Mary.

Annetta is remembered as a mild mannered person. She was very busy taking care of her family, and the only time she left her area was when she visited Orville, who had been kicked in the stomach by a mule while he was in the armed forces.

Myrtle remembers her mother being very particular about her wash. The wash was first, then boiled, then starched, and finally ironed. The sheets and pillowcases had to be blued. They were washed once a week. Myrtle remembers there were 33 white shirts, and they were the whitest around. Clarence, himself, needed seven or eight because he worked in a bank.

The family butchered their own meat. Pork was fried and then covered with lard to store in a crock. Chickens were canned. It took 15 pounds of butter a week for family use. There were always sandwiches to make; usually jelly ones and 24 at a time for the school kids. Later they made their own peanut butter by shelling the peanuts, grinding them, and adding salt.

Myrtle won a piano in a contest. She collected the most coupons from goods purchased by patrons of the Larson Mercantile Company.

Myrtle also worked out a few times, especially during threshing. For one dollar a day she would include baking and cooking two lunches, dinner, and supper. When she helped Emelia Miller, she got twenty-five cents a day.

Before Vivian was born, Annetta had to stay off her feet for three months, so Myrtle helped out. As Annetta cut out baby flannel diapers and kimonos, she taught Myrtle to sew.

The family went to school in Lyon County, which was one mile south. The big event of the year was the Christmas program where everyone had a little piece to recite. They sang songs and did dialogues or plays.

When Norman was 11 years old he stayed at Eddie's (where Grandma Anna Reishus and Lettie were), and helped with chores and carrying wood and cobs. Dirty cobs that had been in the pig pen burned longer! Freshly shelled cobs didn't last long enough. The farm had 14 to 16 cows to milk. Cows were milked in an open pen, and the flies were bad, coupled with the cows' tails switching. Once Norman tied two tails together, but one cow started pulling, and a tail came off.

Norman helped thresh with the crew run by Olai Aamodt for four years. The grain had been bundled, and then about five loads of bundles were put into a peaked stack built so it would shed water. At the Knute Reishus farm they had close to 100 stacks. It took about 40 days for the threshing crew to go around to the various farms. Sometimes they were still threshing at Thanksgiving.

Cousins Lestof Miller, Alfred Reishus, and Norman Reishus had a good singing trio. Nettie Brenden Mauland was their pianist. Sometimes they would go help out the Islandic Choir, which was directed by Mrs. Anton Kompelien. Alfred, Norman, and Orville joined their uncles Martin and Olaus Miller and

Pete Thoreson, Neil Kise, and H. L. Kolhei to form a "Mons Kor" (Men's Octet), which sang in St. Lucas Church. Alfred, Martin, and Norman sang in the men's chorus directed by Sybil Dahl, and Alfred was in many bands. He also did some directing of choirs, especially at St. Lucas Church.

In the 50s when television was new, Stan was a sneaky salesman. When he knew someone was away from home, he went in and installed an antenna and TV set and would leave it turned on. When the owners came home, they wondered who was inside. They then would find the TV and get hooked watching it, so they bought it. Today Stan would be charged for breaking and entering.

Vivian worked at Ristvedt's Grocery in Cottonwood and was a bookkeeper at various places. She tells how during World War II she worked for the O.P.A. (Office of Price Administration) in Marshall. Vivian was in charge of the sugar rationing stamps and coupon books. Individuals had to register for coupons for sugar, tires, and gas. When you went to buy these items, which were in short supply, you had to turn in your stamps. Usually you wanted more items than you had stamps for. White flour also was in short supply, so you could only buy some if you also took some barley flour. When Stanley was delivering gas, he had to paste these stamps into his book.

During these days, brothers Knute, Ted, and Eddie each took a team and sleigh to get coal in Ghent. In the grocery there they asked how much sugar they could get. The grocer there didn't follow regulations on sugar rationing, so they each brought back 100 pounds of sugar with their coal.

Two and one half miles from the home place where Vivian now lives, Alfred would take two teams over to plant at 5:00 in the morning. Someone would bring him a change of teams at 10:00. Dinner was brought out to him, therefore the whole 65 acres was planted in two days.

Alfred's main instrument was the tuba, which he played in several brass bands. Alfred also played the accordion and mouth organ, so at house parties he, or his uncle Oscar Erickson on the accordion, would accompany the waltzes or square dances.

Annetta's brother Hans Miller was out hunting one day. He crawled up to the slough, which was saturated with ducks. After one shot of his 10-gauge gun, he picked up 43 ducks. This feat made Ripley's "Believe It or Not" column.

Annetta's father, Ole Miller, had a fish trap set in the Yellow Medicine River (illegal, but often done). One morning when he went to check the trap, he discovered a great big fish—a sturgeon that was over five feet long. When he carried it home over his shoulder with a pitchfork through its mouth, the fish dragged on the ground.

Stanley wrote from Mesa, Arizona. "It's 1982, and 55 years ago I moved to Cottonwood to sell Model T Fords. About 1912–15 Uncle Eddie sold a few Karter cars. Times have changed a lot since I started selling cars. Standard Fords and Chevrolets sold for less than $600."

When Leslie Larson was in the café business, he saved a certain kind of a 25-cent piece. He had $425 worth in a box, and he told me he would give these quarters and his used car for a new Chevrolet two-door. I said, "Okay, we'll trade." I guess I should have kept that silver until now.

Another time I was trying to sell a truck to a farmer east of town, and he said I had to take a horse in trade, which I did. When I got back to town, I called Andrew Severson to come in and look at the horse. Sure enough I sold him the horse.

In 1930 I sold Fred a new Chevrolet Sedan for $800, and he paid for it with all $20 bills. When I got back to town, I heard the Green Valley Bank had been robbed of $800. So I went into our bank with my wad of $800 in paper money, and I said, "Well, here is what was left of the Green Valley Bank." They counted it to be $800, and they didn't know whether they should give me credit for it or not."

I remember Dad used to start us kids out with a three-section drag and three horses. Whenever I got tired of walking, I would jump up on the evener and drive the horses from there. One day I turned too short, and the evener went into the ground, and I turned the whole drag over slick and clean. For me, at that time, I had a puzzle on my hands to get it back together again.

Another time Dad helped me hook up six lively horses on a disk in the yard. Vivian at that time was around four or five years old, and she wanted to sit on the end of the disk to get a ride. I said, "No, you'd better not." I started out holding four lines and two lunch pails, and before I got off the yard, the horses were going full gallop. I dropped the lunch pails and held onto the seat; otherwise I'd have fallen off into the disk. Anyway I turned them into a barley field, and we went round and round until I got the disk in full gear. Dad came running over, and all I could hear him say was, "Keep them away from the fence." Vivian was lucky she didn't get on for a ride.

When we were young kids, Mother made Bill and me go down in the basement to churn butter. Before it was close to done, we took the lid off to see, and over it went on the floor. Just then Mother came down. Bill took off for the grove, and I got caught. Wham!

For 15 years Stanley Reishus hauled mail for Kelly and Foley whenever they took vacations. The first year, 1927, I drove a model T Ford and also a Buick touring car I had traded in. It was just like the Buick cousin Victor Reishus used to drive when he was selling woolen goods. At that time postcards cost one cent and a letter three cents.

One year some of us boys had been to the State Fair, and one thing we saw was a motorcycle inside a big wooden silo going up on the sides. When we got home, we told Franklin about it. I said, "It's too bad our silo is full, otherwise we would get a motorcycle and try it." Franklin said, "Couldn't we try it on the outside?"

A lady came to look at a new home one day, and she said there were seven in the family, so they needed a big house. I said, "Seven isn't very many, in our family we had nine brothers and each brother had two sisters." She said, "My God, 18 girls?"

It seemed like every few months Dad would come home from town with a full bushel basket of shoes, overshoes, or coveralls for all us kids. The storekeeper asked him, "How do you know they'll fit?" Dad told him, "Aw, they'll certainly fit somebody."

Knute must have had a good business head to feed and raise his family and also accumulate land. Knute helped Orville start carpentering; Alfred, Myrtle, Norman, Franklin, and Vivian each got 40 acres. Martin now lives on Knute and Annetta's original farm. So Knute and Annetta were generous in sharing their property.

The following descriptions are short remembrances. Each of these families will have to continue their own generation's story. Norma Dovre and her Dad, Norman Reishus compiled this information in 1982, with help from Stan Reishus, Myrtle Olson, and Vivian Wendshuh.

Orville (2-25-1895 to 10-3-1967) finished St. Paul Ag School, was in World War I, graduated William Hood Dunwoody Industrial Institute, studied carpentry, was a builder for many years, operated Coast-to-Coast store, suffered from arthritis, and married Mabelle Ree (7-26-01 to 2-7-65).

Clarence (9-18-1896 to 12-17-1964) Ag School, Mankato Business School, worked in banks, bought out Kolhei Insurance, Lions Club named Cottonwood Lake Park in his honor, killed in train accident, married Mayme Gullickson (8-18-02 to 2003).

Alfred (4-17-1898 to 7-2-1962) Ag School, Kansas City Engineer School, mechanic of family, farmer, tease, perfectionist, on REA Board, director of Men's Choir, died of cancer, married Edna Berre (5-17-09).

Myrtle (12-19-1899) Ag School, worker, baked 16 loaves of bread three times a week at Reishus home, speaking voice carried well, church worker, pieced hundreds of quilts, married Nuel Olson (8-14-1896 to 12-29-1972).

Norman (11-1-01 to 4-1-1983) Ag School, farmer, Township Board, Farm Program Committeeman, Cottonwood Elevator Board, Creamery Boards, Yellow Medicine County Commissioner, tease, soloist, sports fan, died of kidney failure, married Leverna Severson at her bridal shower to everyone's surprise (9-22-10 to 1-16-1980).

Bill (William) (8-12-03 to 5-25-1978) strong, Cottonwood Oil Station attendant, teased kids and brought them treats when he delivered gas, helped at fertilizer plant, died of heart attack.

Stanley (4-12-05) Ag School, had chickens, oil company, salesman of cars and TVs, etc., story teller, practical joker, married Eloise Siechrist (5-16-05).

Martin (11-14-06) quiet, good ball player, good smile, always worked on home farm, married Ardith Kompelien (2-3-26).

Franklin (1-3-09) farmed, John Deere Implement Dealer in Clarksfield, handyman, jack of all trades, owned and operated a motel in Rapid City, married Helen Sharkey (5-20-15).

George Tungland, 2 Rudolph Tungland, 3 Aletha, 4 Annanias, 5 Anna, 6 Gunhild, 7 Even Tungland, 8 Magnus Reishus, 9 John Reishus, 10 Even Reishus, 11 Emma Reishus, 12 Adeline, 13 Clara, 14 Anna Reishus, 15 Edward Reishus, 16 Aletha Reishus, 17 Anna Johnston, 18 John Wangsness, 19 Agnes Wangsness Reishus, 20 Anna Wangsness, 21 Marie Reishus Wangsness, 22 Ole Reishus, 23 Agness Reishus, 24 Brita Kjos Reishus, 24 Ole Madland

REISHUS ANCESTORS

CHAPTER 40 / *The Family of Knute T. Reishus and Annette Miller* 335

Howard (3-21-12 to 10-12-43) farmed at home, died of kidney disease when he was 31; it was detected when he was called for Army.

Vivian (6-20-16) youngest, only one to finish high school (Cottonwood), store clerk and bookkeeper, struggled with M.S., married Kurt Wendshuh (8-5-14 to 11-4-83).

PAGE FROM CHURCH RECORDS IN NORWAY
RECORDING THE BIRTH OF EVEN OLSEN

EPILOGUE

Service above Self
—ROTARY CLUB

MY EPILOGUE IS BASED ON many things I have learned firsthand along with the rich heritage passed down to me from my parents, grandparents, and beyond the shores of America, to my ancestors in Norway. My philosophy, that I touch on here, has worked in my professional and my personal life. Some experiences came from firsthand knowledge, and in other cases, I've learned from my mistakes. In either case these are the foundations of my philosophy. A number of special interest items are highlighted in the following categories.

Church

Attend church regularly, and get involved. Many of your best friends will come from church.

Give to your church every week. Be generous with your time, your talents, and your money.

Enroll your children in Sunday school, church choir, and church youth activities.

Social Organizations

Get involved with at least one social organization. Be generous to them.

Join a couples club, be it with your church or in your community.

Kids

Spend quality time with your kids. Get involved with their activities, including sports.

Know where your kids are. Get to know your kids' friends and their friends' parents.

Savings

Sign up with your company's 401k. It is best to put in the maximum, but at least put in enough to get the matching amount. Then increase the amount you invest in your 401k every year until you are investing the maximum allowable.

If your company does not have a 401k or equivalent, invest in an IRA.

Always spend less than you make. Save something out of every paycheck. Don't let yourself live from paycheck to paycheck.

Credit Cards

Do not have more than two credit cards. Anything more than two is unnecessary and tempts you to buy things that you don't need. If you have a credit card, always pay the amount due *in full* and *on time*.

Do not allow yourself to get in a position that you have to pay interest or late charges.

If you cannot pay your bills in full and on time, put your credit cards away, and do not use them until your balance on all the cards is zero.

If you are tempted to use the cards anyway, when you have a balance due, cut the card up and go without. When you get everything paid off, get a debit card.

Don't buy anything on credit unless you can pay for it *in full* when the bill comes due. *Exceptions:*

1. A car bought before age thirty-five or forty. After that you should try to save enough before you buy. Many in every income bracket do just that. It is not too hard to do.
2. A home to be used as your personal residence.
3. A business from which you intend to make a profit.

On Cars

Don't buy a new car. Buy one that is two or three years old, and save big time.

Buy a car that gets great mileage and uses regular gas.

When you get older and your children's college expenses are

behind you, and your retirement account is funded and secure, then you can buy that new car you always wanted.

On Home Equity Loans

Do not buy anything on a home equity loan except home improvements. In other words, do not buy home electronics, Christmas presents, or use for monthly expenses or such.

Schedule a payment plan on your home equity loan so that it is paid off *in full* in no more than five or six years. Some banks do not require you to pay on your home equity loan every month. Do not fall for this trap. Pay on it every month.

Your Time

Operate on Lombardi time. Vince Lombardi, head coach of the Green Bay Packers and the Washington Redskins, said that if you aren't ten minutes early for a meeting, or anything else that matters, you're late. He fined players for being nine minutes early for a meeting. He said they were late. Lombardi carried this over in business too. This philosophy pays off in business big time.

Live by the Four Way Test

Whether you are a Rotarian or not, live by the four-way test in both your personal and your professional career.

- Is it the truth?
- Is it fair to all concerned?
- Will it build good will and better friendship?
- Will it be beneficial to all concerned?

Live by the four-way test, and you will have a successful and wonderful career and family life.

My Final Words

I have said many times in this book, "If it is to be it is up to me." Now, with my final words I say,

IF IT IS TO BE IT IS UP TO YOU.

Appendixes

Appendix A

OUR MANY MOVES

At the time of our marriage on February 1, 1953, I was still in the Army and Marg was in nursing school. We had our first home together some seven months later in the fall of 1953. Since then we have had a total of 21 primary residences.

Date	Description
10/53–2/54	Cary Dahl house. We moved to our first apartment. It was the upstairs of an old house in Cottonwood with an outside stairway.
2/54–9/54	Ted Reishus house. This was a small two-bedroom house with single garage. It was a wonderful house for us to start with.
9/54–11/54	Branch Avenue in Anoka, Minnesota. We lived with Helen and Earl Olson while I started at the "U" and waited for Kathy to be born, thus enabling us to qualify for married student housing.
11/54–7/57	University Grove East. Married student housing on edge of the St. Paul Campus. We lived in this metal roof, metal siding building, which was for married students. Every time it rained it sounded like hail. Marg's mother would call every time it was really cold to see if we were warm and we always were, as the buildings were well insulated. The apartment had two doors, one to the bathroom and one to the outside.
7/57–8/57	Canton, Ohio for three weeks. Furnished apartment where we lived while we looked for an apartment in Alliance, Ohio where my Student Engineer classes were held.

8/57–12/57	Alliance, Ohio. Marg would put old clothes on Kathy and Eric because the basement laundry was so dirty. I changed the vents, without the landlord's knowledge to get heat upstairs. He controlled the only thermostat. When I bought our first used television, he charged $1 extra per month for the extra electricity it would use.
12/57–10/58	Grandview Avenue. Wadsworth, Ohio. Upstairs in the split level duplex. A very nice home.
10/58–6/60	Grandview Avenue. Wadsworth, Ohio. Downstairs in the same split level house. It was larger, plus it had a basement.
6/60–6/62	Wolf Avenue. Wadsworth, Ohio. The first house we owned we purchased for $13,500. It was originally a two-bedroom house with an addition, making it a three bedroom, one-bath, with a single garage under the new bedroom addition. Good schools for the kids.
6/62–9/63	Coon Rapids, Minnesota. A rented house with only two bedrooms. The kid's bedroom was large enough to allow three single beds, plus ample play space. It was a great place in the woods. The Anoka Hennepin school district was very good.
9/63–5/64	Lake Minnetonka, Minnesota. A fairly new rented house, as we knew we were to be transferred to Des Moines, Iowa. It was a good house with good schools.
5/64–8/64	West Des Moines, Iowa. A furnished house while our second owned house was being built. It was a really hot summer with no A. C.
8/64–2/66	Des Moines, Iowa. This was our first new house and was across the street form the elementary school. A good neighborhood and good schools.
2/66–4/67	Davenport, Iowa. A very modern, contemporary house that looked new but was 25 years old. Some 42 years later, it still looks like a new very contemporary house. Good schools.
4/67–11/74	Aspen Ct. Naperville, IL. Seven years in this house. Great neighborhood, close to our church, and a fantastic school system.

11/74–3/75	North Canton, Ohio. We rented this furnished house while our new house was being built. Well water stunk of sulfa something terrible.
3/75–7/76	North Canton, Ohio. We had this new split level built. We enjoyed a great church, but the school system was so bad that almost immediately after joining Diebold, I started a new job search.
7/76–10/84	Huntington Ct., Naperville, IL. New job with R. R. Donnelley, a very professional company and a great place to work. Glad to be back to Naperville with its outstanding school system.
10/84–11/02	Peppertree Ct., Lisle, IL. (Next door to Naperville and in the Naperville school district) The best house we ever owned. We lived there for 18 years.
11/02–8/06	Charlestown Woods, Naperville, IL. Empty nesters, we moved to a townhouse complex in Naperville, our hometown.
8/06-present	Cottonwood Ct., Naperville IL. We moved to Monarch Landing, a retirement community. Marg and I agree that this is the best move we have ever made, and this is our last and final move. We started out in Cottonwood, Minnesota, and we now live on Cottonwood Court. What goes around comes around.

Appendix B

BURGER KING STORES

Here is a listing of all our stores. As you see we were quite busy. We were involved in ownership and running of the businesses for 36 stores.

REICER, INC.

	Location	Built	Acquired	Date Sold
1	Fox Valley Aurora	January 22, 1980		March 1, 1988
2	Naperville	September 1980		March 1, 1988
3	West Chicago		September 1981	March 1, 1988
4	Hoffman Estates		September 1981	March 1, 1988
5	Warrenville	June 1986		March 1, 1988
6	Hoffman Estates 2	November 1987		March 1, 1988

ME, INC.

	Location	Built	Acquired	Date Sold
7	Lockport		April 10, 1986	January 20, 2006
8	Palos Heights		April 10, 1986	August 22, 1997
9	Streator	June 27, 1989		January 20, 2006
10	Lombard		August 1, 1990	January 20, 2006
11	Elmhurst		January 18, 1991	January 20, 2006
12	Richton Park		November 2, 1992	March 19, 1998
13	Aurora	September 3, 1993		January 20, 2006
14	Tinley Park	December 20, 1994		January 20, 2006
15	Wenona	November 4, 1995		January 20, 2006
16	Peru	October 2, 1995		February 14, 1997
17	Florissant, MO.		December 1, 1995	September 30, 1999
18	Shorewood	February 13, 1996		January 20, 2006
19	St. Ann, MO.	July 30, 1996		September 30, 1999

20	Joliet Mall	September 25, 1996		January 20, 2006
21	Naperville 95 TH	October 20, 1996		September 1, 2006
22	Chicago Heights	May 28, 1997		March 19, 1998
23	Blue Island	June 23, 1997		January 20, 2006
24	Marseilles	May 19, 1997		January 20, 2006
25	St. Charles, MO		February 7, 1997	September 30, 1999
26	Naperville DT		January 16, 1998	January 20, 2006
27	Joliet Houbolt	June 1, 1999		January 20, 2006
28	Oglesby	May 14, 1999		January 20, 2006
29	Princeton	July 7, 2000		January 20, 2006
30	Ferguson, MO	October 7, 1997		September 30, 1999
31	CHGO Ridge Mall		November 5, 2001	January 20, 2006
32	Bradley		November 5, 2001	January 20, 2006
33	Burbank		November 5, 2001	January 20, 2006

L.M. FOODS, INC.

34	Harvey		November 5, 1992	August 22, 1997

GEMR INC.

35	Rochelle	February 12, 1995		1999
36	Dixon	October 26, 1995		January 20, 2006

Enjoy —
from Grandma Reishus
Dec 2020